HOME
FREE

HOME FREE

Adventures of a Child of the Sixties

by

RIFKA KREITER

SHE WRITES PRESS

Published 2017
Printed in the United States of America
Print ISBN: 978-1-63152-176-8
E-ISBN: 978-1-63152-177-5
Library of Congress Control Number: 2016961324

For information, address:
She Writes Press
1563 Solano Ave #546
Berkeley, CA 94707

Every effort has been made to obtain permissions for pieces quoted in this work. If any required acknowledgments have been omitted, or any rights overlooked, it is unintentional. Please notify the publisher of any omission.

Cover design © Julie Metz, Ltd./metzdesign.com
Book design by Stacey Aaronson

She Writes Press is a division of SparkPoint Studio, LLC.

Names and identifying characteristics have been changed to protect the privacy of certain individuals.

This book is dedicated to you, Reader.
Enjoy!

An unexamined life is not worth living.

—Socrates

God is alive, magic is afoot . . .

—Leonard Cohen

TABLE OF CONTENTS

*S*cruffy men with beards and long hair, women mostly my age, many wearing long skirts. About forty people milling around on a midtown street corner on a cool afternoon, waiting to board a chartered bus. I recognize some of them from the introductory meeting I attended last week. Many are speaking excitedly to one another but I'm happy to keep to myself. When I go to meet a new spiritual teacher, I like to stay centered so I can tune in to my inner bullshit detector. So I can be open to whatever I may glean of value from the adventure at hand. I pride myself on my well-worn bell-bottom jeans and work shirt, which distinguish me from the women, many with hair in plain buns, who seem to be wearing spiritual costumes. My shoulder-length hair, whipping in the cool breeze, is barely combed.

Someone taps me on the shoulder. I look down to see a pretty young woman, only five feet tall, smiling up at me from limpid gray eyes.

"Hi," she says. "I don't know if you remember me—you were in my est Training last year. I'm Olga."

"Yes, I do remember you," I murmur. "I'm Rifka."

Olga's soft eyes glow as she says, "And now we're both going to meet Swamiji at the same time." Swamiji is the latest Indian guru to arrive in the spiritual marketplace of mid-seventies New York. We'll be traveling to his upstate ashram in the defunct Lido Hotel, where a welcome program is to be held when he arrives later this evening. I guess he'll be like the sixth or seventh teacher I've checked out since my breathtaking acid trip last year. If our free ride ever shows up.

Finally, a bus that appears to have barely survived a long career in the sixties, shudders to a halt on the curb in front of us. The image of a lithe Greyhound is almost obscured by the name of the charter company painted over it.

"Shall we sit together?" asks Olga.

"Sure," I say, hoping my terse reply reveals my disinclination to talk.

We shuffle halfway down the aisle to find two seats together. I take the window seat without asking Olga if she wants it, only slightly ashamed of being so rude.

"Did you have to take a day off work?" asks Olga.

"No, I'm just doing temp work right now. How about you?"

"I'm a freelance textile designer. I make my own hours."

"Mm," I answer, praying this will exhaust our small talk.

After a pause Olga says, "I was so excited last night, I couldn't sleep. Maybe I can sleep a little now." Great!

The driver pulls the door closed with a squeak and the bus begins to make its way uptown.

We enter the West Side Highway on 72nd Street, in view of my own apartment, and seem to hit our top speed at fifty miles per hour. Though I'm not sure exactly where the Lido is, I can tell it's gonna be a long ride. Watching the city pass by my window, I reflexively tick off memories associated with virtually every street I see. The Esquire on 86th, the sublet on 93rd; first kisses parked at the Spry Club (I'm nostalgic—the neon sign for Spry shortening no longer sparkles across the river); my father's old apartment on 98th. A million fleeting incidents peppered throughout the years.

CHAPTER 1
The Ties That Bind

M ommy and I tiptoe out of the apartment so we won't wake up Freddie the Jeweler. I am confused; where are we going? Still, Mommy and I haven't had our own secret since Freddie moved in with us last year when I was in first grade. I'm excited, holding her hand as we walk down Broadway. The autumn sun makes our eyes squint as we turn onto 78th Street and go down a few stone steps to a basement office. The room is crowded with people speaking loudly in German and other languages. Mommy says this is a special agency to help Jewish people. She talks to a man behind a glass window and then we sit down on some folding chairs to wait. Glancing at the lady sitting next to me, I almost stop breathing. I nudge my mother, whispering, "Look at her arm, Mommy." Then I notice a lot of the people in the room have those ugly black numbers written on their arms. How come? Mommy frowns and tears come to her eyes.

"Shh, Rickie. I'll explain when we get home." I don't like this place.

Finally, our name is called and Mommy says to wait for her while she speaks to a lady in the office. Something about me going to a special place in the country to live for a while. What could *that* mean?

When we get home, we tiptoe past the bedrooms down the long hallway, thinking Freddie is still asleep. But when we reach the kitchen, the light is on. Suddenly he's walking towards us from the dining room, a look of fury on his face. He's shouting in German. I don't understand; is he angry because we went to that place without him?

Our boarder, Ingrid, comes out of her room and puts her hands on my shoulders protectively. Mommy is yelling back at Freddie in German, crying and banging her fists on his chest. He pushes her to the floor and takes off his belt. The scene blurs through my tears. From the kitchen floor, Mommy turns her head towards us and screams, "Ingrid, take Rickie away." Ingrid takes me to my room and tries to comfort me.

• • •

I BEGAN KEEPING A diary when I was in the eighth grade. "Thought Lines," I called it at first. Later I personified it as "Niki," a sort of alter ego to me, Riki.

March 19, 1959—Dear Niki, I have been reading Anne Frank's diary over and have decided to fashion mine after hers. Of course it isn't easy to express one's deepest feelings on paper but I can try.

I had not always been "Riki." I was born Rifka Batya Kreiter on November 8, 1945—11:31 p.m. for the astrologically inclined. This momentous event was documented with dubious accuracy at Grace Hospital in Detroit. Yes, my mother was twenty and my father forty-six years old and yes, their color was "W." Our address was the Seville Hotel. My father was with the USO, stationed in Detroit. However, both my parents' first names were misspelled. Instead of Samuel, "Father's Name" appears as "Manuel." They also dropped the final h from Mom's palindromic Hannah. Rifka, a transliteration of the Hebrew for Rebecca, is usually rendered with a *v*, Rivka. Following Jewish custom, I was named for my father's mother who died ten days before I was born.

My mother immediately began to call me Ricky. She was trying so hard to be American. (Not to say she wanted a boy.) So, I was Ricky until first grade, when the other kids began to tease me.

"Ricky is a *boy's* name," I wailed when my mother came home from work one day. She was standing at the stove, spooning coffee into the aluminum percolator.

"It is not," she said, displaying her preferred mode of dealing with irritating realities. I promise you, in 1951 only boys were called Ricky. When I pressed the point, Mommy said we could change the spelling to "Rickie." That would make it a girl's name. I was mollified.

By the fifth grade, however, I was captive to the notion that I had to be "different." Unilaterally, which is how I like to do things, I started signing myself "Riki." This suited my romantic fantasies for four more years. Then in ninth grade my friend Sue Haberman suggested I spell my name with a *q*. By age thirteen, among my friends, being different was a universally acknowledged good. Sue was sure that there would be no other Rickys in the world spelled "Riqui." I remained Riqui until I was twenty-nine.

After a powerful acid trip in 1975, I *knew* I needed a new

name. And there it was, right on my birth certificate: Rifka Batya. Batya means daughter of God.

Later I heard that certain Native American tribes have the custom of adding new names as one grows older, each name a milestone on the individual's progress through life.

MY FATHER WAS A handsome man, though not as tall as I thought he was, with thick salt-and-pepper hair and a mellifluous voice. Sam was a freelance writer, Yiddish translator, and sometime fundraiser for Jewish organizations. I never knew much for sure about his life, past or present. He was secretive (not to say paranoid) and answered personal questions with vague generalizations or another question. My parents were separated when I was three, and at first I looked forward to Daddy's visitation days with passionate anticipation. He appeared at our door dressed like a Damon Runyon character, wearing, perhaps, a black shirt and white tie with a sharp pinstriped suit. And a fedora. He smoked gold-tipped Turkish cigarettes that came in rainbow colors. When I got to be six or seven, I felt honored when he held out the pack to me so I could select which color he should smoke. If our conversation lagged, he'd ask me, "So, do you like this country?" which always made me giggle.

When I was in my twenties, my father gave me this unforgettable advice about how to attract a man: "Wear a hat with a veil. Allow the smoke from your cigarette to drift mysteriously from your lips. Say very little."

What little I discovered about Dad is largely gleaned from the voluminous papers we found in his closet when he died in 1978. There was a biographical piece, scrawled with revisions, called "Mother's Search for the Messiah" about my namesake, his mother. He also had a trunk full of letters dating back to the 1930s, including carbon copies of some of his own letters. Most of these were to and from various women and we learned from them of his *nom d'amour*, as he always signed himself "Sven." I had to chuckle. He wass an inveterate womanizer, which was not so amusing to his three wives, the first of whom, we think, committed suicide back in the twenties. A 1937 letter to an unknown woman, with the salutation "Charming Evelyn," says:

> *I am not trying to appear mysterious. Only that I don't feel the need to speak of myself to anybody. I live fully. And my experiences are so crowded, gratifying, rarely disillusioning, always absorbing, that they leave neither room nor reason for bitterness.*

My father could be exquisitely tender or hard as a rock. In another missive to Evelyn he writes that her letter "gives me a gratifying impression of your essential honesty, a trait of character that few women possess, and freedom from any repulsive trickery that seems to be the masthead of most women's equipment."

He was born Shmuel in 1899 in Buczacz, Eastern Galicia (part of the Austria-Hungary empire) and came to New York in 1913 with his mother and older brother. They settled in a railroad flat under the Williamsburg Bridge. Years later, Dad described his first impressions of the Lower East Side:

> *A smell of fish fouled the air pierced by squealing fowl. The sidewalks steamed with strolling Jews, sweaty, bearded and clean-shaven, wearing skullcaps or panamas. Women huddled in front of shaded tenement stoops, fanning themselves with folded newspapers. Boys played handball in the street, braving honking cars and trucks. All ignored the rancid open garbage cans festering at the curbstone. As we passed,*

people smiled, waved, exclaimed: "Shalom Aleichem, Yidn! *Where do you hail from?*"

Like so many others, my father and his brother rejected in short order the Old World pieties of their Orthodox parents and embraced the secular Yiddish culture thriving in New York. No greenhorns they.

I have only one reprint of my father's published work, "Notes on Yiddish Poetry," from the Literary Review (undated, but after 1957). In this article, he bemoans the loss of "what was left of Yiddish culture after World War II." I remember days out with him in the early fifties when he took me to the Café Royale on 12th Street, a famous hangout for Jewish artists. From there you could still see a row of Yiddish theaters down Second Avenue.

Daddy loved to hang out. On our weekly visitation days—if he actually showed up—he'd take me to the Automat or one of various cafeterias around town where we always ran into people he knew, regulars who came to sit and schmooze for hours—or read, or write—over a cup of coffee and a piece of cheesecake. Of course the best cheesecake was famously at Lindy's on Broadway. When Daddy took me there as a special treat, we'd sit in a booth and watch the people revolving in and out of the busy restaurant: tourists with cameras, men with shifty eyes under fedoras with racing forms folded under their arms, women wearing fur jackets and lots of makeup.

WHILE I HAVE VIRTUALLY no memories of my father's relatives, my mother's family filled my early childhood. Hannah and her twin, Naomi, were born in Berlin, October 27, 1925. My ability to state this with clarity is hard-won. When I was growing up, Mother always told me that she was Swiss, and that she was nineteen, not twenty, when I was born in November of '45. (When confronted with this years later, she quipped, "I was sick a year.") As children will, I accepted what she told me without question. I must have been nineteen myself before I stopped to think that if Mommy's fraternal twin, Noni, was born in Berlin. . . . My grandmother *did* move fast but not, I reasoned, that fast.

My maternal grandfather, Bernhard Schapiro, was a pioneering physician in the field of sexology. From 1922 to 1933 he directed the Department of Disturbances of Potency at the Institute for Sexology in Berlin. The Institute was radical, not only in its field of study and treatment, but also in its defense of homosexuals and transvestites at a time when they were considered criminals. Opapa developed and patented a medication for impotence which was marketed until 1989.

The brilliant Dr. Schapiro, who was also deeply religious and learned in Talmud, married Thekla Feuchtwanger, a young woman from a prosperous Orthodox family. My grandmother was something of a beauty who, as far as I can tell, was never in her long life photographed without a string of pearls— except at the beach at Ostend, or on skis in the Alps. She was an intellectual, independent enough to have become a teacher in an age where this could almost be characterized as rebellion for a young Jewish woman of high culture. Omama's cousin, the novelist Lion Feuchtwanger, issued a prescient warning in 1933 about National Socialism in his novel *The Oppermans*. In it, he describes the growing threat to a successful extended family not unlike his own, Jewish but with a proud Bavarian identity. According to the family genealogy, almost eight hundred Feuchtwangers (including "consorts") emigrated from Germany between 1933 and 1945. Eighty were murdered by the Nazis.

Three months after Hitler came to power, the Institute for Sexology was ransacked by a mob of Nazi "students" and its library burned. Opapa, Omama, and their four children moved to Zurich. This was possible because my grandfather had obtained Swiss citizenship while a medical student in Switzerland. Omama's father, Felix Feuchtwanger, was sent to Dachau concentration camp, outside his native Munich where there is a street bearing his family name. The ailing seventy-one-year-old was released to die in 1938, when a Jew could still get a marked grave. I saw it myself in 1999 when an amazing number of local residents went out of their way to help me find "the old Jewish Cemetery" in Munich, apparently eager to be of some assistance to a living Jew. I was told that the cemetery had escaped desecration because of a valiant Gentile caretaker who had refused entrance to Nazi vandals.

In May 1940, as England stood alone against Hitler, Opapa finally obtained visas and the Schapiros sailed to New York. What must it have been like for my mother, age fifteen, escaping from Europe with the shadow of the Holocaust looming? All her life she was full of fears. When I was little, if sirens sounded from fire engines passing under our apartment windows, she would run from window to window, pulling down the shades as if it were an air raid. Like so many first-generation children, the terror of the Nazis has always been very real for me, an integral part of my *zeitgeist*. I never believed it couldn't happen *here*, or to me.

My Aunt Noni recalled high school as torture for the strictly reared girls who wanted desperately to fit in with their peers but were forbidden to wear lipstick. She said she would lie awake nights, wondering, "When will I ever learn English?" Both Mother and Noni left their authoritarian home at eighteen, going to work right out of high school. I have no idea how my mother met the dapper Sam Kreiter. Perhaps it was at a USO function. My grandparents were scandalized when she married him, a non-observant Jew the age of her own mother! But Mommy was a rebel, the black sheep of the family.

In his last years, Daddy grew sentimental about the eighteen-year-old Hannah, whom he divorced when she was twenty-three. "She was so innocent," he said with misty eyes, over coffee at Dubrow's Cafeteria.

SHE MAY HAVE BEEN innocent, but life with mother was no picnic. We lived in sixteen different places during my first eighteen years; of these, only two were houses. The first house was in Lynbrook, a small Long Island suburb. There, I attended Happy House preschool and rode my tricycle up and down our dead-end street. I still have a scar from the gash I got on my left knee the time I fell off my tricycle.

Daddy was away a lot of the time, on whatever his business was, but I was crazy about the accordion-fold picture postcards he sent from cities across the United States and the towels he brought home with different hotel names. When he was there, my parents did a lot of shouting. I would hide in the closet, pressing a pillow around my ears to drown out their angry voices. Sometimes, my father got mad at me too; he shook me and made me cry and Mommy would scream at him and cry also. But I still adored my Daddy.

I have no actual memory of the divorce, but when I turn my attention within and revisit my three-year-old self, what comes up is the feeling of my Daddy being wrenched out of my arms.

• • •

I AM FOUR YEARS old. Mommy and I live in the city now, in a big room on the third floor. The house has five floors with a shiny wooden staircase. Mommy works as a dental assistant.

When she goes to work in the morning, I stay downstairs at the preschool run by the two ladies who own the house. They are German, like us. One of them, Niecie, is very strict. At lunchtime she makes the kids eat liver, stupidly "hidden" in mashed potatoes. I hate liver and throw up on purpose. When Niecie catches me making drawings with my left hand, she tears them up and tells me I must draw only with my right hand. But I won't.

On Friday nights, Mommy and I walk down Broadway to Omama and Opapa's apartment on 81st Street for Shabbat. I love Shabbat because my aunts and uncles come over and everyone talks and kids around. They make a big fuss over me. I am the only grandchild and they all think I am cute and funny and smart. Mommy is pleased when they praise me.

Tonight Omama is finishing dinner in the kitchen as the rest of us wait for sunset in the living room. Aunt Mina says, "Ricky, would you like to dance together?" Of course I would! I love to dance more than anything. Mina puts a thick black disc on the Victrola and winds the handle that makes the record turn. I let the pretty music move me as Mina taught me, and she and I float around the living room on our toes, gently waving our arms, smiling at one another while the others look on.

"You're so graceful, Ricky," Aunt Ruthie says warmly.

I want to be a dancer when I grow up.

As the sun sets, we line up with our backs to the dining room windows. Oma and Opa do the *benschen*. One by one they go down the line of their children, holding cupped hands above our heads, muttering barely audible prayers in Hebrew. First, there is handsome Uncle Ray, home from MIT. Tall and thin, he has boundless energy and a hearty laugh that always makes me feel good. His wife, Mina, is a teacher in a "progressive" school. Then come Aunt Noni and Uncle Billy. Pretty Noni always speaks to me thoughtfully and asks me what I think about things. Billy likes to tease me. He was buddies with Ray in the Army, on Guam, which is an island. That's how Billy came to be Uncle Billy. I was the flower girl at their wedding. Noni is Mommy's twin, but she is smaller, like Ruthie, Mommy's kid sister who goes to Hunter High School. Ruthie picks me up from Hebrew School every Saturday and together we walk up the nine flights to my grandparents' apartment. You're not allowed to take the elevator on Shabbat. Ruthie makes the hard climb fun—we pretend we're climbing up to heaven.

Next in the line is my mommy, so glamorous with her thick brown hair and generous figure. I watch my grandparents as they make their way toward me at the end of the line. When they bless me, the top of my head feels warm. *Benschen* is mysterious and thrilling.

Afterward, we gather at the round oak table to sing the Shabbat songs and bless the meal. I stand on a chair next to my Opapa, so I'm as tall as he is. The smell of dinner, which had to be fully cooked before sundown, wafts through from the kitchen, making my mouth water. As we sing, Opapa lifts my hand to his face. I smile as he gently presses the back of my hand into the warm, soft skin over his eye. When we say the blessing over the wine, he gives me a little sip.

At last, Omama brings a platter of pot roast through the swinging door. Omama is not gentle like Opa but she shows me lots of interesting things, like the big art book with the picture of the yellow drawbridge and then we saw the real painting in the museum. Wow. I love going to the Metropolitan Museum with its grand staircase and beautiful art.

I try to copy the way Omama eats her dinner. I turn the fork so it points down. Then I put some pot roast, salad, and potato on my fork, all at the same time. I like the way the crunchy salad tastes together with the rich meat and mushy potato.

Soon I am full and the dining room feels warm; the French doors to the living room are closed. My eyes are heavy. I try not to look at the big, dark painting over the wooden sideboard. It shows a boy and a girl in a stormy forest, fleeing from a vague, threatening figure.

When we get home, Mommy tucks me in and we sing "*Sh'ma Yisroel . . .*" which means God is One, and we pray for the whole family and everyone who is unfortunate.

IN OUR ROOM AT Niecie's, lace curtains lie flat against the cold windowpane. Dark wood furniture is set around the walls of the room, leaving plenty of space for dancing in the center of the carpet. Mommy likes to watch me dance, too.

I am sick today and must stay in bed instead of going downstairs. Mommy has to go to work at the dentist's office but Mrs. Schoenfeld will come up to check on me during the day. Now Mommy tucks me in with my teddy bear and Snooky, the hard rubber doll who pees when you give her water from her bottle. She kisses me tenderly and sings our song:

> *I don't care if the sun don't shine,*
> *I get my loving in the evening time,*
> *When I'm with my—ba-a-by!*

She always tickles my tummy when she says "ba-a-by" and I still giggle even though I'm a big girl now. It's our game.

I wish Mommy wouldn't leave, but I don't want to cry. When I cry Mommy feels so bad she cries too; she holds me close and begs me, "Please don't cry, Ricky." Then I feel like I'm falling and falling and there's no bottom. So I swallow hard to keep the tears down.

After Mommy closes the door, the room feels too big so I close my eyes tightly and pray.

"Dear God, please stay with me until Mommy comes home."

All of a sudden a thought washes over me like a big wave at the beach. What if God is not really there? As soon as I think it, I am certain that it is true. Now blackness is all around me, just blackness and nothing else.

I pull the covers over my head and hug the teddy bear to my chest.

Soon I hear the words, "I'm home, dear." It's George. Mommy calls George "Ricky's imaginary husband."

"Oh, Sweetheart," I say in my mind, "did you remember to bring the bread?"

"Of course I did, Darling," George answers. "I brought ice cream, too."

"Oh, thank you, Sweetheart. That means that after I make your favorite supper, spaghetti and tomato sauce, we can have ice cream for dessert."

"Yes, dear," says George. He comes over and gives me a hug and kiss. Then he lies down with me and we fall asleep.

• • •

IN 1951 MY GRANDPARENTS finally fulfilled Opapa's Zionist dream and made the move to Jerusalem. In their stateroom on the *Queen Mary*, I remember walking waist-high to all the black clad well-wishers who were eating canapés and drinking champagne. Now and then a powdered face appeared at my eye level and red-tipped fingers pinched my cheek hard as someone said "*zehr schön*." Each time the foghorn blasted I tried to pull my mother away, fearing the ship would go out to sea with us still on board.

As the chartered bus crosses the George Washington Bridge, I gaze absently at the trees on the Palisades, fuzzy with early spring growth, and wonder what tonight will bring. So many of the teachers I respect—and many I doubt—speak of this Swami as the real thing.

Olga sleeps quietly beside me, her mouth slightly open. The hum of the engine acts as a soporific and the scenery of the passing towns doesn't engage me. Despite the fact that I lived here for a while (or because of it), the sights of New Jersey hold little interest. When the bus turns north, I try to determine where we are by referencing things on the other side of the river. In my New Yorker's view of the world, everything north of the Bronx jumbles together in my mind under the label "upstate."

We might be parallel with Ardsley right now, for all I know . . .

CHAPTER 2

Ardsley

Mommy and I are living in Omama and Opapa's old apartment. I am in the first grade now and Mommy is letting me stay up to watch her poker game with her girl-friends. They play at the dining room table where we used to have Shabbat dinner. Each one has a pile of pennies in front of her and during the hand they make bets and put the pennies in the pot. I like to watch all the hands like Seven Card Stud or Baseball, where threes and nines are wild.

Ingrid comes in through the swinging door from the kitchen and says, "We're out of soda."

Mommy says, "Ricky can get us some from the store."

Everyone talks and murmurs at the same time. "Oh, no, Hannah, she's too young." "It's too late . . ." "We don't really need it . . ."

"I can go," I tell them. I jump at the chance to show what a big girl I am.

"It's okay," says Mommy, "she doesn't have to cross the street. Ricky's done it before."

Mommy gives me a dollar from her purse and I practically run down the long hallway and out the door. Reaching up, I open the elevator door and press "1" to go down. Out in the big courtyard I'm startled to see it is already dark. I falter a little as I step out onto 81st Street and walk quickly toward Amsterdam. The block seems much longer tonight. A few people turn their heads to look at me. I go around the corner to John's Grocery Store where we get our food and am relieved to find John there as usual. Stepping up to the dusty counter, I say, feeling very grown up, "Can I have a bottle of ginger ale, please." You should always say please when you ask for something.

"You're out late, young lady," says John as he puts the big glass bottle in a paper bag.

"My mommy sent me," I tell him proudly. I give him the dollar bill, a little damp now, and he hands down the change. My green plaid dress has no pockets so I clutch the coins in my left hand and put both arms around the bag to carry it home.

It's a little heavy.

Walking back down 81st Street, I feel the bottle start to slip. Uh-oh. Our building looks very far away. I try to shift the awkward weight around in my arms but, like slow motion in the movies, the bottle slips through the bag and crashes to the sidewalk.

Oh no! Oh no! I bend down to pick it up and a thick piece of glass cuts me on the hand. I can't believe this is happening. A lot of blood is dripping from my hand and I've dropped my change. I burst into tears, crying really loud. I can't help it. A lady comes over and asks me where I live; she'll take me home. I want to pick up the bottle but it's all in pieces and ginger ale is spreading out on the sidewalk. The lady puts her handkerchief around my hand and helps me get my change before taking me upstairs to my house.

Mommy and her friends make a big fuss when they see me. I cannot stop crying so Mommy cries too, her forehead wrinkled and tears on her cheeks.

"I dropped it," I wail, but Mommy says, "It's all right, Ricky," and puts iodine on my hand, which makes me cry even harder. She puts on a bandage and hugs me tight.

I am so ashamed.

· · ·

MY MOTHER LIKED FINDING euphemisms for things to assuage her characteristic guilt feelings. Cohabiting with Freddie the Jeweler was a "trial marriage" because, she said, her parents—consulted, presumably, via air mail—had approved of the arrangement. The imprimatur of her parents' approval (fabricated by her, I now imagine) was meant to neutralize the stigma of such an arrangement in 1952. I believed her as I always did when I was a small child: hook, line, and sinker.

Freddie was German, a harsh man, and I hated him. Of course, I probably would have hated any man my mother took up with. Like most children of divorce, I secretly clung to the hope that somehow my father would return to me, despite the fact that my mother hurled curses at him whenever they were in the same room for more than two minutes.

When Freddie gave me a watch for my birthday, I threw it out the window. He had a mean daughter who was twelve. When she came over and we played in my room, she frightened me with her bossy attitude. Once she made my head bleed when she pushed me hard against the wall. Mommy got very upset. "She gave Rickie a hole in the head," she yelled at Freddie as she held ice to the wound through my matted hair.

Before Freddie, I used to be free to climb into Mommy's bed and cuddle anytime I wanted. She hated sleeping alone and always kept a night-light on, afraid of the dark. After Freddie moved in I would try to sneak into their bed when they fell asleep. But Freddie was a light sleeper. If a board creaked as I crawled on hands and knees across the bedroom floor, he would wake up and get angry. Picking me up roughly, he'd carry me back to my own bed. If I made it across to my mother's side of the bed, she'd take me in her arms and under the covers without even waking up. This made the risk of incurring Freddie's anger worthwhile.

Then one day, she took me back to that agency, and before I knew it, I was brought to live with Hans and Ruth Krause in the sleepy little town of Ardsley, New York, forty-five minutes from the city. My mother told me that Hans and Ruth were friends of my grandparents. For years, I believed her. She said she sent me away because—since she was of course looking for a husband after breaking off with Freddie (what else would a single woman do?)—the family told her it was bad for me to witness "a parade of men" in her life. In 1953 the divorce rate in the United States was only 25 percent. And that was when most people got married. Affordable child care was virtually nonexistent.

IN THE RED BRICK house on Euclid Avenue, everything seemed large and strange. I cried desperately when I realized my mother was leaving me there. She cried too.

"It's just until I find a husband," she begged. "Then we'll have a big wedding and we'll be together always."

From then on, I lived for that wedding day. Meanwhile, I was determined to hate it in Ardsley.

The Krauses were a Jewish couple who had emigrated from Germany in the '30s. Hans, a bald man, perhaps fifty, with soft features and a roundish body, was a furrier who commuted by train to his business in Manhattan's fur district. Ruth must have been around forty. She was rugged, with a strong, unmade-up face. She usually wore slacks so she could work freely in the house and garden. Her thick black hair was clipped at the nape of her neck with a barrette. Beneath her gruffness she was filled with longings—for children, for music, for romance. Hans was a gentle soul, as tender as Ruth was strict. He could sit playing songs on the grand piano in the living room for an hour.

I loved Hans and thought Ruth was mean to him, often speaking contemptuously about his failing fur business. Hans was overtly loving and affectionate. I was afraid of Ruth, though I sensed that she cared for me in her own way. Still, in my misery, I could not soften toward her. I regret that now. Then, I was seven years old.

The Krauses had two dachshunds, Hazel and Heidi, and two tabby cats, former strays named Percy and Peter. I had never had a pet and I delighted in brushing those frankfurter dogs and in how Percy, way friskier than stolid Peter, came running when he heard the noise of the can opener mounted on the wall in the basement pantry, knowing this meant his dinner would be served immediately.

I remember the living room best. There was a large Oriental carpet. In one corner stood the piano, unscratched and polished to a shine. A wooden console housed the television, then just beginning to appear in most homes. We always watched *Your Hit Parade* and *Ed Sullivan* on Sunday nights. The rest of the living room was crowded with heavy mahogany furniture, reminiscent of my grandparents' apartment. Also on the ground floor were the dining room, Hans and Ruth's bedroom, and a large kitchen with a breakfast nook where we ate our meals on a Formica and chrome table, sitting on vinyl chairs. On the infrequent occasions when there was company for dinner, we ate in the dining room. The table would be covered in a white cloth and we used the good china, exactly like Omama's. Conversation was stilted and if it was my mother who was visiting, I would be dreading the time when the meal ended and she would leave.

For a while I was the only child there, but after some months another girl my age, Judy, came to live with us, placed by her single mother for reasons similar to my mother's. Judy and I shared a slant-ceilinged bedroom upstairs with a window facing out onto the quiet street.

I only remember Judy's black ponytail and that she was my colleague in misery as well as my rival. At night, we whispered together across the chilly bedroom, trying to outdo one another in bragging about our mothers.

"My mother has dates every weekend."

"My mother has a rich boyfriend—they'll probably get married soon and I'll be going home."

Hans and Ruth told us that they kept foster kids because they wanted children but couldn't have any. One girl, Connie, had stayed with them for five years. Her mother had disappeared after two years, and the Krauses raised Connie as their own daughter. Then her mother reappeared and took Connie away. They never heard from her again and we could tell they were bitter about it. Judy and I thought Connie was terrible to be so ungrateful and vowed that we would never be so thoughtless, even though all we wished for was to go home.

At the Krauses' we had chores and discipline, something totally foreign to my experience. We had to set the table and clear the dishes. There was a half-acre garden and we had to weed the flower beds every day, in season. The garden was pretty, and wild raspberries grew at the edge of it. On the slope beneath the flagstone patio, Ruth had planted a rock garden. I learned names of flowers like pansies and rhododendron. I learned that crocuses grow so early that they peek up through the snow! Still, I hated weeding and always malingered until Ruth yelled at me and threatened to send me to my room without supper. Sometimes I took the punishment, just because.

The Krauses listened to different kinds of music on the radio and they had records: German *lieder*, big bands, opera. Hans bought sheet music so he could play popular songs such as "Wish You Were Here" on the piano.

I resented Ruth, as if it were her fault that she was not my mother. I constantly compared her to my mother as in, "My mommy doesn't make me do that," to which she responded by saying that my mother had no discipline and was overweight. This infuriated me. Every few weeks when Mommy came to see me, I would cry and tell her all the bad things Ruth said about her. She said Ruth was just jealous. Before each visit I would harbor the hope that, this time, Mommy would surely take me home. When I begged her, she always said, "It's just until I find us a husband."

Hannah was twenty-seven then.

In the winter, Hans started teaching me and Judy how to play the piano. We each had to practice for an hour a day. Whenever I thought I could get away with it, or maybe just to make Ruth mad, I would spend the time playing with Hazel and Heidi instead of practicing. But I can still pick out the two simple German folk songs I learned from Hans.

. . .

IT IS ABRAHAM LINCOLN'S Birthday and Judy and I are off from school. Hans is late coming home from work. Fat old Peter is curled up on the living room windowsill, studying the snow falling on the deserted street. Finished with chores, Ruth puts a record on the Victrola and Perry Como croons a dreamy love song. I begin to dance around the room on tiptoe, more aware of how I look to Judy and Ruth than really listening to the music. Heidi, standing in the doorway, tilts her head quizzically and wags her tail. Soon enough, the familiar pleasure of dancing overtakes me and I let myself go, making little leaps with arms circling over my head.

Ruth bursts out laughing. "You look like a little elephant," she chortles. Judy guffaws at this.

"We should call you elephant foot," says Ruth, and the two of them laugh harder.

Shocked out of my reverie, I restrain hot tears. I hate them but I won't show them they've hurt me. I continue dancing 'til the record ends, feeling ugly and fat.

. . .

SOMETIMES ON SUNDAYS, THE Krauses took us down to Riverdale to visit their friends Irv and Sylvia Feinstein in their high-rise apartment. Both the Feinsteins were tall and elegant, with well-groomed silver hair. Their home had plush white carpeting and thick cut crystal glasses on a rolling bar with glass shelves and brass trim. The liquor was kept in matching crystal decanters. The grown-ups listened to music and drank highballs, talking and laughing while Judy and I played in the bedroom.

It was at Sylvia and Irv's place that Ruth first met the handsome opera singer Mario Castelli. We saw him there several times. Later, Judy and I would hear Ruth talk to him on the telephone when Hans was at work. After a while, we both noticed something funny about her tone of voice. We spent many hours alone with Ruth in the house and sensed, as children do, that she was lonely and frustrated.

One day during Easter vacation, the phone rang and we heard Ruth speaking intensely for a long time, covering the receiver with her hand so we couldn't hear. Judy and I looked at each other, trying to imagine what it could be about. When she hung up, Ruth piled us into the backseat of the black Oldsmobile and drove to the city. This was extremely unusual. Ruth was distracted and seemed not to notice when Judy and I whispered to each other, wondering where we were going. She parked near the City Center Theater and told us to wait in the car and keep the doors locked. Judy and I now knew she was doing something naughty—it must have something to do with

Mario who, we remembered, sang in the opera here. We giggled together nervously as we watched people hurry by on the busy midtown street.

After a little while Ruth returned. She sat in silence behind the wheel for a moment. Then she began to cry softly, bending her head toward her hands which gripped the steering wheel. Judy and I looked at each other in fear and amazement. We did not utter a sound. After a few minutes, not saying a word, Ruth dried her eyes and turned on the ignition. On the way home, she told us we should not tell Hans that we had gone to the city. I was too disturbed by the whole event to dream of prolonging it in any way. I preferred to pretend it never happened.

SO I LIVED ON at Hans and Ruth's and settled in, in a way. Despite myself, I was experiencing a new sense of safety at the Krauses', thanks to their consistent routines and their real concern for my welfare. In second and third grade I went to Ardsley Elementary School, a rectangular brick building just erected to accommodate all the kids born since the war ended. In Mrs. Ruotolo's third grade class, I learned US geography from a puzzle kept on a windowsill near my desk. Each state was a different colored piece. To this day, I picture those pieces when I think geographically of Nevada (purple) or Tennessee (yellow). I had a crush on Mrs. Ruotolo, who was tall and slim with auburn hair. She once told us she lived at 3030 Valentine Avenue (in the Bronx), which I thought was perfect, since she was my perfect valentine.

I made two good friends at school, Mary Ann Greer and Laurie Feldman. Visiting their comfortable homes, I experienced, for an evening or an afternoon, what an intact family was like. Mary's father came home for dinner and spoke respectfully to her mother, complimenting her cooking. Laurie's parents teased each other affectionately and fed their collie from the dinner table. They all spoke to me in sympathetic tones that made me feel I was a sad case.

On New Year's Eve, 1952, the Krauses gave a party. Sylvia and Irv and three or four other well-dressed European couples ate canapés, sipped cocktails, and danced cheek to cheek to Hans's records. I was so excited because tonight Judy and I would stay up late to perform for the company. Hans had written some special poems and we had been practicing and practicing.

As midnight neared, the guests took seats in the living room and Hans played a few songs on the piano. Then, after he said some words of introduction, Judy entered the room dressed in a long, dark skirt and shawl, bent over and walking with a cane. As rehearsed, she spoke in a quavering voice:

I am 1952,
I'm old and tired and almost through . . .

Shivering in my costume, I listened through the kitchen door. Judy's part took a long time—she finished just before midnight. Then Hans played "Auld Lang Syne" on the piano and everybody sang along. When the last strains of music faded out, and everybody had kissed everybody else, I burst into the room, wearing only a diaper and a ribbon across my chest emblazoned with the numbers of the New Year. With great energy, I recited:

I am 1953,
I just was born as you can see . . .

I remembered all the right words and basked in the admiration I felt from the grown-ups. Hans's doggerel must have been clever enough. We were much acclaimed.

SOMETIMES HANS TOOK US down to his store in the West 30s. Seventh Avenue was lined with shops whose windows displayed black coats of curly Persian lamb, mink stoles, ermine muffs. Hans's name was written in big gold letters on the window of his store, along with those of his partners. This was most impressive.

I loved hanging around the store, where pelts were sold to the trade. When you walked in, there were several large tables heaped with mink and sometimes sable or chinchilla. Over the tables hung green, cone-shaped lamps. There was a particular musty smell which I found comforting. I would walk around the tables and bury my head in the piles of soft fur. Russian sable was my favorite—it was the softest. Even though the mink pelts often had the heads still attached, it never occurred to me that minks were conscious animals, like Percy and Peter.

I waited for Hans while he worked in his office upstairs with his brother Paul, who was also his partner. I watched whatever was going on, which wasn't much. Business, which had been lucrative for many years, was down. I knew this to be a source of friction between Hans and Ruth because I heard Ruth yell at him about it.

One winter day, Paul and I were seated alone in the car, parked on Seventh Avenue, waiting for Hans to come out. I was wearing my red wool coat and earmuffs and our breath made the windshield fog up. Paul took me on his lap. "Come, I'll keep you warm," he cooed in a high-pitched voice that made me wince. He put his hands under my coat and dress, rubbing my white tights between my legs! I tried to squirm away but he held me firmly, saying affectionately, "It's OK, don't worry." Where was Hans? I wished he would hurry. But I knew I couldn't tell him this shameful thing. It never happened again but I knew it was bad and that somehow it must be my fault.

AFTER JUDY HAD BEEN at the Krauses' for a year and a half, her mother remarried and took her back. So Judy had won our contest. I was beside myself with pain and jealousy, which were swiftly followed by rage. Now I was often alone in the house when Ruth was in the garden or at the grocer's.

One day, I watched myself as I turned the handle of the can opener, making the noise that always brought Percy running to the basement. Percy was the youngest of the four animals in the house. I loved him best and usually showered him with affection. This time, I grabbed him and beat him with a hairbrush, which was how Ruth punished him when he was naughty. He squirmed in my arms, but I would not let him go. When I stopped hitting him, I burst into tears, hugging and petting him and cooing endearments before I let him go. I'm ashamed to say that I did this more than once. Looking back, I think the worst part was that Percy always forgave me.

Hell may simply be the state of fully realizing the harm you have inflicted on another when you can no longer do anything to make amends.

MY FATHER SHOWED UP to visit me now and then. He usually brought a date, always a much younger woman. They would take me to restaurants in the city like Mike's Ship-Ahoy, where the tables were set inside real boats and the bar was made out of the side of a large yacht, complete with portholes. As was common in restaurants then, there was a roving photographer. I have several pictures of these outings, showing my handsome father in suit and tie, a lock of thick hair falling over his forehead and a lit cigarette dangling from his lips. A buxom woman sits across the table and next to her is me, a waiflike girl with wispy bangs and sad eyes above a Peter Pan collar, all dressed up for a date with Daddy.

At Mike's Ship-Ahoy with Daddy and his date

During my second year at Hans and Ruth's, my father brought the same woman, Fanya, several times in a row. She was Polish, my mother's age, and she was always very kind to me. I could tell when she talked to me that she felt sorry for me, just like my friends' parents did. Fanya and my father were married in 1953.

Soon after that, my mother's quest for a husband finally bore fruit. She met a man named Irving Freed and told me we were going to be married at last. Not only that, we were going to live in California! She would go first and send for me after the wedding. Although I was bitterly disappointed not to be at the ceremony as she had always promised, I was so happy that at last I would live with my mommy again. I was rescued!

At her small wedding, performed by a judge in Los Angeles, my mother wore a close-fitting, V-necked dress of white jersey, which showed her new suntan to advantage. It was cinched at the waist, the cocktail-length skirt flared by crinolines. She had lost a lot of weight and she looked radiant. The little white cloche on her head was sequined. From the pictures, it looked like a good party.

Bonnie and Riki in California

CHAPTER 3

LA, 1955

"Coffee and cigarettes, coffee and cigarettes." This was Irving Freed's constant refrain in his campaign to have my mother give up two of her favorite things. We lived with Irving in Los Angeles from 1954 until 1957, when I turned twelve. Our first home was in a Spanish-style two-family house on Bedford Avenue, a half block from the Beverly Hills city line; later, we moved to a snazzy new apartment with a balcony and a swimming pool. "Snazzy" was my mother's favorite word of approval then.

Irving was a man ahead of his time, a health food nut. He

got me to drink malteds made with eggs and Ovaltine—no sugary Bosco for us. We ate yogurt sprinkled with wheat germ, which Mommy and I had never heard of, and neither had anybody else. Irving said nicotine and caffeine were poisons, which proved to us that he was a fanatic. With his friend Charlie, Irving had developed his own formula for a multivitamin that he hoped would make his fortune in the Golden West. He loved tennis and spent much of his time at the Beverly Hills Tennis Courts, where he played chess for hours with the other men who hung out there. He taught me how to play chess, too. On weekends, we all went to watch tennis matches, where we saw famous players like Pancho Segura and Pancho Gonzales. It almost seemed we were a family. But as I relaxed into this new life, my resentment at having been sent to live in Ardsley began to bubble up. And I didn't like having to share Mommy with this boyish husband.

Irving had a grinning, suntanned face dotted with freckles, and red hair thinning around a shiny bald spot on top of his head. I liked him well enough, at first. He must have been around thirty-five. He called my mother first "Boopsie," then "Schnoozer." When he first arrived in California, before she joined him to get married, he sent letters back to New York addressed to Hannah Boopsie Kreiter. She saved them.

Our "snazzy" upstairs apartment was on Bedford. We rented it from the Lefkowitz family, who owned the house and lived downstairs. Esther, the mother, was a cousin of Irving's. Her son Neil became my playmate and partner in countless conspiracies. In the backseat of the car on our way to the beach, we'd crack each other up with our made-up word, "dahzee," which we repeated in response to everything and anything. We shared hours of hysteria dialing numbers from the phone book and informing whoever answered the phone that they were on the air, and could they answer the following question:

Who was buried in Grant's Tomb? The confused stranger might stammer, "uh, Grant," to which we shouted, "Mr. Gordon you have just won a new washing machine." Or we might just say "dah-zee," and hang up, convulsed with laughter.

Mommy loved California and I guess she loved Irving, too. It was during this time that she changed her name in her ongoing quest to be more American. I don't remember what explanation, if any, she gave but suddenly (or was it gradually?) everyone had to call her Bonnie—a much more American name than Hannah which, in German, is pronounced with a guttural first consonant. She never spoke German anymore and worked hard at losing her slight accent. She remained Bonnie until the day she died, in 1991. At my new school, she registered me with Irving's last name. It would avoid confusion, she said, so people wouldn't wonder why my last name was different from hers. So I was now Riki Freed.

Bonnie looked sensational in those years, with her wavy brown hair cut short, large eyes, and expressive features. In photos from that period she is thin, fit, and movie-star gorgeous. Once, in our local grocery store, we saw Charles Bronson. We recognized the then little-known actor from his TV role in an episode of *The Millionaire*, in which he portrayed that week's unsuspecting recipient of an anonymous gift of a million dollars from the reclusive benefactor John Beresford Tipton. I was thrilled to hear the admiring Bronson ask my mother out as they flirted over their shopping baskets. She blushed and said, "Oh, no. I'm married. This is my daughter," as if that explained everything.

During our first year in LA, Mother and Irving often took me along when they went folk dancing. Folk dancing took place in various gymnasia and halls around the city, where large numbers of white people met to do native dances from around the world: Slavic, Israeli, Austrian. Some people dressed in peasant costumes. Though I was too shy to try the dances myself, they were fun to watch. Through the newspapers we joined up with a large group, young families as well as singles, who went on monthly outings. In Irving's sky blue '52 Mercury convertible (a snazzy car) we drove to barbecues or picnics held at different ranches and estates in the area, or at the beach. On other weekends, we might just drive around the Hollywood Hills, looking at the mansions with the help of a map of movie stars' homes. LA was not a megalopolis then but a manageable—if you had a car—palm-lined city filled with stucco and tile architecture and only occasional smog.

We ate out often and had a favorite steak house in West Hollywood. There was a piano bar there; people drank cocktails. I liked my steak really rare and it was a standing joke among the three of us that I liked it *so* rare that the cow just walked through the fire. We didn't think of the cow as a sentient being. 'Til the end of her days, my mother subscribed to the all-American idea that eating steak was synonymous with good living.

On Bedford Avenue, there were three bedrooms in our upstairs half of the house. We rented one of them to a young actress who was trying to get into the movies and was having an affair with a famous married director. She would confide in my mother about this painful relationship as they sat at the kitchen table for hours, drinking coffee and smoking. Not infrequently, she cried. All her life, Bonnie had people, women and men, who poured their hearts out to her at the kitchen table. As long as she felt you were a victim, she was the most compassionate listener in the world.

By the age of eleven I was really into entertaining the grown-ups. Mommy was a great audience and Irving laughed too. On Sunday mornings we would sleep late, then read the newspapers. (It was a time in our life when we read the funnies—this was Irving's influence.) I would perform skits for them as they sat up in bed with the *LA Times* strewn around them. Mommy always cracked up when, after some silly monologue, I clapped my hand to my forehead and said in a melodramatic voice, "I must be gone," pivoting abruptly and marching out of the room.

She called me Sarah Heartburn.

When I was alone after school, I played records and danced around the living room, singing along with the scores of my favorite musicals, like *Seven Brides for Seven Brothers.* When Mommy and Irving had parties, sometimes she woke me up to come out and sing for their guests. Though I had only a middling voice, I sang with verve and I always believed the applause was enthusiastic. Once, I went on TV with my best friend, Joanne Handelman. There was a show called *Rocket to Stardom*, broadcast live every weekend from the Pan Pacific Auditorium. It began early Saturday morning and went on for thirty-six hours, to Sunday night. Anyone could go on stage in front of the cameras and sing, dance, or do any kind of act, even if you were eleven years old. There were judges who picked a winner every hour; these people later competed for the big prize. We thought you could get a movie contract. After all, Lana Turner had been discovered and became a star not that long ago, just sipping a soda in Schwab's drugstore on Sunset Boulevard. Joanne and I got her mother to drive us to Schwab's once. We had ice cream sodas at the counter, but nothing happened.

On *Rocket to Stardom*, Joanne sang the current Tony Bennett hit "Rags to Riches" in her pretty soprano voice. I sang "If I Were a Bell" from *Guys and Dolls.* I wore a navy blue satin dress with white polka dots and a stiff crinoline. Joanne's family, watching at home, said I was so pretty, they predicted I would be Miss America of 1963. We didn't win anything, but I felt very glamorous.

In LA, life was good for a while.

Since Irving's vitamin formula didn't take off, he got a job selling vacuum cleaners door to door. However, this didn't seem to interfere too much with his time at the tennis courts. I would see his car there when I walked by on my way to Carthay Circle Elementary School. Often the car was still there when I passed by again on my way back to Bedford Avenue.

• • •

I'M AMBLING HOME AT a leisurely pace in the California sunshine, my feet scraping the sidewalk. I turn right at La Cienega, "Restaurant Row," and go into Lawry's. La Cienega is lined with famous restaurants, only a few in our price range. At Lawry's, for twenty cents, I can order a waxed paper bag of crisp, hot French fries, with plenty of that delicious seasoned salt. Back on the street I savor them one by one as I continue my walk down Gregory Way. It's too nice out to hurry home to the empty apartment. I turn in at the tennis courts when I spot Irving's blue Merc in the parking lot, top down of course.

Sure enough, I find Irving at one of the stone tables inlaid with chessboards, immersed in a game with one of the other regulars, Louis Jean Heydt, the character actor. I played one of my first games with him when he came over to our house. Later I saw him on Million Dollar Movie with Humphrey Bogart in *The Big Sleep*. And I played chess with him!

Irving and Mr. Heydt greet me amicably before returning their attention to their game. I watch for a while, trying to follow, careful not to comment. Irving has taught me no one likes *kibitzers*. Mr. Heydt calls checkmate and Irving groans in a good-natured way. I decide I won't stay to watch the next game. I take the four blocks home at a quicker pace, hoping Neil is at the house.

• • •

I WAS ONLY HALF AWARE at first that Irving was supposed to be out selling vacuum cleaners, which he did on commission. My mother blew her stack whenever I mentioned I'd seen him at the courts. She was now working as a waitress in coffee shops, where she made good money in tips. Since she always expected a man to take care of us, she must have been angry that she had to work at all, though she was a really good waitress and took pride in that. It was one of the few things in her life she allowed herself to excel in.

In 1956 we moved to the newly built Buena Vista Apartments in Palms, just south of the Westwood Village and UCLA, so I guess Irving did make some money. Mommy decorated with her adored wrought iron furniture that included ultra-modern chairs, wing-shaped iron slung with brightly colored canvas seats. "Ultra-modern" was now the highest praise, even better than "snazzy."

I learned to swim like a fish in the pool with a girlfriend who lived in one of the other pastel-painted buildings set among winding flagstone walks. For supper, we grilled steaks on the balcony on a hibachi. After dinner Mommy, Irving, and I might play Rummy 500, an open-ended card game that could go on for hours. A particularly stealthy ploy in this game was known as a "Rickaroozer" because of my success using it to rack up points.

I loved watching the Million Dollar Movie. The same movie was on TV each day for a whole week, at seven each night plus matinees on Wednesday and Saturday. Sometimes, I'd watch every showing. (It's because of this that I saw Cary

Grant and Shirley Temple in *The Bachelor and the Bobby Soxer* nine times.) While I still loved to read, movies were my passion and I would go as often as I could. The only rule my mother made, as far as I recall, was that I could only go to one show a week. But she couldn't enforce it; she was at work when I came home from school and I always had the thirty-five cents it cost at the theater on Pico if you were under twelve. If I only saw a movie twice it meant I didn't like it that much.

I was going to be an actress, definitely. I had a "leather" bound scrapbook with my stage name, Viki Reed, carefully lettered on the first page. I filled its leaves with photos of stars like Elizabeth Taylor and Montgomery Clift, cut from movie magazines. One of my favorite pictures was Joan Collins reading in her bubble bath in a scene from *The Opposite Sex*. Movies showed how catty women were, especially Joan Collins. I vowed I'd never be like *them*.

• • •

IT'S A SATURDAY MORNING in spring and I am eleven-and-a half. I'm barely awake, stretching languidly in the early light, when I realize my body is covered in scratchy red bumps—hives. I'm about to panic when I hear the door close as Mommy returns from working the graveyard shift. I rush to the living room to show her.

"My God, Riki," she says as she whisks me into the car, still in my blue nylon shorty pajamas, clutching a blanket. The pediatrician's office is fifteen minutes away. When we arrive, the office isn't open yet. We wait in the car but after a few minutes the hives disappear. Mystified but relieved, Mommy starts to drive home. Stopping at an intersection, she glances over at me and a look of horror spreads across her face. My lower lip has swelled up to the size of a saucer. It doesn't hurt, though.

"My God, Riki," she screams, turning back toward the doctor's office. By the time we pull into the parking lot, my lip has returned to normal size. The doctor cannot find anything wrong with me.

On the way home, we stop at a drive-in for breakfast, to help us recover from these exhausting adventures. After the waitress on roller skates fastens the tray to the car door, my mother starts kidding me about my "Ubangi lip," referring to the African tribe we've seen in newsreels who stretch their lower lips on purpose. This tickles her funny bone; every time she says "Ubangi," she breaks up. By the time we get home we are both hysterical, laughing about my hives and my "Ubangi lip." We repair to our respective beds, she to join Irving, who is still asleep, me to read *War and Peace.* An hour later, feeling something wet, I find blood in the crotch of my pajamas. I jump up and burst into their bedroom.

"Mommy, Mommy!"

She sits up and I show her my hands, bloody from where I was touching myself. She explained everything about menstruation and sex years ago but my heart is pounding in response to the actuality of warm blood.

Her face lights up. "Oh, my God, Riki," she says in a delighted voice. "That's what's been happening. You got your period. I can't believe it! Irving, she got her period . . ."

I look at her in wonder as she laughs and gives me a big hug. A warm feeling spreads through me. It seems I have done something good.

• • •

IT WAS AROUND THIS time that family life turned sour again. Mother and Irving were fighting more and more. She wanted to have a baby but he said he wouldn't until she quit smoking and drinking coffee. He would shout at her in frustration, "Please, Schnoozer!" which I imitated to mock him when my mother and I were alone.

I escaped into fantasy as much as possible, reading or lying awake late into the night, imagining everything I would do if John Beresford Tipton gave *me* a million dollars. And when I was not escaping, I took it upon myself to make as much trouble as possible. I knew I was taking revenge for my two years at the Krauses'. Whatever she'd ask me to do, I'd say no, justifying it with some lawyerly argument. "Why do we have to eat steak on the patio every night? Why can't we just eat slop in the kitchen?" I would demand of my mother when she asked me to set the table.

I was driving her crazy, she said, screaming at me. Later, she blamed me for the breakup of the marriage.

he brakes squeal at a red light in Sloatsburg, one of the shabbier towns along Route 17. Olga sighs in her sleep and shifts in her seat to face the aisle. Run-down houses sit close to the road, nearly flush with the narrow sidewalks, and I try to peek through the windows as the bus lumbers by. Ever the voyeur. Unsuccessful, I lapse back into my thoughts. When was it that I realized that my time at the Krauses' had some surprising benefits? In therapy? In the est *Training? No, it was seeing my brother and sister beset by weight problems from such a young age. That certainly didn't come from their dad. Don was always skinny and more interested in drink than food. Despite the mocking resonance of "elephant foot," the disciplined meals and balanced "home" life in Ardsley saved me from the food issue. Every time I see those kids in Vegas, I witness my mother pile their plates high with food, yell at them if they don't eat it all, then tell them to conceal themselves behind someone else when posing for family pictures so they won't look fat. I grit my teeth remembering the shame on the face of my eleven-year-old sister.*

I always took my good-enough figure for granted . . .

CHAPTER 4
New Frontiers

B onnie and I moved back to New York from LA in December
1957. I had just turned twelve but people usually took me
for fourteen or fifteen. I had already been kissed by a sixteen-
year-old friend of Joanne Handelman's brother, who was
aghast when I told him my true age.

At first we stayed in the Upper West Side building where
my father lived with Fanya and their two kids, renting a room
in someone's apartment. Bonnie had taken up drinking when
her marriage with Irving collapsed and, like so many mothers
and daughters, she and I were more and more locked in mortal
combat. I was also angry on a semi-permanent basis with my
father, to whom Mommy still referred as "Sam, that bastard."
When his child support checks were late—almost every
month—she badgered me into calling him about it. He would
then accuse me of only seeing him when I wanted money.

And the endless questions he would ask! "Does your
mother have a lot of boyfriends? Does she give you fresh vegetables or do you only eat canned? You can tell me, darling."
(What was it with Bonnie and these health food nuts?) While I
often subsisted on spaghetti with Del Monte tomato sauce or
fried bologna and Minute Rice, cooking for myself while
Mommy was at work or at the bar, I balked at what I saw as my
father's attempts to control me. I'd be damned if I'd let *anyone*
control me—especially either one of my so-called parents.

Later I realized that Sam's harping on my questionable diet was his way of trying to be a good father.

BACK IN THE CITY, I pretty much felt I was at the center of the universe. Something was always going on, yet whatever it was seemed always just out of reach. The Upper West Side at that time was a heterogeneous neighborhood whose main avenues defined its cultures. The massive prewar apartment buildings on Central Park West, West End Avenue, and Riverside Drive were home to middle- and upper-middle-class Jewish families. Working class Irish- and Italian-Americans lived in brownstones on Amsterdam Avenue and its side streets. The other tenements in the neighborhood were filled with Puerto Ricans, who overflowed onto their stoops and fire escapes in the summer. On Columbus, men standing in front of the pungent-smelling *bodegas* would regale any passing woman between the ages of thirteen and sixty with lewd kissing noises and exclamations of "*mira, chiquita,*" or "*que linda* baby, can I help you carry your packages?" While I was intimidated by these unwelcome intrusions upon my privacy and dignity, I soon learned to ignore them.

I hated Joan of Arc Junior High School, from which I was frequently truant. As one of the middle-class Jewish kids, ghettoized in the "Enriched Learning" classes, I was routinely taunted by the tough Puerto Rican kids who outnumbered us by about twenty to one. But I was much more angry than afraid. I gradually developed a street-smart persona of my own and won the grudging respect of the aggressive girls in gym class. A yellowing report card from the eighth grade indicates that I was absent seventy full and twenty-one half days that year. The half days accrued when, unable to bear being in school, I would sneak down a back stairway at lunchtime, fling open the door onto 92nd Street and race toward Broadway and freedom, spirits soaring. When teachers and administrators spoke earnestly to me about being an underachiever, clucking sympathetically about my "difficult home life," it only made me want to cut school more. Except for getting 90s in French, which I loved, my marks were barely passing.

Although my grades suffered, I continued to read omnivorously. Reading was always a way of shutting out the realities of life with Mother. I also hung out in the street a lot, building an alternative family of friends.

MY BEST FRIEND, WHOM I met in seventh grade, was Ronnie Primus, a shy, well-bred blonde who suffered leers and other humiliations at school due to her already well-developed bust. Like me, Ronnie dreamed of being an actress. Her brother Barry was a professional actor at the start of a long career in television, theater, and movies.

Ronnie was close with her mother, a dowdy, overweight woman with thick glasses. Mrs. Primus was warm and understanding. I believe she had a master's degree in psychology, though she did not work. When we weren't dancing around the living room to *Johnny Mathis' Greatest Hits*, we girls spent hours talking with Ronnie's mother at the gray Formica table in their kitchen. I felt I could tell her everything. When things got unbearable at home, I sometimes called Mrs. Primus and asked if I could come over. She usually said yes.

Yet my mother and I still had our moments. In June of 1958, we sublet a two-bedroom apartment from a Czech couple who were going home to Europe for six months. Now, at least, we had our own place. It was in one of the gray stone prewar buildings on Riverside Drive. The apartment was filled with old rugs and heavy furniture, so like my grandparents' and the

Krauses'. Sitting at the table in the long narrow kitchen, we could talk for hours, Mommy still in her waitress uniform, listening attentively as I confided in her about my ever more engrossing social life. After taking off her thick white shoes with a sigh of relief, she'd sip scotch and milk out of one of our jelly jar glasses. Sometimes, she let me have a taste, knowing how I liked to feel grown-up. I'd tell her everything—how I worried about Ronnie getting picked on by the tough girls in gym, how I hated my social studies teacher. She was most interested when I talked about boys: who I had a crush on or when a boy flirted with me. She said I was going to be a heartbreaker because I was so pretty, and remember, "It's just as easy to love a rich man as a poor man, Riki."

Which was funny, because she never went out with rich men. She was currently dating the pipe-smoking son of our landlords, whom she had met through her international group of friends who worked at the UN. She told me he was nice but she wasn't in love with him. His name was Ivan but it was pronounced *ee-von*, like Yvonne Athens, one of the girls in the crowd of older kids who hung out in front of the Esquire Coffee Shop on 86th Street and Broadway.

Ronnie and I spent the summer of '58 scheming to ingratiate ourselves with this crowd of older kids who loitered regularly in front of the Esquire. On carefully picked evenings in July we would just happen to walk by that corner at seven o'clock, when ten or fifteen boys and girls would be standing around for an hour or two before (Ronnie and I were certain) they went off to do something terribly exciting. As we walked by, we casually smoked our Marlboros in the cool way we had practiced together, hoping one of the kids who knew us from school would stop us to talk. If that didn't happen, we would have to continue walking downtown, since we were pretending to be going somewhere, which we rarely were.

During the steamy afternoons, we stayed in my mother's air-conditioned bedroom while Bonnie was at work. There, between cigarettes, we drank iced tea and read Herman Wouk's *Marjorie Morningstar,* the story of a West Side Jewish girl like us who met an exciting artist, Noel, and won him. In our view, and to our scorn, she sold out in the end when she gave up Noel to marry good old Wally.

When we weren't reading, we rehearsed skits we made up and performed to some acclaim from our respective families. In one of them, Ronnie, costumed in a bathrobe with cold cream all over her face, played a distraught mother waiting up late for her errant teenage daughter (me). In another sketch, Ronnie played a therapist and I was her patient. The theme, which was repeated several times in our dialogue, to roars of laughter, was "A psychological question? A psychological answer!" I was a bit disgruntled, however, when the audiences laughed almost as much at the dramatic scenes as they did the comedic ones.

By the end of that summer, we were fully accepted by the Esquire crowd and became its youngest members, embroiled in the intricate relationships between boyfriends and girlfriends, best friends and "first-and-a-half" best friends and all the attendant dramas to which we had so fervently aspired. August days were passed with large groups of girls sitting in the grass at "The Courts" in Riverside Park, talking while the guys played basketball. Nights, we milled around in front of the Esquire, asking each other, "What do you want to do tonight?" Usually, we spent the whole evening this way. Sometimes, bored out of our minds, a group of us walked from The Esquire through Central Park to Madison Avenue where the rich kids hung out in front of the Croydon Coffee Shop after dates or parties on Saturday night. We knew them from dances we sometimes attended at their affluent Upper East Side synagogues. We called them the King Shits. They went to private schools and the girls wore forty-dollar sweaters. At these dances, I always stood against the wall, pretending I was too cool to dance when, in fact, my arms and legs stiffened with self-consciousness if I ever tried.

I still loved the movies and my friends and I went often. Loew's 83rd Street was that lost haven, an ornately decorated movie palace showing double features, with real butter for your popcorn and smoking in the balcony.

With my long auburn hair and big hazel eyes, I was called pretty despite the acne which plagued me throughout adolescence. It flattered me that people always thought I was older than my age but, as a matter of pride, I never lied about it, except if I were getting served in a bar. This happened first when I was fourteen. I was with Ellen Schwartz, who was a year older and had fake ID. For a lark, I ordered a 7 and 7 at Wilby's, a neighborhood bar that smelled of stale beer and cigarettes. I was amazed when the bartender didn't even blink. Even after turning eighteen, I continued to feel I might be caught out when ordering a drink.

I wanted to learn how to be cool from my older friends, and my wide-eyed eagerness attracted protectors. The boys in our crowd became my big brothers. Steve, a sweet, hulking guy of seventeen or eighteen, was *everybody's* big brother. One day, when I was fourteen, I was standing on 86th with Steve's arm draped over my shoulder. He was probably lecturing me about taking better care of myself, not drinking so much, etc. I didn't notice my father walk by on Broadway but a few days later, my mother announced that Daddy refused to send any child support checks until I was tested by a doctor to see if I was still a virgin.

"Bastard," she hissed.

"Bastard," I agreed, humiliated. My anger toward my father froze into hatred, but I had to go to the doctor: we needed the money.

SOMETIMES, WHEN WE CRASHED the King Shits' parties, a couple of our guys—like Pete Hartz, who later died of a heroin overdose, and Barry Taylor, who always wore a studded black leather jacket—would get into fights with the private school boys. We girls were embarrassed and indignant about such fights and would swear to have nothing to do with those goons ever again. For a while, the girls would just visit each other at home, meeting at Renee's big apartment on Central Park West or at Rochelle's on 98th Street. We formed a club called the Loc-ettes and started to write a play together. But soon the irresistible lure of boys worked its spell on our pubescent minds. One Saturday night, we nonchalantly ambled by the Esquire just to see who might be there, and soon we were all passing the hours together again.

Another hangout was on Broadway between 91st and 92nd. You'd go through a littered doorway and grimy vestibule past Bernie the Bookie, a stocky, middle-aged man in a brown suit and fedora, always standing there with the pad and pencil with which he conducted his business. Upstairs was the West End Bowling Alley. Here, at least, was a structured activity, if anyone had the sixty-five cents for a game. But if you sat around and weren't bowling you might get "carded," which meant the cops would give you a JD card. This identified you as a juvenile delinquent. I guess it was because liquor was served at the bar up there, though God knows we almost never had enough money to buy a drink. I never actually saw anyone get carded, but left in a hurry more than once when someone said in an urgent voice, "The cops are coming."

That summer our crowd got our own assigned social

worker, which I thought made us cool, like the Jets in *West Side Story*. This man hung out with us at the Courts as we lounged on the grass, chatting amiably, unobtrusively exerting a good influence on me by just listening and seeming to understand my world. At a local synagogue, an actor named Byrne Piven worked with kids in an after-school program. Years later, his son Jeremy became a well-known actor. In the spring, Byrne directed some of us in a Purim play, effectively keeping us off the street for a while. In the tradition of Purim, the boys played the female roles and vice versa. Ronnie was a smashing King Ahasuerus in the manner of Yul Brynner in *The King and I* with a lot of "et cetera, et cetera, et ceteras." I played wicked Haman of the three-cornered hat for whom the pastry is named. When I was acting, I felt like I was doing what I was best at. When the time came, Byrne coached Ronnie and me in the monologues required to audition for the High School of Performing Arts.

• • •

ELLEN, RONNIE, AND I climb up the subway steps and emerge into a Saturday night on Sheridan Square. Greenwich Village! I'm dressed in black Capri pants and a turtleneck and we're all wearing white lipstick and dangling copper earrings. We mingle with the crowds on MacDougal Street, indistinguishable, we hope, from real Beatniks. Walking past the Caffe Reggio I'm thinking that, for all I know, the bearded man in a beret, writing at a table in the window, is one of Jack Kerouac's thrilling friends.

"How much money have you got?" asks Ellen.

"Four dollars," says Ronnie.

"Three," say I.

"That's enough," says Ellen. "Let's go to the Café Wha."

We descend the stairs into a dark, low-ceilinged room full of exciting men—oh, and women too. As we edge our way to a table, I can feel the heads turning toward us: blond bombshell Ellen, her hair in a French twist (not very hep); Ronnie, with her stunning figure, always smoking; and me appearing more bohemian, I imagine, with my long hair falling over one eye.

We order coffee from a waitress in a black leotard. It's just like that café in *Funny Face* with Audrey Hepburn. Ronnie and I exchange excited smiles. Now a man dressed in black walks out into a spotlight in the center of the room. Another guy in shades sits down beside him and thwacks some bongo drums with a flourish. The buzz of conversation stills and the man begins to recite some free verse in a monotone with the bongos beating counterpoint. I'm not really following the words but respond to the jungle rhythm of the piece. When he finishes, the whole audience snaps their fingers together in appreciation and of course, we join in.

This is so groovy.

• • •

JUST AS OUR SUBLET ended, my mother fell in love with a man called Eddie and we moved to the Clifton, a comfortable residential hotel on 79th Street that had the advantage of requiring no security deposit, no month's rent in advance. Eddie was a good-time Charlie, an erstwhile musician who spent lavishly at the bar without regard to mundane niceties like the rent. He once treated Ronnie and me to an evening at the famous Copacabana nightclub to see Mickey Rooney perform. We both got a Copa matchbook with our picture on it. A few days later, when I came home from school, I found the lock to our door was stuffed so my key didn't work. They told me at the desk the lock would be unplugged when we paid the rent.

Humiliated and scared, I called Mommy at whatever coffee shop she worked in then. She said to call my father and go to his place for a couple of days. Eddie was gone. We moved down the block to the Lucerne. It was cheaper, but we soon got locked out of there, too.

AT THE BEGINNING OF ninth grade, Mommy and I were living in one big room in the Euclid Hall Hotel on 86th and Broadway, where we shared a bathroom with five or six neighbors on our floor. When you switched on the bathroom light at night, the whole floor moved: an undulating carpet of wall-to-wall cockroaches.

When I felt like cutting school, I would leave the room at 8:00 a.m. to meet Ellen at Gurner's, where we had toast and coffee each morning. I went back home after my mother left for work, spending hours reading in bed before going back to Gurner's to meet the girls when they got out of school. I played hooky for three weeks straight that winter. At the end of the third week, someone knocked on our door at seven thirty one morning. I opened it to find a stern Puerto Rican man wearing a hat and trench coat. He said he was a truant officer. My mother threw a fit when she learned she'd have to miss work to come to school with me and meet with Miss Gaines, the assistant principal. At the meeting, Mommy defended me, saying the schoolwork was too easy for me and they should have skipped me a grade, as she'd told them to when I first entered Joan of Arc. I said the right things about being sorry, turning over a new leaf, etc.

Miss Gaines, a well-groomed black woman in the style of Condoleeza Rice, walked me back to class, saying, "You're not one of the middling students, Riqui. You could do so well if you applied yourself. But I know how hard things are at home, dear." I listened with dull disinterest. What did school have to do with me, really?

Miss Gaines spoke with Mr. Kaye, my new Core teacher. He was a dynamic man with a crew cut of graying hair, and I sort of liked him. Core included major subjects like social studies and English, so we spent several hours a day in his classroom. Miss Gaines asked him to put together some work to help me catch up with the rest of the class, which he did, giving me detailed assignments. After about a week, I went truant again, missing three days of school in a row. The next time I walked into Mr. Kaye's class, I was surprised to find him glaring at me. The room was empty.

"Come here, Riqui," he said curtly. I walked over to his desk. "You know, I went to a lot of trouble to help you make up the work you missed and you didn't even have the courtesy to make an effort to do it." His ears were red. I was shocked—he was really angry at me! Like a laser piercing the fog, a light dawned. He had indeed gone out of his way to create the makeup assignments and I suddenly felt embarrassed that I'd ignored them. Mr. Kaye's anger—or the fact that he respected me enough to hold me responsible for my actions—catapulted me into a new relationship with my schoolwork. My work habits changed dramatically as I spent hours in the library writing a report on the history of Argentina.

In the spring, when the whole school was studying Japan, I was assigned to do a presentation on Buddhism. I found the subject fascinating and read numerous books, including classics like Alan Watts's *The Way of Zen*. When I studied the doctrine of reincarnation, I immediately felt it was true. With some bitterness I assented, "Yes, life *is* suffering, and we have to do it again and again." My oral presentation at the end of the year was crammed with too much information as I tried, in my enthusiasm, to explain everything I had learned to the class. I went on for far too long. Smiling, Mr. Kaye said I'd have to cut it short to give the other students a chance. On my final report card I got a "90" in Core. From then on, school became a source of satisfaction for me, especially when Ronnie and I finally got out of Joan of Arc and into the fascinating world of Performing Arts.

•   •   •

IT'S NOVEMBER 8, 1960, my fifteenth birthday. Election Day. At my party that evening, we're waiting to learn if our next president will be John F. Kennedy or Richard Nixon.

Don, the local bartender mom fell for while she was getting over Eddie, now lives with us. In the new "suite" we moved into upstairs, we have our own bathroom. A tiny vestibule opens onto the living room. There, atop Mommy and Don's dresser, is the *pièce de résistance* of my presents, a stuffed panda with fifteen one-dollar bills pinned down his chest and on his arms like buttons. (We had a tradition that I would get as many dollars as my age each birthday. I didn't know then that, because my age would soon outstrip my mother's budget, this would be the last time I'd get the full amount.)

Through the vestibule, in the spacious main room, a kitchen table sits on the right, set near the alcove where a stove, sink, and waist-high refrigerator can be concealed behind venetian blinds when not in use. The refrigerator is decorated with flowery decals, and various *tchotchkes* are placed around the room, as there always are in places we live in for more than one or two months. Mommy and Don's double bed, strewn with throw cushions, serves as the couch. A pair of gaily painted red maracas hang crossed on the wall over the fake fireplace. This is typical of my mother's idea of interior decoration, paid for with her waitress earnings.

Our hi-fi console stands on the left as you enter the room. We bought it cheap from a guy who had to leave town in a hurry, a friend of Mommy and Don's from the bar. The hi-fi came with something like five hundred LPs in mint condition. I still can't get over the fact that this guy had so many records without a single rock 'n' roll, jazz, or classical album, and barely a show score among them. His collection consists primarily of albums by Lawrence Welk, Montovani, and their ilk. However, the eleven Frank Sinatra albums make it all worthwhile for me.

French doors lead into my small bedroom and then the bathroom. Everyone has to go through my room to use the bathroom. My single bed faces the window overlooking Broadway. A dresser and mirror stand near a portable phonograph on a rickety metal stand. I spend hours lip-synching in front of the mirror to original cast recordings of *Gypsy* and *West Side Story*. Next to the window, a wooden wardrobe holds clothing I am ashamed to wear, mostly hand-me-downs. But tonight I have on a new black sheath dress with short puffed sleeves and faux leopard buttons and belt. I feel pretty.

All my girlfriends come to my party: Rochelle, with her fastidious ways; Renee, wearing a matching lavender skirt and vest over a pressed white shirt; Ellen Schwartz, of course; both Ronnies. Yvonne comes late, very upset because she's just broken up with Brucie Gordon (again!). Ronnie Primus is still my best friend; Unterman my first-and-a-half; Ellen is my second best, I guess. These things have a way of shifting monthly, like dunes in a Sahara sandstorm, which is what most of my adolescence feels like so far.

Later, in the many photos Uncle Bill will take, I'll be amazed at how sophisticated we girls appear. We are all wearing sheath dresses or sharply pleated skirts with stockings and high heels. (Stockings mean garter belts or girdles, too.) Ellen's blond hair is teased and sprayed into a French twist. Everyone is holding a cigarette in one shot or another, except my nine-year-old cousin Frank. Despite the black dress I look innocent, which I mostly am, though I spent hours one night last year sitting in a coffee shop, titillated as I listened to Rochelle and Ellen (both a year older) describe their heavy petting sessions with their boyfriends. As best friends, they have a sacred pact that when one of them loses her virginity, she'll immediately call the other one, no matter where she is, and say "Bingo." I think this is so cool. But I have vowed to stay a virgin 'til I am sixteen.

Tonight, Renee has brought her 45s and my girlfriends dance to the latest rock hits. Rochelle and Ellen show off the routines they practice after school while Ronnie watches languidly from a chair near the table, doing the French inhale which is now second nature. Renee dances the Philly with Yvonne. The Philly is a version of the Lindy danced on *American Bandstand*, a live TV show broadcast every afternoon from Philadelphia. I don't Lindy tonight, still painfully inhibited by paralyzing self-consciousness any time I try to dance socially.

.   .   .

IT TOOK FIVE YEARS of therapy in my twenties, and plenty of marijuana, to restore my deep and natural joy in dancing. Nevertheless, that night I was happy. I've always liked my birthdays, and I loved my girlfriends in an easy way and felt loved by them. My mother was crazy about parties and this one was a triumph. At nine o'clock, she unveiled a bakery cake with "Happy Birthday Riqui" written on it in pink icing, and everyone sang to me.

From time to time I went into my room, where Don had moved the TV, to watch as Chet Huntley and David Brinkley reported on the election results. I wanted Kennedy to win, of course, even though I had canvassed door-to-door for my mother's adored Adlai Stevenson to get the nomination. God knows we didn't want Nixon. At least Kennedy was a Democrat; he was young and handsome. If he won, the future might hold some promise.

Checking out the records on my fifteenth birthday

CHAPTER 5

Stagestruck

My love affair with the theater grew white-hot when I was twelve. The occasion was a visit by my grandmother from Israel. Uncle Ray and Aunt Mina took Omama, my mother, and me to see the original Broadway production of *West Side Story*. As the orchestra launched into that gorgeous overture, the hair on my arms prickled. By the time the curtain rose on the handsome Jets singing Sondheim's emotional song of life on my own streets, I was in ecstasy. And the dancing!

When we left LA, one of the carrots Mommy held out was that I could go to the High School of Performing Arts, unique in the country as a public school with professional training in the arts. In 1960, I knew I would die if I didn't get in.

To be accepted into the Drama Department, you had to prepare two monologues and do a cold reading with a senior drama major. Byrne Piven coached me on pieces from Shaw's *Saint Joan* and something from Ibsen. Only high drama for me, of course. Ronnie and I hugged each other with joy when we were both accepted. Perhaps it was emblematic that it was Joan herself who got me off the mean streets of Joan of Arc Junior High and into the hallowed precincts of Performing Arts. I felt I had finally found a place where I could be myself and thrive.

The school, later made famous in the movie and TV series *Fame*, was located on 46th Street, in the heart of the Theater District. At PA they taught the Stanislavski Method of acting, which Ronnie and I considered the only approach worthy of a true actress. To me the theater was, as Stanislavski had called it, "the Cathedral," and acting was its holy rite. I aspired to be its priestess.

I was no longer the only one in my class who came from a broken home. More important, the other kids at PA loved what I loved: Art. We disdained movies as lowbrow except, of course, the films of Bergman, Truffaut & Co. We spent hours in a booth in the Cup & Saucer Coffee Shop, arguing about Ayn Rand. (One kid, Skip, was an acolyte of hers and had to be dissuaded.) Lewis Cole, a student in the short-lived Playwriting Department, was our resident Marxist. At fourteen he was 6'3", as pimply as I was, and able to give a splendid Marxist analysis of anything, including *Hamlet*. He remained my friend for years, one of many treasured male friends I've had in my life.

PA students spent half the school day in academic courses, the other half in acting, dance, or music classes. Murray Perahia, later called by one critic "the finest concert pianist of his generation," was in my homeroom. We were privileged to hear him play often in our weekly assemblies in the dingy old auditorium.

The drama faculty taught us to take ourselves seriously as actors and held us to high standards. The course work was intensive, beginning with exercises like sense-memory, animal improvisations—even playing inanimate objects. (I still recall the stiff, metallic sensation of being a can opener.) We learned to break scenes down into beats and use our own experiences to find the truth of a part, stretching our bodies, imagination, and emotions.

After school I often went with classmates to plays on and

off-Broadway, thanks to student rates which almost all the theaters offered at that time. By the time I graduated, I had a stack of Playbills to my waist. I still rue discarding them in my 1975 post-*est* cleanout.

One performance I need no Playbill to recall is Uta Hagen's in Edward Albee's *Who's Afraid of Virginia Woolf?* The play was electrifying, not least because destructive, vulnerable Martha with her passion for mind games reminded me of my mother. Hagen gave a breathtaking performance of power and pathos that left sixteen-year-old me swooning in the last row of the balcony. For months after seeing it, I would pause to marvel on an evening or a Saturday afternoon, thinking, "My God, she's doing it again right now."

The old school had no gymnasium, a fact I loved. Instead of required gym class, drama majors got to study modern dance. Twice a week for three years, we practiced Martha Graham's challenging techniques in the small cafeteria, which doubled as our studio when we pushed the lunch tables against the walls. I'm still proud that, as a leotard-clad senior, I was finally able to touch my chest to the bumpy linoleum floor, between legs spread out 170 degrees, while holding the bottoms of my outstretched feet as our teacher, the long-legged Miss Trigg, intoned, "point, flex . . . point, flex."

PA students didn't perform in front of an outside audience until Senior Production, just before graduation. The faculty believed that premature public performance would detract from our artistic development. While some kids wished there were more public performances, for me, the audience was never primary. My satisfaction came from expressing myself on so many different levels. When a scene or even an exercise ("be an oyster") worked, I often felt wildly joyful.

Junior year I was in Mr. Olvin's acting class. Many students were afraid of him—he could be very harsh. In fact, he was the model for "Mr. Carp" in Priscilla Lopez's autobiographical song from *A Chorus Line*. Carp was an inspired alias for Olvin who, when engrossed while watching students do a scene, would unconsciously round his mouth, just like a fish, emphatically nodding his bald head up and down on the rare occasions when the work pleased him. Lopez sang about attending PA and being told by "Carp" that she would never be an actress. She was a year behind me in school but, thanks to Olvin's discouragement, she transferred to her neighborhood high school. Ten years later, she created a leading role in one of the biggest hits in Broadway history. In 2003 I saw her give a masterful performance, playing six different characters in a one-woman show written for her, called *Class Mothers of '68*.

Priscilla Lopez's story illustrates the destructive aspect of the training at PA: the experience of having one's youthful abilities evaluated on a scale of 100, as if it were a scientifically measurable quantity. Luckily, my teachers saw me as talented. The department asked four or five kids in my class to leave at the end of sophomore year due to their alleged lack of potential. One boy was so stagestruck he couldn't bear to go; since it was a public school, they couldn't force him to transfer. For the next two years he worked so hard, and improved so much that he was given the boys' acting award at graduation. (I lost out on the girls' award to Dorothy Smith.)

Dr. Marjorie Dycke, chairman of the Drama Department, was our Voice & Diction teacher. She was tall, handsome, and elegantly coiffed, with steely gray hair and a perfectly modulated voice. She called us "cherubs" in honeyed tones while instilling in us the pristine rules of Eastern Standard Speech. She always wore a fresh rose pinned to her tailored dress in a tiny little bud vase. From time to time she would drop a reference to "Sir Larry," meaning Olivier, whom we all had to grudgingly admire, even though he was not a Method Actor.

One end-of-the-year assignment in Voice & Diction was to find a recitation piece to demonstrate correct pronunciation of all the vowels, consonants, and diphthongs—while breathing deeply from the diaphragm, of course. My text was an anecdote taken from *Reader's Digest*:

> *George Bernard Shaw had been bored for several hours by a man who was trying to impress him. Finally, Shaw said, "You know, between the two of us we know all there is to be known."*
>
> *"How's that?" said the man.*
>
> *"Well," said Shaw, "you seem to know everything, except that you're a bore—and I know that."*

MY RELATIONSHIP WITH MY mother continued to deteriorate throughout high school. Between 1958 and 1962 we lived in seven places, mostly residential hotels. To avoid facing her pervasive guilt, shame, and rage, Bonnie drank heavily and created crisis after crisis, losing jobs, having unhappy love affairs, defeating herself and—by extension—me, at every turn. She liked to say, passionately, that I was part of her, intending this as a statement of how much she loved me. But when she was angry, her eyes narrowed with hatred and she called me a bitch or "a rotten egg." (Years later, it was my Freudian therapist who pointed out the resonance of this projection, coming from the fraternal twin who was identified as the bad one in contrast to her sister Noni, the product of the other "egg.")

One day, during the calm that followed a big fight she'd had with Don, I begged my mother to go into therapy. We were in the bedroom of Ellen Schwartz's apartment, which we were subletting while Ellen and her mother were in Florida, where they were planning to relocate. Don had stormed out before I got home and Bonnie was sitting up in bed, spent, with a gauze bandage wrapped around her wrist. After the worst happened, she tended to be calm and reasonable. Smoke drifted up from her Newport, burning on the edge of the blond wood night table, which, like the matching bureau, was dotted with scars from cigarettes placed on their sides when Bonnie was too distracted to find an ashtray. A long cylinder of ash was about to hit the carpet.

"Why won't you just try seeing a therapist?" I implored.

"Better to let sleeping dogs lie, Riqui," she said ominously, closing her eyes and sighing for emphasis. I knew what she meant. Inside, she felt like she was an exquisitely sensitive lump of seething flesh, organs without skin, all exposed nerves. Or was that me?

In my heart, I ached for the beloved Mommy of my childhood; I wished I could make her feel safe and happy. But I knew from experience that this was impossible.

AS AN ANTIDOTE TO life with mother, there were boys.

Since I'd turned twelve—or five, if you count my father—boys had been telling me how pretty I was: complimenting my thick hair and long-lashed eyes, my sultry voice. I was always taken to be three or four years older than my age, so these attentions also came from older men.

Of course, Bonnie thought this was great. Her approval, however, was not unmixed with jealousy. She often flirted with the boys who picked me up at the house. After all, any female's worth rose or fell in direct proportion to her power over the opposite sex, didn't it? And rebellious as I was, I was still my mother's daughter.

In LA, I had "made out" a little with Joanne's sixteen-year-old brother and, another time, with a handsome blond friend of his in a car at the beach. In junior high, I learned to love long necking sessions. At parties I endured dancing the fish with some boy droning in your ear—*Tears on my pillow, pain in my heart* . . .—feeling that scary hardness as he pressed his groin against mine. When the lights were turned down, couples grew silent on all the chairs and sofas; we'd find out the next day who got to first or second base. I loved losing myself in the backseat of some King Shit's car, in the wet warmth of lips and tongue, in the glow of hearing how delicious I was. This was a revelation of how life could be, almost like in the movies I ate up with insatiable gusto.

One day during junior year, as I was walking home from a movie, I bumped into Steve Simon, an older boy I knew peripherally from the neighborhood. I'd heard he'd married Georgia who, I knew from neighborhood gossip, had been crazy about him and suffered over it. They were the first couple I'd known of to marry. Now, Steve told me their marriage was over and he'd moved back in with his mother and younger brother. He wasn't exactly a King Shit but he had grown up on Central Park West and gone to private school. Steve was twenty, and instead of going to college he was working downtown as a film editor—impressive. He was about 5'6", with a soft face and a tendency to fat. In an attempt to have more *gravitas* at work, he sprayed silver hair color at his temples. As we chatted that day, he kept laughing at my wry comments in a flattering way and telling me how pretty I was. He said I had to go out with him.

Steve was my first real boyfriend. In our early months together, he often told me I was the best thing to happen to him. I was enchanted by his affection and near-constant praise. He seemed to me a person of great sensitivity, too. He lived in a high-rent prewar building across from Central Park. Since returning home, he stayed in the tiny maid's room next to the kitchen. I would go over to his place almost every evening and all weekend, spending so much time there, I almost lost my self-consciousness when I said hello to the doorman in his white gloves and uniform.

His mother, a Slavic blonde who reminded me of Zsa Zsa Gabor, worked as a stock broker and was seldom home. Steve's brother was out a lot, too; even when they were home, their bedrooms were so far away from Steve's I can barely remember seeing them at all. They seldom ate or watched TV together. The sunken living room with deep white carpeting and white sofas covered in plastic was used only on the rare occasions when there was company. Steve hated his mother but spoke often of his father, who'd died a couple of years earlier. His dad had been a musician and part owner of the famous Latin Quarter nightclub, but had had financial reverses before his death at age forty-seven. In Steve's mind his father was a hero, a titan brought down by a selfish wife who couldn't forgive him for losing his fortune. Steve's warm brown eyes welled with tears when he spoke of his father, and I cried with him. When he wanted something from me, say, to spend New Year's Day with him instead of with my mother, Steve would, when all else failed, look at me intensely and say, "Don't you understand? My father is dead!" So of course I'd try to comfort him as best I could and agree to stay, bracing for the screaming fight with my mother who was, by then (since she'd split up with Don), in full-blown competition with Steve. "You're spending too much time with him, Riqui," shouted Bonnie. "What about your family, Riqui? I want you to come to Noni and Billy's on New Year's."

Steve and I spent hours necking and petting while he feverishly declared how much he loved me, how he needed me, how painful it was for him not to have sexual release. After months of this, the urgency of his entreaties persuaded me that it was about time to "go all the way." After all, I knew he loved me and I was in thrall to his passion. He'd even given me his father's pinky ring to wear around my neck, a heavy gold band with the initials "SS" set in a square, spelled out in diamonds. And I *was* sixteen, the age I'd said I'd wait for.

So it was that, on a rainy evening in March, we finally made love. We'd planned it so that I could spend the night, telling my mother I was sleeping at Rochelle's. What—you should excuse the expression—an anticlimax! A bit of pain, some hasty activity (which felt good while it lasted) and then the whole thing was over. Afterward, I lay on my back in the narrow bed in the dark while Steve went to get the pint of Breyer's ice cream he ate every night before bed. The kitchen light angled through the half-open door. I felt like I could almost see the question marks bobbing above my head.

This was *it?*

Later, as he fed me vanilla fudge from his spoon, Steve declared how wonderful it had been, how happy he was, so of course I felt a warm glow. Our five-minute couplings went on for the next few months. He taught me that the reason he always ejaculated so quickly was that I was so great in bed. The best thing about sex was how it evoked Steve's praise and declarations of undying love.

But as months passed, his extravagant praise abated. Soon there were reasons why he couldn't see me after work. I couldn't believe this was happening and begged him to tell me what was wrong. The good thing was that he *did* say tenderly, "You're beautiful when you cry," so that was reassuring, right? But he continued to cut short our dates.

One Saturday afternoon, he told me he had to go back to work on a big project that evening. We said good-bye in front of his building on Central Park West. He explained again why he couldn't see me tomorrow. I protested, begging him to see me again after work. Making an impatient gesture with his hand, he said with distaste, "You're so possessive. I don't think we should see each other anymore."

What? Could he really be saying this to me?

"What do you mean?"

"I'm under enough pressure at work. I don't need more from you."

I sobbed, I entreated. He walked away.

I staggered home in a dumbfounded state, buckling to the living room floor in tears as soon as I got through the door. My mother was working the swing shift so she wouldn't be home 'til after midnight. So I just lay there on my back. Ellen's apartment was on the ground floor. Every time I heard the lobby doors open I'd think, is that him? It must be him coming back. Seven o'clock. Nine o'clock. I continued to sob until crying felt like a permanent state. Wait, I heard the door. Was that him? Eventually, I fell asleep. It wasn't until thirty years later that I learned Steve had been dating one of my classmates at that time.

A SHORT TIME AFTER this, I came home from school one day with my friend Alice to find empty rooms and our belongings dumped in the middle of the floor in both bedrooms. I called my mother at work to tell her, my voice trembling. It seemed Ellen's mother had come home unexpectedly and, infuriated by the damage we'd done to their furniture, had removed everything. Mommy said I should call my father to see if I could stay with him for a while. She got us a new hotel room within a few days and life went on.

Throughout junior year, I stayed out with my friends as much as possible. When I was home, I criticized Bonnie at every turn, contemptuously refusing to do anything she asked of me. After living in this battle zone for two years, Don, who was kind but ineffectual, moved out. So, in the summer of '62, my mother and I were sharing a small bedroom in a two-room suite at the Kimberly Hotel on 74th and Broadway. I got a job selling fashion accessories at Franklin Simon, a downtown department store, so now at least I had my own spending money. When senior year started, I continued to work on Monday and Thursday nights and all day Saturday. By October, Bonnie and I rarely talked to each other without sniping or screaming. The fights became so bad that she finally agreed to let me move out, saying if we continued to live together, one of us would probably end up dead, by murder or suicide. I thought so, too. I was sixteen.

I MOVED IN WITH Stephanie Davis, my twenty-one-year-old supervisor at Franklin Simon. My father's sixty-five-dollars-a-month child support check covered the rent; my mother, aunts, and uncles helped me with the rest of my living expenses.

Stephanie's apartment was in a three-story walkup in a quiet Bronx neighborhood, where you commonly heard the musical mix of Irish brogues in the local markets. It took me almost an hour to get to school on the D train, but at last I felt I had real freedom and control over my own life. The furnished apartment had two small bedrooms, a tiny kitchen, and a living room with a linoleum floor where we had our Formica table, a couch, and a fake fireplace—well, really just a painted wooden mantelpiece placed against one wall. With my earnings from Franklin Simon, I bought a little hi-fi to play the beloved records I'd brought from home.

Stephanie was cheerful and easy to get along with, though we had little in common. She was a tidy blonde with a short, no nonsense haircut. She wore straight skirts with soft nylon blouses and low-heeled pumps which flattered her shapely legs. She spoke with a limited vocabulary in the broad accent of her native Massachusetts. Though I could never discuss a book with her, or the psychology of a relationship, I admired the capable way she dealt with practical matters as manager of the Fashion Accessories Department. We did share a lusty appreciation of men and had bonded when we realized, while gossiping at the fashion accessories counter one slow, rainy evening, that we both had had an affair with the same married store manager.

When I first moved in, Stephanie was protective of me, teaching me how to prepare meals, do laundry, manage shopping, and pay the bills on time. It felt good to have a peaceful home. Having my own apartment pretty much made me the queen of cool among my friends at school. By senior year, I hung out less and less with Ronnie Primus, whom I viewed now as pathetically sheltered, and spent more time with Alice and Rose, faster girls more in tune with my taste for liquor and older men. Alice had also gone to Joan of Arc. She was a skinny, voluble girl with huge black eyes and a husky voice. Rose was blond and *zaftig*, with sensuous lips and seductive ways.

Even though I loved school now and was getting good grades, I was occasionally inspired to cut classes with Alice after lingering over morning coffee at the Cup & Saucer. We'd walk the four blocks to Radio City to catch the 11:00 a.m. movie, stopping on the way to pick up a half pint of Kentucky Gentleman Bourbon, easily concealed in a pocketbook. Several flights up the grand staircase, in the balcony which we often had entirely to ourselves, we'd prop our legs on the seats in front of us, smoking and drinking bourbon and Coke as we watched the elaborate stage show, Rockettes and all, performed between each showing of the movie, even if there were only thirty people in the palatial theater.

My friends also shared cozy afternoons in my Bronx

apartment, sitting around the living room listening to Barbra Streisand records, smoking Marlboros, and having long, earnest talks. Ronnie even came up a couple of times. It is hard to remember now how splendid it was to hear Barbra Streisand for the first time, before she became a phenomenon. I was blown away by her fresh, passionate style as well as her matchless voice. And of course, the drama of the songs she chose. I wore out her first three albums, along with Sammy Davis, Jr.'s *Showstoppers* and the albums of my perennial love, Frank Sinatra.

ONE TUESDAY NIGHT IN March, the phone rang in my Bronx apartment.

"Hello."

"Riqui? This is Sylvia Primus."

"Hi," I said, mystified by this unexpected call. I hadn't seen Ronnie's mother since sophomore year.

"Riqui, dear, I'm calling to ask that you stay away from Ronnie. I'm afraid you've become a bad influence on her."

I felt my face flush. Hot tears sprang to my eyes. Holding my voice as steady as I could, I murmured, "Oh."

"I understand you encourage the girls not to listen to their mothers."

This was true. I had taken to lumping all mothers together in my mind, and arguing to one and all that mothers were the enemies of free spirits. I suppose I was jealous of girls who had better relationships with their moms than I did. Apparently, Ronnie still told Mrs. Primus everything, as I had done myself not that long ago.

"It's nothing against you, dear," she continued. "I know you're very angry with Mother, and with good reason." I hated the way she used "Mother" as a proper noun, and the saccharine sound of "dear."

"You know how impressionable Ronnie is," she continued in an even voice. "It is very important for her to have a good relationship with me. Will you promise me to stay away from her?"

I managed to squeeze out "Yes" through my constricted throat.

"I don't mean to hurt you, dear. I just want to protect Ronnie."

After saying good-bye, I threw myself on the bed, sobbing. I always knew I was too dirty to be friends with wholesome Ronnie. I just wished I could disappear.

I DID STOP SEEING Ronnie Primus, but we became friendly again when I was in college and she moved in across the street from me. She had married at nineteen—the only way she could get out of her house, I thought—and was divorced soon after. Later, she became a columnist for the trade paper *Back Stage*, writing under her middle name, Francesca. In our thirties, reconnecting at a class reunion, we got together a few times and even met for lunch once, at The Rose Cafe in Venice, California, when we both happened to be in LA at the same time. After that, I lost touch with her again. Later, I read this in *Back Stage*:

> *Theatre writer, critic, and dramaturge Francesca Primus died of lung cancer in New York City in 1992 at the age of 45. She wrote eloquently on the role of women in theatre and the regional theatre movement in her monthly column, "Cross-Country Stages," for Back Stage.*

I was stunned when I heard of her death. For months, obsessively, I replayed in my mind scenes in Riverside Park when we were thirteen where, at her request, I taught Ronnie how to do the French inhale. This consisted of letting cigarette smoke drift gracefully over your upper lip to the nostrils before you blew it out.

We just wanted to be Bette Davis.

Now there is a Francesca Ronnie Primus Prize for pioneering new plays written by a woman.

AS GRADUATION APPROACHED, I became more and more anxious. Soon I would have to leave Performing Arts, the oasis of safety where I had experienced approval and a sense of mastery of the work I loved.

I started going to more and more parties, hanging out with older boys and men. I developed a taste for scotch. I felt quite sophisticated when I ordered "Dewars on the rocks with a twist," copying Ellen Schwartz. When I was drunk, I didn't care about my pain or anything else.

• • •

IT IS EARLY JUNE and I find myself at an after-hours party on the ninth floor of an East Side apartment building. Rose and I are here with Vinnie, a seedy man in his thirties or forties who is "an associate" of a girlfriend's father. The sun is just rising over the East River. I am aware that I am in something of a drunken haze.

I sit in a corner watching the others, adults who are talking too loudly, pouring drinks, dropping ashes on the rug. On the hi-fi, Sinatra croons. I glance out the window and think how peaceful it looks out there. I've always loved sunrise.

No one notices when I climb up on the windowsill and step outside—not even me. I'm surprised at how easy it is, finding a place to escape the noise. The stone ledge is several inches longer than my feet. Moving to the side of the window, I lean back against the rough wall of the building. The sky is a lovely rosy color and the morning air is cool. I can hardly hear the cars, nine stories below. I look over at the ironwork of the 59th Street Bridge, starkly outlined against the pink and gold sky, and take in a deep breath. For once, I feel at peace.

Suddenly, Rose's round face appears through the window near my feet.

"Riqui! What are you doing? Get in here!"

I'm startled. "I'm fine," I assure her. "It's great out here."

"Goddammit, Riqui," she hisses.

Rose withdraws and is replaced by Vinnie, his pasty face even whiter than it was before. "Come back in, honey—I'll help you." I realize now they think I might jump. How ignorant they are. Vinnie reaches his arm out toward me. "Here, take my hand." He glances fearfully down toward the street, where traffic is beginning to pick up, and I look down for the first time.

My chest tightens. Suddenly, it's hard to breathe. "No, no. I can do it," I stammer as I make my way back into the room. The party has stopped and everyone is looking at me as I crawl in over the windowsill. I'm unnerved by all the fuss.

"I just wanted to see what it felt like," I tell them in a shaking voice, embarrassed. But truth be told, I do enjoy the attention.

 · · ·

ROSE, ALICE, AND I were also hanging out with some college guys, smart, cynical boys I knew from my old neighborhood who thought it was cool to compete to see who the biggest "low-life" was. Stephanie had slept with one of them; she had a crush on him but he treated her with contempt. Dean, the one I liked, drove a Corvette.

I remember one rowdy dinner for five in our living room.

It must have been May of senior year—the guys were already out of school for the summer. Rose was there but Stephanie was working that night. The table was set around a candle burning in a straw-covered Chianti bottle already layered with multicolored wax drippings. The spicy fragrance of marijuana hung in the air. We were all stoned and drunk on red wine. As the jokes came fast and furious, Bobby was ostentatiously slobbering over his food, which only made the rest of us laugh louder. When we were done, we stubbed our cigarettes out in the remains of our spaghetti and meat sauce. Stephanie came home around ten thirty and, while polite as ever, she retreated quickly, closing the door to her bedroom, which couldn't possibly have shut out the noise of our carousing.

Not long after this I came home from school to find a note from Stephanie, informing me that she had moved out. She included her new address and phone number in Manhattan. *Déjà vu.* I sat in her bedroom, opening and closing the empty bureau drawers one by one. I took this as another confirmation of my unwholesomeness—I was just like my mother. However, Stephanie and I stayed in touch. It was just my friends she couldn't stand, she assured me.

Stephanie soon married a young guy who worked as a stock boy in Franklin Simon. He worshiped her and they lived together in apparent harmony for some years, neighbors of mine when I was in college. In 1970, when I was living in California, I got a call from Stephanie's sister in Andover, asking me if I knew where Stephanie was. It seemed her husband had come home one night to find that Stephanie had run off with a shoe salesman from Bamberger's, the New Jersey department store where she was then working as a floor manager. The shoe salesman had a pregnant wife. Stephanie's sister said that their mother had died and if I ever heard from Stephanie, would I please let her know.

. . .

MEANWHILE, BACK IN HIGH school, I was caught drinking in the girls' room on Senior Day and sent to see the principal, who told me I would graduate over his dead body. But I did graduate and I took special satisfaction in receiving the French Award—a one-year membership in the *Alliance Française*—from his hand during the commencement ceremony.

A few weeks after Stephanie decamped I got a call from Laurie Evans, whom I'd known slightly from PA. She was finishing her first year at the Bronx campus of NYU and had heard I was looking for a roommate. So Laurie moved in and shared the rent for my last few months in the Bronx.

MY FATHER'S CHILD SUPPORT obligation (and thus, my rent money) would end when I turned eighteen in November. I needed a place to live while I saved enough money to get my own place in Manhattan. Meanwhile, my mother and Don had reconciled and were now married. Bonnie had given birth to a little girl and seemed happy at last. So in the fall of 1963, I went to live with this new family in their apartment in the basement of a big private house on an ocean block in Manhattan Beach, Brooklyn. I shared a room with my baby sister, who smiled in delight when I dandled her on my knee. Perhaps, unconsciously, I hoped that now I could have the "normal" family life I had longed for. But, as my eighteenth birthday approached, I was depressed. I wrote to Lewis Cole, who was spending a lonely first semester at McGill in Montreal. Like my father, I kept copies of my letters:

> *Saturday night I was very depressed in an unusual way. . . .*
> *I just started to cry and wanted to die. Then my mother got*

very sad and said that you never know what the next year will bring. "If you would have told me last year," she said, "that I would be so happy this year . . ." and she trailed off thoughtfully. "Last year I had nothing. This year I have you and Don and a brand-new baby. I have a home and I don't have to work. One never knows."

That autumn, Alice, Rose, and I took a professional acting class with Michael Kahn at the Circle in the Square Theater. (Kahn was later the longtime head of the Drama Department at Julliard.) For his class, Michael suggested I do a scene from *A Streetcar Named Desire*. It wasn't the first time I'd been cast as one of Tennessee Williams's desperately vulnerable heroines.

A woman named Louise played Stella in the reunion scene between the Southern sisters. I was Blanche, who guiltily tells Stella (married to the earthy Stanley Kowalski) of the loss of their family estate, after the deaths of other members of their family.

At the end of the speech when Blanche's anguish rises to a crescendo, she slaps Stella. When we did the scene in class, a wanton anger seized me. Instead of the staged slap we had rehearsed, my right arm swung back and, without my willing it, struck my partner full in the face. Fingerprints appeared on her cheek. Louise was very professional, and just went on with the scene.

*O*lga wakens when the bus pulls into *The Red Apple Rest*, just past all the faux Tudor buildings of Tuxedo, New York. "I fell asleep," she announces.

We debark with the other spiritual seekers to use the restrooms and to get a snack in the dingy eatery, a historic milestone on the NYC–Catskill route. I remember how glamorous I thought it when, in senior year, Dean drove me up here at 2:00 a.m. after a party, just to take a ride in his red Corvette. Then, it was crowded and we had to wait on line to get coffee and a thin, greasy hamburger. We drove home, no longer high, to see the sun rising over the Manhattan skyline, visible in the distance from the hilly parts of Route 17.

Today, there are few customers and the tables are littered with empty paper cups and crumbs. To forestall any friendly overtures, I take my coffee outside. The coffee is as bad as I remember and, still my mother's daughter, I take pleasure in the immortal combination of coffee and cigarette. I draw deeply on my Marlboro as I recall the hot sex I had with Dean that summer before he went back to college and I moved on to ever more desperate grabs at—what? Relief from the inner demons, yes, but more—finding a home. Yes, home.

At least now, perhaps I'm looking in the right places.

CHAPTER 6
JFK & Me

I n the spring of 1960, the street corners of the Upper West Side sprouted card tables with petitions to get Adlai Stevenson the nomination as the Democratic candidate for president. Stevenson was the darling of my mother and the whole neighborhood, as he had been in '52 and '56. I was recruited to help by canvassing door-to-door in the big apartment buildings, clipboard with petition in hand. Despite our somewhat quixotic efforts, John F. Kennedy became the Democratic candidate.

Because of my participation in the Stevenson campaign, I once saw Kennedy in person. My name must have been on some list of Democratic volunteers because, that September, I received an invitation to attend a Democratic fundraiser and rally to unify the party, to be held at the Waldorf Astoria. It was the first time I had ever been to the Waldorf and I could hardly get over *that* to begin with. I arrived late, clutching my invitation, gawking at everything and tiptoeing in awe around the plush-carpeted lobbies. I expected to be thrown out at any moment.

In a balcony above the Grand Ballroom, I craned my neck to catch a glimpse, between the shoulders of the adults in front of me, of Kennedy on the stage far below. Even from that far away I could feel the palpable shock of his charisma. He was movie-star handsome. His hair was redder than I'd thought and the glamour of his young wife, standing beside him in her perfectly tailored suit, enhanced that impression. Truman and Eisenhower had been the only presidents in my life. This man was a totally different species from those gray-suited, gray-faced politicians of the fifties. Despite my passionate loyalty to Stevenson, I couldn't help but be wowed by the Kennedys that night.

• • •

IT IS NOVEMBER 22, 1963. I'm working at the Julius Matthews Special Agency in a brand-new office building at 757 Third Avenue, still only half occupied. This is my first full-time job, obtained a few weeks after graduating from PA last June. The agency is in the business of selling advertising space for a variety of small-market newspapers, including the fledgling Gannett chain of six papers. The owner is a blond, suntanned man in button-down shirts and expensive suits. Thanks to having dropped chemistry for typing during my last year in high school, I am now secretary to one of the three sales reps. My job consists of little more than screening his phone calls, typing a few simple letters, and making reservations at the Pen & Pencil Restaurant for his three-martini lunches. The rest of the time in the office I spend gossiping with the two other secretaries, Shelley, a wisecracking brunette from Long Island, and Maureen, the owner's secretary, an older woman of twenty-five who doubles as receptionist in the quiet office. From Maureen I learned to use the levers on the monitor board switching system so I can handle incoming calls when she goes to lunch or takes a day off. I like the easy feeling of competence I get from this job.

I am covering the board. It's Friday, payday, so I know Maureen may take some extra time for lunch with her friends from the Bronx. I don't mind.

Line one lights up and I depress the lever.

"Julius Matthews Special Agency . . ."

"Riqui?" It's Alice calling from home. Her voice sounds funny.

"Yeah, Alice. What's wrong?"

"Kennedy's been shot. It's on the news."

Knowing Alice to be given to hysteria, I patiently reply, "Now Alice, if you listen again, you'll see that you're mistaken."

"No, it's true," she insists. "Walter Cronkite's on. He's crying."

"Alice . . ." I say doubtfully.

"Listen," she shrieks, holding the receiver up to the television. Then I hear the nation's preeminent newscaster and father figure reporting, his voice cracking: ". . . thirty-fifth President of the United States died at 1:00 p.m. Central Standard Time . . ."

"My God," I say, stunned.

I arrange to meet Alice right after work. I hang up and tell Shelley. Everyone else is out to lunch. Just then, Maureen walks in and confirms the news has spread through the streets. On Third Avenue, New Yorkers are in tears.

That night, Alice and I go to the movies. The Riverside, my old neighborhood movie house, is packed—it looks like there isn't a single empty seat. As we have done so many times when we cut out of school, Alice and I share a pint of Kentucky Gentleman, which we pour into our Cokes out of a brown paper bag. I have no idea what we are watching; I don't think anyone else knows, either.

• • •

THE TV WAS ON all Saturday morning in my mother's basement apartment in Brooklyn, just like it was everywhere else in America. We followed the unbelievable events as they unfolded. I couldn't begin to take in what had happened. I spent a lot of time on the phone with my friends. Maxine, who had graduated from Performing Arts the year before me, told me that some friends of hers from Queens College were planning to drive to Washington that night; Kennedy's body was to go on view on Sunday morning. I arranged for me, Alice, and Helen, another PA classmate, to ride with them. I hoped that somehow this trip would help me break through the stubborn sense of unreality that enveloped me like a cloud.

We met that evening in the Queens apartment of this guy named Steve Hagen and hung out for a while, waiting for Bill, the other rider, to show up. We set off at ten o'clock. Alice and Helen sat in the back and slept for most of the trip. The car radio was dead, so Bill and I sang all the way to DC to help keep Steve awake at the wheel. Bill knew as many lyrics of the old standards as I did: we sang Gershwin, Cole Porter, the entire score of *West Side Story*, and everything else we could think of. Every once in a while, we'd remember why we were traveling and look at each other with fearful, amazed eyes. Then we quickly started singing again.

It was still dark when we arrived in Washington at around 4:00 a.m. I had never been there before. The monumental buildings seemed ominous to me. There were many people around but an unnatural quiet pervaded the streets as we walked to reach the line that was forming in back of the Capitol. The doors to the Great Rotunda were scheduled to open at eight o'clock. All kinds of people were on line: old and young, black and white. Everyone spoke in hushed tones; I don't remember what we talked about. Alice, usually a nonstop talker, was abnormally silent, and Helen seemed to be in a fugue state. I hadn't slept for twenty-four hours.

We waited on that line for hours in an atmosphere that

was totally surreal. Time slowed to a trickle. People were talking to each other about random things. When it started getting light, some went off to bring back cups of coffee in cardboard containers. Others listened to the news on transistor radios. After a few hours, standing in line came to seem like an end in itself. My mind still refused to grasp what had happened. Such things just didn't happen in America, which was strong and safe and good—everybody knew that.

What I hadn't noticed in the preceding year and a half was how the spirit of Kennedy's presidency had crept up on me, giving me hope for the future despite my habitual resistance to any kind of optimism. The quality of intellect of the men he brought to Washington; the rejuvenating rhetoric; the New Frontier programs. I had gotten goose bumps listening to his inauguration speech, when he said, "Ask not what your country can do for you; ask what you can do for your country" before it was a famous sound bite—before the whole world was filled with hollow sound bites. A few weeks earlier, just before I turned eighteen, I sent away for brochures about joining the Peace Corps. Just having this option made my sad world feel like a better place, a place where my country could be a force to uplift the lives of the downtrodden and dispossessed.

By the time the November morning turned from dark to gray, the line behind the Rotunda stretched back for a mile. The DC police were not prepared for the thousands who had come to Washington. There were some scary moments when cars started passing through a road intersecting the loosely organized line of people. Suddenly, the crowd behind us surged forward to make room for the cars. I almost panicked when it seemed we might be crushed. After a while, the police got things under control as traffic systems were put in place. Calm settled over the line once again.

At one point a middle-aged black man with a transistor

radio started shouting, "Harvey's been shot, Harvey's been shot."

"Who?" people murmured to each other. "Who?"

By the time I realized that he meant Lee Harvey Oswald, it hardly seemed to make a difference. I guess I was in a fugue state, too. People talked in a desultory fashion about Oswald's shooting for a while. Then it became quiet again and the waiting continued.

Finally, the doors to the Capitol opened and the line started to move. At about ten fifteen we entered the Rotunda. The stone floor and imposing space seemed to magnify the silence. The coffin, directly under the huge dome, was surrounded by red velvet ropes and a guard from each branch of the service. Each man in an ornate uniform stood motionless. The mourners moved in steady, single file around both sides of the coffin.

I can still picture him lying there as I passed the coffin. With his red hair and handsome face, JFK looked just as he did when I saw him at the campaign rally at the Waldorf three years earlier. After the strange all-night vigil, the president's death finally became real for me. The deep hush of so many people—though many wept as they shuffled by in the large circle—and most of all seeing that face in its final repose, finally brought home to me that he was dead. No one close to me had ever died before. For the first time, as I saw that handsome, vibrant man lying there, the sense of walking in a dream was dispelled. I started to cry.

As we exited the building, Bill came over and put his arm around me. Standing at the top of the Capitol steps, I leaned into his chest and sobbed.

None of us wanted to stay for the funeral. We just got back in the car and returned to New York. For me, the purpose in going to Washington had been accomplished—the fog had been pierced; I accepted, or at least acknowledged within myself, what had happened. I had seen him in his coffin.

This is what I remembered through the years that followed. However—as I discovered to my shock when I recently reviewed newspaper articles from that day—the coffin was never open. It was closed and covered with the American flag.

THE AUTHORITIES HAD PLANNED to close the doors to the Rotunda at 9:00 p.m. on Sunday. However, due to the unforeseen number of mourners who came to Washington, including thousands of teenagers, it was decided to keep the casket on view as long as people came. By 2:45 a.m., 115,000 people had filed through the Great Rotunda. Three hundred thousand lined the streets for the funeral on Monday, which I watched on television back in Manhattan Beach.

On Tuesday, November 26, next to four columns of reportage on the funeral, the *New York Times* ran a front page article with the headline, "Johnson Affirms Aims in Vietnam—Retains Kennedy's Policy of Aiding War on Reds."

The sixties had begun.

CHAPTER 7

The Loser's Club

After the assassination of JFK, a blanket of hopelessness descended upon me. I still planned to go to college, but first I needed to make enough money to move out of my outer-borough limbo and back to Manhattan where my job and friends were.

When Laurie, my ex-roommate, got a job at the newly opened Playboy Club, I discovered New York's nightlife. Laurie was working her way through NYU, and you could make a hell of a lot more money as a Playboy Bunny than at most other jobs, though it was backbreaking work. Bunnies, highly publicized waitresses in the swank club on East 59th Street, wore tiny satin costumes (low-cut corsets which flattened their stomachs and pushed their breasts up dramatically) with little cotton-ball tails, stiff white collars and cuffs, black stockings, and two-inch stiletto heels. Atop their teased and sprayed hairdos they wore headbands with satin bunny ears.

Laurie introduced me to lots of men and we double dated often, almost always with men at least twice our age. Usually, we enjoyed each other's company more than the men's, though their admiration and flattery were indispensable, not to mention their picking up the checks. Sometimes Laurie told people that she was from France and I would converse with her in French when we could be overheard. I dressed in black and wore sunglasses in the dimly lit lounges we frequented, burying the pain that surfaced whenever my pace slackened by drinking. I liked to see myself as a wild and tortured would-be actress.

Thus, I entered the gritty world of people who work in the city's clubs, restaurants, and bars, and those who frequent them 'til closing time: bartenders, entertainers, and Mafiosi, whom I learned were called "goodfellas" by those in the know. People finishing work at 3:00 or 4:00 a.m. sought a congenial place to socialize and unwind over breakfast. In 1964, the "in" place was the Tower East Coffee Shop, on Third Avenue and 72nd Street. A very large dining room with an adjoining lounge, the Tower East might be dead at midnight, but by 4:00 a.m. the joint was full of night people, many hopping from table to table to gossip and exchange quips.

Before long, Laurie and I were invited to sit at the table of restaurateur Danny Stradella in the back of the coffee shop. Danny's Hideaway was often mentioned in the gossip columns of Earl Wilson or Cindy Adams as a favorite haunt of Frank Sinatra (undisputed monarch of this universe) and other celebrities. Danny held court each morning, presiding over seven or eight people who were "in" enough to be invited to join him for breakfast. These included his current girlfriend, a Bunny named Lisa, a black-haired, single mother with a faraway look; some male cronies; one or two comics, constantly spieling even though they'd done three shows that night; and some pretty young girls like me and Laurie.

Jerry Joseph was a friend of Danny's, a regular at the table. He was night manager and part owner of the Colony Record Store, located in the Brill Building of Tin Pan Alley fame. The Colony stayed open 'til 3:00 a.m. to serve the city's musicians, theater people, and various heirs to the characters of Damon Runyon who were still in evidence on Broadway. Jerry was thirty-three, a swarthy, bearish man with a teasing sense of humor and wistful mien. I was instantly attracted to him. He had recently been featured as one of the town's eligible bachelors in a local column. He walked with a severe limp from a football injury sustained when he was fourteen and this was a dominant factor in his personality, his bitter reason for not having done more with his life. He loved music and this had led him to the Colony, where he had worked for fifteen years; the unique position of the store in the city was due in part to Jerry's knowledge of music and his genial personality.

To my surprise, I learned that Jerry, such a manly man in my eyes, lived with his parents out in Brighton Beach, five minutes from my mother's place. After breakfast, he often drove me home to Brooklyn and we had long talks about the meaning of life as the sun lifted out of the Atlantic to shine upon the Belt Parkway.

I dated Jerry on and off for about six months.

IN THE WINTER OF 1964, as the siren Night Life drew me deeper to her bosom, working in the daytime became impossible. At the Matthews Agency, I was regularly falling asleep at my typewriter. In January, I moved into the Hotel Cameron, a residential hotel back on West 86th Street, where Laurie had a room on a different floor. I got a night job through a girl in my acting class named Chickie, a tough-talking blonde whose vulnerability was painfully apparent in her acting work. This work is best remembered by me for an assignment where we were asked to recreate our morning routines as an acting exercise. Apparently faithful to a Muse who demanded complete authenticity, Chickie performed her morning rituals (which included sipping from a can of beer) for our coed class, dressed in her completely sheer black shorty pajamas. I knew her only slightly when she told me about a waitress job at the place where she worked, a newly opened bar on 68th and Lexington.

It was called The Loser's Club because the owner, a balding, mournful-looking guy named Frankie, had been divorced four times and had tried and failed to make a go of five bars before this one. The place was small, with six or seven tables and two booths. The red walls were decorated with larger-than-life pictures of famous losers such as George Armstrong Custer and Richard Nixon (who had lost most recently to Kennedy in 1960). As at other "joints" around town, the three waitresses at The Loser's Club wore black leotards, fishnet stockings, and high heels, a sort of poor man's Playboy Bunny.

I have always liked bars. One reason is the romance of a smoky haunt where sad souls come to ease the pain, preferably to the cool sounds of a jazz trio, or at least a piano player. To my teenage mind, wearing fishnet stockings was glamorous, as was the necessity to obtain a cabaret license from the Police Department.

Frankie had strict rules about not going out with customers, since one of his joints had been closed down when a waitress was caught turning tricks with men she met there. Nevertheless, after I had been at The Loser's Club for a few weeks, Chickie asked me one night if I wanted to meet men "for gifts, not cash." I said no immediately, trying to act like I was not frightened and appalled. However, she saw that I was. After that, Chickie was always curt with me. I had hurt her feelings.

Another time, a lonely tourist staying at a nearby hotel tried to entice each of the waitresses to his room with large tips, as we later discovered by comparing notes after he left his room key wrapped in a twenty dollar bill at Elaine's station. He had had a drink at each of our stations, leaving Chickie a ten, and me a five.

"I got a twenty-dollar broad, a ten-dollar broad, and a five-dollar broad," quipped Frankie, thinking himself fatherly. We all laughed.

In keeping with Frankie's track record, business at the club was not good. On weeknights there were rarely any customers to serve at the tables, so I had plenty of time to get into conversations, those long out-of-time talks for which so many people frequent bars. I might start by announcing brightly, "A girl loses ten percent of her sex appeal when she lights her own cigarette," as I drew a Marlboro from my pack. When a man held up a flame for me, I leaned forward, touching his hand lightly as I looked into his eyes and took a deep drag, then blew out the match.

One acquaintance thus made was a young writer who frequently begged to take me home. Despite the rules, I could never resist a tormented artist (especially if he claimed he was tormented because of me). After saying no a million times, I finally agreed. I let him kiss me in the cab, but I refused to let him come upstairs. Still, the next night I was fired. It seemed Frankie had had us followed and, even though he knew I had left the young writer longing in the taxi, he said he couldn't take any chances. I was out of The Loser's Club.

Soon enough, I got a job as a hatcheck girl at the Michelangelo, an upscale Northern Italian restaurant next door to the Copacabana. The highlights of that year included seeing shows at the Copa like Sammy Davis, Jr.'s dynamite act, which I got to watch ringside. Oh, the perks of being a pretty girl.

The Michelangelo served potato croquettes, not spaghetti, and was owned by a silver-haired Roman named Marco Sardi. He and his red-headed, mink-clad wife were there every night to welcome the friends who were the largest part of their clientele. When these elegant Italians would enter the carpeted lobby, the Sardis greeted them effusively with hugs, air kisses, and cries of "*Caro!*" I watched all this from my domain just inside the entrance, a narrow coatroom with a half-door over which I took people's wraps and handed them numbered tags. I made a lot of money at this job, often getting exorbitant tips simply because I was a seductive young thing who'd developed some fairly snappy repartee. In the back of the coatroom were a chair and a little ledge with a lamp, wide enough for my textbooks. I was taking College Math and French at Hunter College night school.

Another role I played at Michelangelo was cigarette girl. The maître d' called me when a customer wanted to buy smoking material. Securing a flat wooden box to my waist with a pink satin strap around my neck, I walked among the candlelit tables to offer a choice of cigarettes or expensive cigars. I saw myself as a character in one of the forties movies which had shaped my fantasy life. In fact, more and more, my life seemed to me like a film I was watching—one with an inevitably unhappy ending.

The Twist swept the nation that year, coming out of an unlikely dive on 44th Street called the Peppermint Lounge, which suddenly became *the* place to go. There, for a few months, you'd see celebrities and society swells, vigorously moving their hips to the rock and roll of Joey Dee and the Starlighters. In the Twist, the feet remained largely planted on the ground while the hips swiveled furiously. At the better clubs, attendants in the ladies' rooms were prepared to remove splinters from your feet and sell you a new pair of stockings, since women were ruining their hose when they took off their high heels to dance.

Most days I'd sleep until 3:00 or 4:00 p.m., rising just in time to get ready for school. I took a cab to Hunter, then to work after class. I'd leave the Michelangelo at 2:00 or 3:00 a.m. to go out with Jerry or some other man, or meet Laurie for breakfast at the Tower East, sharing a cab home at 6:00 or 7:00 a.m. I found daylight depressing.

This was an intoxicating life, in more ways than one. The

constant attention of men was a drug I required, a salve to my open wounds. I longed for someone who would love me, convinced that I was inherently unlovable. Underneath my desperation, I was full of venom and ire. I suffered in what I thought of as the Russian way, wallowing in the drama of my anguish while despising myself for my self-dramatization. The only respite from these inner demons was sensory pleasure. "Live fast, die young, and have a good-looking corpse" had long been my favorite quotation, my motto in fact.

In May, when spring semester ended, I received As in both my courses and lost my job at Michelangelo, since New Yorkers don't wear coats in summer. Laurie got us both jobs as bar waitresses at the Granville, one of the famous Catskill Mountain resort hotels, two hours from the city. We gave up our rooms at the Cameron and took the bus to Montgomery for the summer.

AT THE GRANVILLE, EMPLOYEES were given room and board. Laurie and I shared a tiny room with a sink (bathroom in the hall) in a staff bungalow across the road from the main buildings of the hotel. I felt entirely out of place in the country, blind to the natural beauty of the mountains. I often joked that I was allergic to fresh air. But I felt I had nowhere else to go. I had no home — I certainly didn't want to go back to Brooklyn. My mother didn't really have room for me anyway except to share that room with my little sister. I knew my aunts and uncles would help me if I asked them but a huge chasm seemed to yawn between their orderly middle-class world and mine.

Like all the Borscht Belt hotels, the Granville was Full American Plan, serving three meals a day to their guests. Bar waiters and waitresses served cocktails first at lunch, returning around five to work in the small bar near the dining room, then at the tables during dinner. After that we served in the nightclub, which was in a separate building. The waitresses were pressured by the two corrupt bartenders, who got a percentage of our tips, to shortchange the guests, of whom everyone spoke with contempt. Most people never noticed that, unless they ordered premium brand liquor, they were served the cheapest brands no matter what label they asked for. The bartenders rang up the cheaper brands and split the difference with us.

There was a different nightclub show each night, followed by a lounge act in the bar next to the nightclub. Laurie and I finished our shifts at around 3:00 a.m., and we usually socialized over a few drinks when the lounge business died down.

I detested the clientele I was serving, mostly rowdy groups of drunken men and their wives, up for spring conventions of Lions Clubs and other fraternal organizations. Unlike Laurie, who could handle vast numbers of tables on her station with no apparent effort, I was a terrible waitress. Once, serving a particularly obnoxious man, I deliberately spilled a drink on him, taking satisfaction in his dismay. This was proof to me of how low I had sunk. On my days off, I begged any ride I could get to the city where I'd meet up with a married guy I'd been seeing.

An inner voice was constantly hissing in my ear, "You're rotten, no good, and you know it. That's the real truth, not all your phony aspirations to be a great actress. . . ." I could picture only one escape from that tormentor—death. A line from Keats repeated itself in my mind again and again: "Now more than ever seems it rich to die."

Death beckoned me like a friend.

One day, I went to see a doctor in the little town near the Granville about a skin rash. I mentioned, almost as an afterthought, that I had been having trouble sleeping. This was untrue. The doctor prescribed "a mild sleeping pill" and I filled the prescription at the drugstore, just in case.

• • •

IT'S ABOUT TEN TO six on the evening of July 4. I'm standing in the hotel dining room, waiting for the doors to open for dinner. Bright sun shines through the picture windows and all the tables are sparkling with white linen and heavy stainless cutlery. Waiters and busboys are scurrying around, placing trays heaped with pickles on the tables.

I'm trying to remember the conversation I had last night with Rodney Dangerfield. I know we talked for a long time after he finished his act, and I was surprised by how thoughtful and compassionate he seemed, none of the endless *shtick* I was used to from other comedians. But what did we talk about? I must've drunk a lot of scotch.

My reverie is abruptly interrupted.

"Riqui, what are you doing?" It's Mr. Slimowitz, the greasy dining room supervisor speaking through the half-smoked cigar clenched between his teeth. "Why don't you go help them set up in the bar?" he sneers. "We're not paying you to stand around with your head up your ass."

In an instant, rage envelops me. How dare he speak to me that way?

"Oh, really," I spit back, glaring at him. "Well, Mr. Slimowitz, I quit!" With a flourish, I throw my order pad on the nearest table and march out of the dining room. I almost chortle with pleasure in the knowledge that I am leaving them shorthanded for the busiest weekend of the season.

I leave the building in a huff and cross the road to the staff bungalow, without even stopping in the bar to tell Laurie what happened. As I sit on my bed in our little room, it dawns on me that now I have to leave the hotel and my chest clenches with fear. Where will I go? What can I do now?

Then, as if in a dream, I jump up and put my Barbra Streisand album on the portable record player we brought up from the city. All at once, I know what I'm going to do. I take off my black skirt and white blouse and slip my nightgown over my head. Passionless, as if watching from a distance, I take the sleeping pills from the medicine chest above the sink. The white tablets look pretty in my palm. Early evening sunlight fights its way through the scraggly trees outside the window, doing little to relieve the stale gloom of the bungalow's dusty floors and overused furniture.

Like a straw in the wind, I keep whirling around . . .

Streisand's singing could fracture your heart.

I swallow the pills in three handfuls, gulping down water chasers. Then, afraid they won't be strong enough, I remove the double-edged blade from the safety razor I use to shave my legs.

I line the empty metal wastebasket with clean white towels and fill the rusty sink with warm water. Immersing my right forearm, I carefully begin to slice my wrist, watching with fascination as the blood seeps out to make graceful curlicues, the slender red lines gradually tinting the water pink. My head feels heavy—the bed behind me is beckoning with its covers neatly folded down.

I see Bonnie's face as if in a cartoon circle above my head, a face contorted with hate, spitting epithets at me. At last, I will shut her up. As I glance into dark eyes in the stained mirror on the medicine chest, my throat tightens suddenly: I am witnessing an act of murder. Jolted, I quickly look down and slice the razor blade again across the thin white skin of my forearm 'til another line of red appears. I know I should cut deeper but damn, it hurts more than I expected and I can't make my hand bear down. So I make another long slit; this makes six on each wrist. It'll have to do.

I drop the double-edged blade, walk unsteadily the few feet to the bed, and crawl under the covers.

Pitched from pillar to post, so helplessly.
What I wanted the most winds up a ghostly memory . . .

I reach for the pad on the night table. The high from the pills keeps coming on as I scribble a note to my mother, smiling as I date it Independence Day. But my mind is getting foggier and I just have to lay my head on the pillow. I pull the lined pail onto my stomach and place the slightly bleeding arms on the white terrycloth. I don't want to make a mess.

. . .

LAURIE WOULD NORMALLY HAVE not returned to the room before 4:00 a.m. on a busy night like July 4. However, she unexpectedly got her period and came back to get a sanitary napkin. She found me in a coma. I was taken to the hospital in Montgomery, where my stomach was pumped several times. I was placed in an oxygen tent. At first, the doctors told Noni and Bill, who arrived with my mother soon after Laurie called them, that I was likely to die. I remained in a coma for three days. While they said that the drug I had taken should not have this strong an effect, and that the damage from the cuts was negligible, the doctors told my family that even if I lived, I might sustain brain damage from being in a coma for that long.

I first realized I was still alive when I opened my eyes to see the blurred form of a nurse through the plastic oxygen tent around me on the bed.

"I can't do anything right," I murmured miserably before passing out again.

My family rallied around me. My mother, pale and, for

once, not making a display of her emotions, said that I must choose to live with her or with one of my aunts and uncles. Also, the family insisted that I go into psychotherapy immediately. Willingly, I agreed. I went to live in suburban New Jersey with Noni, Billy, and my cousin Frank, who was twelve. And I started therapy.

THIS WAS UNQUESTIONABLY A turning point of my life. Perhaps because I sensed that I had avenged myself on my parents—even my father said he had "gotten [me] wrong"—I was able to let go of some of the rage that had been eating me alive. For the next five years, with the unflagging moral and financial support of the family, I worked hard in therapy to climb out of the darkness which had been my only reality. Gradually, painfully, I learned to understand my own mind and began to value myself as a human being.

Maybe I wasn't a loser after all.

April 1965

I toss the rest of my coffee and throw the paper cup in the dirty trash can outside the door of the Red Apple Rest. Climbing back on the bus behind Olga, I ask her if she'd like the window seat but she declines.

"You take it," she says. "I think I'll just meditate for a while."

The bus shudders as it accelerates painfully up the winding road past the woods of Harriman State Park. My reflection in the window shows I forgot to comb my hair. Typical. Idly, I begin to count how many long bus trips I have taken in my time. Several. Which was the first one? Mississippi, I guess . . .

CHAPTER 8

March On

My Aunt Noni and Uncle Bill's apartment was in Teaneck, New Jersey; a mere three miles from the George
Washington Bridge, it was so *not* New York. With their solid
marriage and deep affection for me, Noni and Bill were the
parents I'd always needed, at a time when I was ready to allow
myself to be nurtured. For the rest of their lives, they offered
me unstinting love and support which no amount of gratitude could repay. That summer, I rested in their garden
apartment. Twice a week I took the bus to a local clinic to see
Dr. Gregory Heimarck, a Freudian psychiatrist with whom I
would work for the next five years.

In September, I commuted to New York to attend night
classes at Hunter College, hoping to transfer to City College
the following year. I also took an acting class at the Uta Hagen/
Herbert Berghof Studio in the city, studying with Bill Hickey.
(Remember him in *Prizzi's Honor?*) But he and I did not hit it
off—I was perhaps too fragile at the time to do any solid acting
work. So, for a year, I did my course work, helped out in Billy's
office, and saved money to get my own place.

In September 1965, I landed a job as commercial continuity
director at WHN Radio in New York, 1150 on the AM dial,
with offices on Park Avenue. The title, impressive to me, went
with an eighty-five-dollars-a-week salary, which was the exact

cost of the rent-controlled studio apartment I found in December, a fourth-floor walkup on West 87th Street.

. . .

IT'S CHRISTMAS EVE. I'M lying on my back on my newly purchased couch. There's a pullout bed underneath—you roll it out and it pops up to make a double when the occasion calls for it. Behind me, a spring-loaded floor-to-ceiling lamp has three plastic cones you can adjust in any direction, toward the bed or desk. I am surrounded by cartons as yet unpacked and am reading *A Movable Feast*, Hemingway's account of his early days in Paris. My mouth is watering at his descriptions of French food, visions of escargots and white wine beckoning. And then it hits me: I'm in New York!

It's 11:00 p.m. and freezing outside, but I bundle up and take the crosstown bus to Fifth Avenue. From 86th Street I walk downtown, stopping along with the tourists to admire the holiday displays in the department store windows. It's almost midnight when I reach the Brasserie, the big French restaurant that stays open all night. Sitting at the counter in the brightly lit dining room, I relish an order of garlicky escargots, sopping up the extra butter sauce with French bread from the little scoops in the metal dish. I wash it all down with a glass of crisp Chablis. Only in New York.

. . .

MY JOB AT WHN consisted primarily of screening all the ads. With my trusty stopwatch, I timed recorded ads to be sure a thirty-second spot didn't run to thirty-one seconds; and I edited written copy to be read by the announcers, not only for length but for words such as "cocktail," unacceptable according to the standards of Storer Broadcasting, WHN's owner. (Storer was one of the few media organizations to support Barry Goldwater in the 1964 presidential election. I, of course, cast my first vote for Dick Gregory, the liberal black comedian who ran as a write-in candidate several times in the sixties and seventies.) WHN was an "MOR" station, playing middle-of-the-road vocals and the bland instrumentals of Mitch Miller, Montovani, Lawrence Welk. The young people on staff made fun of this music to each other when we went out for drinks after work on Fridays. These evenings often stretched happily 'til ten or eleven o'clock.

I enjoyed my job and coworkers. It felt cool to get to know the radio personalities, some of whom were household names. There were numerous perks to working for a New York radio station. I went to a recording session of a comedy album called *The Bunch*, a satire of Mary McCarthy's *The Group*, starring (among others) Linda Lavin and Renee Taylor. Before the staged recording began, the audience was plied with liquor at an open bar for the benefit of the laugh track. Another time, I went to a party to promote the newly released original cast album of *On a Clear Day* at the Hotel Americana. I loved seeing the waiflike Barbara Harris, whose acting work I admired. And the buffet was lavish—free food!

Once, I got a chance to write a one-minute theater review when Roy Schwartz, WHN's station manager, offered me reviewer's tickets to a short-lived Broadway play starring Geraldine Page. However, my career as a critic was not to be. "Too many big words," said Roy.

At the staff Christmas party, I had my first taste of corporate hospitality in Storer's own townhouse on East 72nd Street. In addition to generous Christmas bonuses, each employee got a set of six leaded crystal rocks glasses with "WHN" embossed on each one.

I felt better about myself and my life than I ever had before. I was supporting myself and I loved my little apartment. I received a lot of respect for the job I was doing and I liked the work. Then, on June 8, 1966, all this came to an unexpected and, as it turned out, abrupt end.

Sitting at my desk that morning before delving into the pile of new copy to be screened, I skimmed *The New York Times* and was gripped by the photo on the front page. Two days earlier, James Meredith, the maverick civil rights activist who had been the first black student at the University of Mississippi, had embarked upon a one-man walk through his home state to prove to black Mississippians that they did not have to be afraid to register to vote. The next day he was shot in the back, though not seriously injured. Civil rights leaders from around the nation were gathering to continue his march to Jackson, the state capital. By June 8, they had been joined by about a hundred others. The state police were demanding that they walk on the shoulder of the road, but the marchers insisted on walking on the pavement. The *Times* photo showed the leaders: Martin Luther King, Jr. of the Southern Christian Leadership Conference (SCLC); Stokely Carmichael of the Student Nonviolent Coordinating Committee, or SNCC; Floyd McKissick, Director of the Congress of Racial Equality (CORE); and others. Recently at odds with each other over strategy and tactics, these men were shown walking in the road, arms linked, being shoved toward the shoulder by a big state trooper. Dr. King was stumbling to his knees.

When I saw this, I was outraged. I hated racism and segregation, and I had a lot of admiration for King, who was obviously a man of great integrity. It was unconscionable that he be pushed around so disrespectfully by some yahoo with a badge. I felt I had to do something. I put down the paper and called CORE in New York. They told me that I could catch a ride to Mississippi in a car that was leaving that afternoon. I decided to go. I thought that Roy Schwartz, a closet liberal, would applaud my high motives when I explained to him (which I did, no doubt, with great excitement) that conscience demanded I leave right away. I'd only be gone for a few days.

Roy reluctantly agreed that I could take a few days off.

· · ·

I'M CLIMBING THE STAIRS in an old office building on lower Sixth Avenue, clammy from the heat and humidity. The door, with "CORE" stenciled on its bubbled glass pane, creaks as I enter the office to see mostly empty desks. The only light is the sun coming in through the tall windows facing Sixth Ave. I surmise that the lights are off to keep it cool, though to little effect. The only sounds are the whirring of an overhead fan and the clicking of a manual typewriter outside an office marked Floyd McKissick. The typist is a white woman, about twenty-five, tall and big boned with straight brown hair and fair skin, her freckled arms extending from a sleeveless white blouse. Beside her typewriter is an open bottle of Coca-Cola.

"Hi, I'm Emma," she says. "I'm Floyd's secretary. You're Riqui?"

"Yes."

"We're just waiting for the guy with the car and one other guy," says Emma. I notice small beads of sweat above her upper lip as she takes a swig of her Coke.

"Where is everybody?" I ask.

"They're all down south already. We'll lock up the office when we leave."

The squeaking door announces the arrival of James, a lanky black guy also in his twenties. He speaks in a kind of languid voice and moves with an easy grace. I like him immediately. He and I chat as Emma finishes her typing. Seems he's a grad student in philosophy at the New School, originally from Cairo, Illinois.

"I've never been south before," I blurt.

"Neither have I," says James, swallowing. "I sure am looking forward to it," he adds with wry sarcasm.

After another few minutes, our driver arrives. Peter is a sandy-haired WASP, a senior at Williams, with tortoiseshell glasses. He's wearing white pants and a white shirt. I immediately feel self-conscious in the face of this upper-class refinement.

Emma finishes up her work, dons a little straw hat, and locks the office door behind us. We clatter down the stairs and out to Peter's parked car, a late-model Volvo, though all models look the same to me, with the round-backed design that seems to scorn sleek, ephemeral fashion. Emma and I sit in the back. When I volunteer to share the driving, Peter says that's OK, he loves to drive. I'm glad I'm in the back 'cause my jaw drops when he pulls on a pair of leather driving gloves, buttoned at the wrist. He tells us he belongs to a "driving club" at school. I picture this as some sort of country club but am too embarrassed by my middle-class ignorance to ask for clarification.

It is late afternoon as we head down the New Jersey Turnpike, driving straight through Pennsylvania. We stop to eat and find gas when we reach West Virginia. The cheap roadside hamburgers we devour taste delicious. Emma has been on previous marches so she seems less excited than the rest of us. Normally, I would tend to dismiss Peter as a different species, from an elite Christian world impenetrable to a New York Jew like me. But as we talk over greasy French fries, I see we all share a righteous anger at the stubborn continuation of Jim Crow, at the use of violence and intimidation to keep our fellow citizens from exercising their most basic right, the right to vote. And the determination to do something about it. I feel

I'm putting my money where my mouth is and am exhilarated to find people similarly motivated. The injustice of the situation demands that I stand up for what I believe; if I didn't, I would deem myself a hypocrite. That following my conscience seems to be leading to a great adventure doesn't hurt at all.

Through the night hours, unfamiliar sights glide by the windows as Peter, James, and I talk. Emma sleeps a lot, waking only to use the bathroom when we stop for gas, and buy another Coke, which makes me giggle to my sleepless self.

The deeper south we get, the hotter and more humid it becomes, even though it's still dark. When we cross into Kentucky, James grows quiet, his fear increasing palpably. I'm also afraid, feeling that we're entering a foreign country. It's only been two years since Schwerner, Chaney, and Goodman, three CORE workers in Philadelphia, Mississippi, were disinterred after weeks of searching by the FBI. The body of Chaney, the black one of the three, had been dismembered. Recently, the Department of Justice had announced it would bring sixteen Mississippians to trial for the crime, including the county sheriff.

But underlying my fear there's an almost exultant feeling to be facing this danger for such a worthy cause. I wonder what Dr. Heimarck will think of this. Are my self-destructive impulses at play?

In the afternoon, we stop for gas somewhere in rural Tennessee. The scrawny guy in overalls who pumps our gas eyes with equal suspicion the foreign car, the Connecticut plates, and the interracial group of Yankees. I can hardly wait for Emma to pull her Coke out of its round slot in the red cooler so we can be on our way.

It is still light when we reach Batesville, Mississippi, thirty miles south of the Tennessee border, where the marchers have stopped for the night. We learn that people are being put up by local black families. The night air is hot and close. I am so tired, I can't remember how Emma and I got to this tiny cottage on a dirt lane, where a large woman in a cotton housedress greets us with great warmth. She shows us to what must be her children's room, though there is no sign of kids. You have to walk sideways between the bed and the only other piece of furniture, a dresser, upon which sits a chipped pitcher and ewer full of water for washing up; she indicates through a loose windowpane where we'll find the outhouse. The waning moon reveals dazzling white sheets on the narrow bed Emma and I are to share. I fall into it, exhausted.

Waking around 7:00 a.m., I dress and open the door to the low-ceilinged kitchen. I can hardly take in what I see. A rickety round table is set with a veritable feast: steaming scrambled eggs, fresh-baked biscuits, grits (which I've never seen before), gravy, a pitcher of fresh milk, and—a big bowl of fried chicken!

Our hostess flashes me a shy smile and invites me to sit. This entire repast is for me and Emma. Our hostess says her husband has already eaten and gone to work in the field. When I thank her again for this hospitality, she repeats, "No, thank *you.* Thank you!"

After my first outhouse experience, a boy of thirteen, the son of the house, comes to take Emma and me to the nearby home where Peter and James are staying. In the bright southern daylight I feel like I've stepped into another world: little shanties, children and dogs playing in dirt yards, the noise of parents and neighbors calling out to each other—and instant fearful expressions upon seeing white faces.

• • •

IT BECAME HABITUAL FOR me, while in Mississippi, to feel a sense of relief when the paved roads gave out to dirt and I knew I was safe in the black section of a town again. We met James and Peter that first morning and joined the march on Highway 51. There were about 150 marchers—the number fluctuated each day as local people arrived and went home. There were young black Mississippians and white northerners, veteran civil rights workers and a lot of first-timers like me, Peter, and James who came from all over the North, Midwest, and later from California.

We walked two by two on the shoulder of the four-lane highway, this being the legal resolution of the earlier dispute with the authorities. Helicopters hovered above and two dozen highway patrolmen and plainclothes state investigators moved along in cars beside us. With fifty to seventy-five news people around, including camera crews, the Mississippi authorities didn't want any more incidents—for a while.

Walking in the ninety-degree heat demanded frequent stops. To prevent dehydration, salt tablets were dispensed from a flatbed truck accompanying the march. We moved at a rate of ten to eighteen miles a day. As we walked, we clapped and sang rousing marching songs which were already anthems of the Movement, many of them set to the tunes of Negro church songs. I remember one, whose staccato refrain was addressed to Mississippi Governor Paul Johnson:

Da de da de dot dut dot de da de dut
De da de da de dut de dut de da de dut
O-oh, Johnson,
You know you can't jail us a-a-a-a-ll,
O-oh, Johnson,
Segregation's bound to fall,
De da de da de dut de dut de da de dut
De da de da de dut de dut de da de dut . . .

The songs were fuel, keeping us going through heat and dust and the curses hurled out of the windows of passing cars by white "crackers."

Local whites came out on foot also, to express their feelings about the march. One day, when we stopped for lunch, Peter, Emma, and I took a side trip to find a country store, which turned out to be far enough away that no one connected us with the march as we purchased our tissues, snacks, and of course, a Coke for Emma. The people in the white-owned store, a husband and wife in their forties, were warm and gracious, revealing to me why the term "southern hospitality" is proverbial.

Later, when we rejoined the march, I saw the same couple standing by the side of the road, faces contorted with hate, shouting "nigger lovers" and so on.

THROUGHOUT THE THREE WEEKS until the march reached Jackson, small groups of civil rights workers left to go into the local towns to encourage and help people to register to vote. In Panola County, where Batesville is located, there were about 7,500 eligible voters of each race; of these, 5,922 whites were registered, and 878 blacks.

The marchers ate lunch off the back of the truck, bologna sandwiches on white bread with mayonnaise, and Kool Aid. (It was years before I could eat bologna again, though I had subsisted on fried bologna and Minute Rice in my days as a latchkey kid.) As our numbers grew, we slept in two large tents pitched along the way. Various leaders gave talks in the evenings, and I began to be aware of their differences. Dr. King, a spellbinding speaker, always stressed nonviolence as a means of struggle, as did his young aides in the church-based SCLC. I was impressed and inspired by Andrew Young, Julian Bond, and Jesse Jackson, who struck me, from their speeches, as men of high principle and deep commitment.

At the same time, SNCC, an organization of younger, grassroots workers, was daily becoming more radical. Their vibrant and articulate leader, Stokely Carmichael, was persuasive when he spoke about the limitations of nonviolence and the need for black people (a new term of pride to replace "Negroes") to take control of their own lives and movement. The meetings always ended when we stood, joined hands crisscrossed in front of us, and sang "We Shall Overcome."

One day, I found myself in a car, going on an errand with five SNCC people. I sat next to a skinny hipster named Willie Ricks, Field Secretary of SNCC. He kept repeating, in a rhythmic way, something like, "I'm tired of that white power, I want my *black* power; it be time for *black* power, now." Though I was a little frightened by his urgency, this new term (recently coined by Ricks) just sounded right to me. How could blacks truly gain self-respect and pride if they felt they owed their civil rights to white "benefactors"?

Peter and James were planning to return to New York and, though I didn't want to leave the march, I thought it was the responsible thing to accept the opportunity to drive home with them. After all, I had a job to go back to. So on June 16 we were back in the Volvo, heading north on the interstate.

• • •

IT'S ABOUT NOON AND the sun's glare is intense through the back window of the Volvo as we head north on Highway 51. I am trying to nap, lulled by the indistinct voices of James and Peter up front, when I notice a dirty old Ford riding beside us without passing. Three beefy men are staring into our Connecticut-licensed car with a black man in the front seat and a white woman in back—a dead giveaway we're Yankee agitators.

They begin shouting at us, mouthing now-familiar epithets that dissipate in the wind before we can hear them. Peter, uttering an epithet of his own, accelerates smoothly, keeping focused on the road ahead. The Ford stays right beside us. I notice the veins standing out in the neck of the cracker in the front passenger seat as his mouth reads "nigger lover" and other choice words.

"Are you OK?" Peter asks me over his shoulder.

"Sure," I lie, heart like a jackhammer. "Don't worry about me." Peter's gloved hands grip the wheel as his steady foot pushes our speed over ninety. The Ford keeps pace and begins to inch over into our lane. My God! They're trying to force us off the road! Remembering Schwerner, Chaney, and Goodman, I am sweating hard now but vow to myself not to panic. James and I speak calmly to encourage Peter.

I say, "Great driving, Peter."

"You got it, man . . . ," adds James in his mellow lilt.

The Ford repeatedly edges a hair's breadth from the side of our car. Boy, am I grateful for Volvo's quality engineering and Peter's driving club skill and experience! When we cross the Tennessee line, the Ford pulls away and passes, its putrid exhaust looking beautiful as the distance between us lengthens. Peter pulls onto the shoulder and stops the car. He takes off his gloves, leans his head on the wheel, and takes a deep breath.

I could've kissed him.

• • •

TEN DAYS AFTER I walked out of WHN, I was back in the city. When I called the station, I learned that Roy Schwartz had fired me. While I was embarrassed about the way it happened, I was secretly happy I could go rejoin the march. I had been planning to quit anyway to attend school full-time in the fall.

I picked up some fresh clothes at my apartment and got a seat on one of two chartered buses organized by a group called the New York Committee for the Meredith March. The buses were filled mostly with students, black and white, going to join the march. That long bus trip was full of singing, laughter, and camaraderie—it took about eighteen hours, but I was able to catch some sleep when we quieted down at night.

Back in Mississippi, the long hours walking stretched into long days of singing and talking as we marched two by two down the highway.

Paul and Silas were bound in jail,
Didn't have the money for to go their bail,
Keep your eyes on the prize,
Hold on, hold on . . .

One day, soon after I rejoined the march, I was paired with a shy girl, about eleven years old. She was one of the local black people who would come to march for a day, or part of it, as we passed near their homes. In hundred-degree weather, she was dressed in her Sunday best, a pink taffeta dress with an organdy sash, too small for her chubby frame. When I asked if she wasn't hot, she said to me earnestly, "If I want my freedom, I got to fight for it. . . ." Her sweet passion touched and inspired me to stay the course.

ON JUNE 23, 2,500 marchers entered the small city of Canton, Mississippi. We pitched the big tents on the grounds of the black elementary school. March leaders warned us there might be trouble, since the Canton City Council had refused us a permit to camp there.

Humph! Couldn't even get permission to camp in their own segregated school grounds. It made me mad!

It was almost dark when twenty state police cars careened into the lot and surrounded us, sirens blaring. As planned, everyone stood in long rows, linking arms in front of the tents as we faced our assailants. Dr. King stood on top of a car with a bullhorn, exhorting us to remain nonviolent. There was a tremendous sense of excitement mixed with fear in the humid twilight.

My blood was boiling, so I pushed my way up to the front row. Those racist crackers weren't going to scare me! I doubt I shall ever forget what I saw before me: a long row of about sixty men wearing gas masks. They looked like Martians. Each one was aiming a rifle with a big round muzzle directly at us. Then I had a thought, which later seemed emblematic of growing up white in America in the 1950s: "I hope the cops get here soon [to help us]." Suddenly, I realized with a gasp: "Those *are* the cops!" It was perhaps in this instant that I changed from a liberal into a radical.

The next moment, the guns were fired and tear gas canisters fell everywhere among the crowd. Two thousand people scattered in all directions, screaming, coughing, crying. I was stunned by how much the noxious fumes stung my eyes and throat as tears streamed down my face. We fanned out into the streets of the black neighborhood around us in pandemonium. That night, I slept in a church basement. Others slept in private homes or cars. There were a lot of angry people and the SNCC men had many derogatory things to say about King and his nonviolent strategy.

The day after the tear gas incident, Dr. King called for volunteers to drive to Philadelphia, Mississippi, the place where

Schwerner, Chaney, and Goodman had been murdered with the collusion of the local sheriff. We were to march through the town and rally at the Neshoba County Courthouse, where a smaller rally had been attacked by locals three days earlier.

I volunteered, along with about three hundred other people, including fifteen or twenty whites. I remember getting out of a car on the outskirts of Philadelphia, where we gathered to form our lines. The entire white population of the town (about two thousand people) appeared to be lining Main Street, waiting for us to come through. They were held in check by one hundred highway patrolmen. I wasn't thinking about how scared I was, but my face must have shown it. Floyd McKissick, who'd been in the car just ahead, took one look at me and came over to put a fatherly arm around my shoulders. With kind words (not one of which I recall), he encouraged me. I mustered the backbone to go forward.

Everyone in the waiting crowd was screaming, jeering, and cursing as we walked the gauntlet. Some were throwing Coke bottles—I remember a marcher in front of me bleeding from the head. My heart leapt to my throat when a white Thunderbird sped through the front of the line at about forty miles per hour. We scrambled out of its way as best we could, caught between the car and the hostile crowd around us. The driver was pulled out of the car and arrested. No one was seriously injured. The march leaders instructed us to hold hands as we walked two by two. My partner was a quiet fourteen-year-old black boy whose hand trembled in mine. At a certain point, we passed a man, swathed in Confederate flags, standing on the roof of a parked car. I saw him look with utter disgust at me, holding the boy's hand. Then his hate-filled eyes met mine.

"Kiss him, why don't you?" he screamed, as though this was the worst insult he could hurl at me.

When we finally reached the relative safety of the square,

Dr. King spoke, telling the townspeople we had returned to show "that we can stand before you without fear after we were beaten and brutalized the other day."

That night, after returning to the safety of the big tent, I felt elated that I had confronted injustice despite my fear.

THE NIGHT BEFORE THE march entered Jackson, there was a rally in the stadium at Tougaloo College, an all-black institution on the outskirts of the city. Several thousand people attended, sitting in the bleachers under the warm night sky. A plane full of celebrities had flown in from Hollywood to support the march. Dick Gregory made us roar with laughter.

Later, I was thrilled to see Burt Lancaster at the microphone. He stood tall, the embodiment of integrity, just as I imagined from his movies. Then he said, speaking with great sincerity about answering the call of conscience, "It has to do with being a man, doesn't it?"

This was a moment of clanging dissonance for me. I actually looked down at myself in some confusion. I wasn't a man, was I?

The next day, Gregory and Marlon Brando were the only stars I saw who actually joined the march and walked the final eight miles into Jackson. I remember Brando, looking quite humble, walking beside a work-worn sharecropper in overalls.

On Sunday, June 26, twelve to fifteen thousand people rallied at the Mississippi State Capitol. Martin Luther King, Jr. declared in his speech that the march and rally "will go down in history as the greatest demonstration for freedom ever held in the state of Mississippi."

To me, the end of the march was anticlimactic. What was significant was that hundreds of black people along the march route had registered to vote.

Back in New York, I did some fund-raising for a CORE project in Meridian, Mississippi, whose coordinator I had marched with for a couple of days. But the Movement had shifted focus and Black Power became the rallying cry, which I respected. The mantra "Black is beautiful" spread and afros replaced straightened hair among most young African-Americans. It was time for white activists to step aside. However, seeing that so many of my generation shared my humanistic values gave me tremendous hope. I began to feel that, together, we could save the world, even in the face of our deepening involvement in Vietnam.

CHAPTER 9

City College

Eighty-Seventh Street between Central Park West and Columbus was a quiet, tree-lined street when I lived there from 1965 to 1969, the longest I'd ever stayed in one place until that time. My apartment was on the top floor of a typical New York brownstone.

You had to walk up four steep flights to arrive, panting, at my door. You stepped into the small kitchen, with its eight square feet of blue and white Dutch-patterned linoleum cheerfully lit by the skylight above. There was a small stove, a half-size fridge under the counter, and a pegboard I mounted on the wall with hooks to hang my pots and pans. The round card table where I ate was on the other side of the wall in the main room, which was about twelve by sixteen feet. The studio was dominated by the handsome, glass-doored bookcases I scavenged from WHN when Roy Schwartz's office was redecorated. My trundle bed served as a couch in the daytime, with its turquoise plaid bolsters and matching slipcovers. The two-toned wood coffee table was another prize from WHN. The cheap but adequate hi-fi I bought for my Bronx apartment stood next to a rolling cart which held a portable TV. The small desk faced the tall window overlooking the gardens of the brownstones on 88th Street.

City College of New York was tuition-free when I attended, as it had been since 1847. Generations of immigrants and their children, including my father, Aunt Mina, and Uncle Bill, had attended there and gone on to accomplished careers in every field. Many CCNY grads became Nobel Laureates. In the 1960s you could still get a great education there, especially if you handpicked your professors as I did, by inquiring about prospective teachers among students and faculty members before registration.

Finally a full-time student at City, I became closer with Roberta Jellinek, whom I'd first met at Performing Arts in 1962. Maxine had introduced us when she appeared one afternoon with Roberta in tow at the smoky booths filled with kids in the back of the Cup & Saucer. We didn't connect right away. Roberta was a year ahead of me, a dance major, but her career goal (from childhood!) was to be a psychologist. Like me, Roberta was a first-generation daughter with a strong European identity who grew up with a tenacious suspicion that Nazis were an ever-present possibility, no matter how safe things appear in this country. After all, just look at history. Although we were very different in style and circumstances (Roberta lived at home until she was twenty-two), in more subtle ways we shared many of the same psychological struggles and interests. For many years, this friendship was my one experience of a long-term relationship and the value of working out conflicts with someone when you'd much rather run away.

Unlike most of my friends, I actually enjoyed college. I was clearly going because *I* wanted to, not for a career goal or parental expectations, though I had imbibed the Schapiro family's love of learning and high culture since childhood. I postponed any acting classes because I felt the professional training I had was better than anything offered by the college theater department. I wanted to use CCNY strictly for the excellent liberal arts education offered there. I resolved never to get a grade lower than a B.

I dove into my studies in humanities and the social sciences. Had it not been that some of my financial aid was contingent upon my majoring in psychology, I would have majored in philosophy, a field which I discovered with joy in City's excellent department. I found deep satisfaction in addressing what were, to me, life's most pressing questions: What is real? What is the purpose of life? How do we know what we know? What is the true nature of the human condition?

As a special treat, I took literature courses when my schedule permitted. Since I also worked temp jobs during school breaks, I usually carried a light course load to avoid feeling pressured. Then I'd take at least six credits during summer session. I told myself I was just going to college for my own pleasure, not for a degree. In this way, I tiptoed past the still-powerful self-destructive tendencies which would, I feared, make me sabotage myself if I admitted to having a goal.

One of my favorite instructors was Margot Bankoff. Any woman who entered a male enclave like the Philosophy Department in those days had to be much better than good. Bankoff was in her late twenties, with a conspicuously low-key presentation. I was won over on the first day of her course in existentialism, which she began by saying, deadpan: "You're probably here to find out where it's at. But we're going to talk about where it's *not* at . . ."—a reference, she explained, to Sartre's idea of reality being defined by what it is not rather than by what it is. In Bankoff's classes the discussions were of such depth, we spent the better part of a semester unpacking the meaning of about ten pages of *Being and Nothingness*. (Later, my good opinion of her was enhanced when I heard she married the comic Milt Kamen. She'd often said not to take life too seriously.)

Reading the existentialists, I came to believe that, since it is impossible to verify whether or not God exists, it is as much a leap of faith to be an atheist as a believer. It was Camus's *Myth of Sisyphus* that seemed to lend, at last, some coherence to my understanding of life. I was captivated by the idea that (a) humans (always referred to as "man," of course) are in the essentially absurd position of seeking meaning in a universe that is inherently without meaning, and (b) we can always opt for suicide, that therefore, (c) if one chooses to stay alive, she must—if she wishes to live with integrity—take full responsibility for her own life, whatever form that takes.

I adopted this as my credo. I would stop thinking of myself as a victim of my unhappy childhood. I consciously chose life over suicide and would take responsibility for my actions on that basis. This stance gave impetus to my therapeutic work with Dr. Heimarck. But adopting a credo and experiencing its truth are two different things.

JIM FRIEDMAN WAS MY new boyfriend. He was forty-one, a misunderstood artist and beatnik, complete with a soft body, a goatee, and a never-cleaned apartment in the Village. He responded with compassion to the victimized child in me. (For years to come I would hear, from virtually every man who was attracted to me, "You have such sad eyes.") He called me Puss. The glamour I felt at having a boyfriend in the Village was enhanced because Jim was a gifted musician and songwriter whose work had been recorded by Judy Collins, Harry Belafonte, and Theodore Bikel. If you asked him nicely, Jim would agree to play you "a medley of my hit." (This would be "Hey Nelly, Nelly" or "The Hills of Shiloh," which he'd written with Shel Silverstein.) Not that his royalties supported him by a long shot. He kept Velveeta on his toast by writing advertising jingles and transcribing sheet music. He was bitter about this, feeling that he was owed a lot more success than he'd found in the fucking music business. So now he was writing a novel called *The Guardians*, about an Eichmann-like war criminal captured and sentenced to live in exile, guarded by four people who were the main characters.

I was proud that Jim was so respected on the music scene by rising stars like Steve Stills, who acknowledged Jim that year in large letters on the back of the new Buffalo Springfield album, as well as mainstream songwriters like Sheldon Harnick. When Judy Collins composed her first songs, she called Jim at 2:00 a.m. to come hear them. We got out of bed and took the subway uptown to Judy's West 79th Street apartment, where she played "Since You Asked" for us on the grand piano in her homey living room. It was beautiful. I remember she was so excited about her breakthrough. Judy was always so warm—effusive, even—but I was too overawed by her celebrity to have a real relationship with her.

However much respect Jim received, he still felt cheated by life, for which he largely blamed his mother, to whom he referred as The Dragon. Of course, I resonated plenty with that. Jim and I were burrowers and spent many hours in his basement pad, making love and playing chess. I loved to listen to the loopy conversations he had with his gray cats in an invented language. He was the first man I went with who I believed was on my side. He supported me in my struggle to climb out of the pits of depression and self-hatred, whether that meant persisting in therapy or following my conscience politically.

NINETEEN SIXTY-SEVEN WAS the year I first bought grass for myself. I would light up after a night of studying and lay in bed, stroking my silky black cat, Lady Flea, who sat Buddha-like on my chest, purring through inscrutable green eyes. As shadows from a candle danced across the high ceiling, we'd listen together to *Sergeant Pepper's Lonely Hearts Club Band*. I wandered through the new Beatles album as if it were a place, gliding and soaring, swimming through rich and exotic inner terrain. I loved marijuana.

Kate Coleman, one of Jim's neighbors on West 4th Street, was a reporter for *Newsweek*. One day, she invited Jim and me upstairs to be photographed for an article *Newsweek* was doing about the spread of marijuana throughout society. In exchange for signed releases permitting publication of our photos (as long as we were not recognizable), we partook of some first-class weed, courtesy of the magazine. Thus it came about that my hand appeared on a *Newsweek* cover, passing a joint to Jim's hand, my bitten cuticles photographically manicured.

• • •

MARCH 26, 1967, EASTER Sunday—a bright mild day with a hint of spring in the air. Jim and I are approaching Central Park's Sheep Meadow, drawn by the psychedelic Peter Max posters around town and the buzz about the Human Be-In, New York's answer to the one they had in Golden Gate Park last January.

The sweet smell of pot reaches us long before the scene appears: almost ten thousand people milling peacefully on the grass. There are hippies in flowing outfits, with painted faces, alongside families who must've come straight from the Easter Parade. One man dressed in a suit and tie and wearing a full-feathered Indian headdress stands, playing a flute. On the edge of the crowd a guy dressed all in white is singing folk songs and strumming a guitar, as friendly onlookers listen politely and pass joints. Although we smoked before heading uptown, I take a toke when one comes my way, just to be communal.

"Looks like this Happening is happening, Puss!" says Jim.

"This is great," I agree.

We amble on through the crowd and soon hear music coming from a sound system all the way across the Meadow. Eventually, we make out the unmistakable Allen Ginsburg, bespectacled and berobed, with long black hair and a longer black beard. He is sitting center stage on a makeshift platform, playing the harmonium, among a group of others playing drums and finger cymbals, all singing some repetitive Sanskrit chant.

More chanting a while later: seven or eight people come dancing through the crowd, carrying a huge papier-mâché mock-up of a bright yellow banana above their heads.

"*Bana-na, Bana-na . . . Ba-na-na,*" they sing calypso-style as the crowd laughs. A hot rumor has it you can get high by smoking the scrapings from the inside of a banana peel, after drying them in a slow oven. Jim and I exchange knowing looks: we tried it last week and just got frustrated by all that work for nothing. Still, we laugh along with everyone else.

Just then we hear a lilting call, "Jim!" An ecstatic Kate throws her arms around us in turn. "Hi, hi," she effuses, "isn't this great?" then adds, "I'm tripping! I finally tried acid and it is *sooo* beautiful."

It's the first time I've been with someone who is actually tripping—I've always been scared of LSD, what it might do to my inner demons if I tried it. But Kate's smile is contagious and all I can say is, "Far out."

● ● ●

THE WAR CONTINUED INEXORABLY. At the end of 1965, there were 184,000 American troops in Vietnam; by the end of '66, 385,000. Virtually all the guys my age had to face the decision about what to do about the draft. You could still get an exemption for being a teacher and many went into education for that reason rather than any desire to teach. Others left the country, most often moving to Canada. These choices were fraught with pain and rage.

Todd Gitlin, in his masterful account of the decade, *The Sixties: Years of Hope, Days of Rage,* asks a question that resonates powerfully for me as I write.

How can I convey the texture of this gone time so that you and I, reader, will be able to grasp, remember, believe that astonishing things actually happened? . . . Statistics are "background," we do not feel them tearing at our flesh. . . . We [young people] felt the violence in the world like a sharp instrument in our psychic skins.

For what was this hell of a war being waged? I became convinced it was for the benefit of what Eisenhower had termed the military-industrial complex, interested only in the rich mineral reserves in Southeast Asia and the victory of capitalism. As I saw it, these sinister powers, in cahoots with the mainstream media, fueled their weapons of empire using the bodies of my brothers, the vital young men I saw all around me, as fodder. It was insupportable. The nightly news reports were like bombs in the pit of my stomach, spurring me to action. I *had* to do everything I could to stop the war.

In the fall of '66, I joined City's small chapter of Students for a Democratic Society. We were a core group of fifteen or twenty, though 120 would turn out for demonstrations. I liked SDS because it upheld the importance of grassroots democracy, which I had glimpsed in action in Mississippi. The members were thoughtful and articulate and, like me, they were angry. From the ideological discussions at SDS meetings, and as I read history and studied political science, I concluded that our society had to be radically restructured into one based upon humane principles such as Rousseau's "enlightened self-interest"—the understanding that one's own long-term well-being is irrevocably tied to the well-being of fellow humans.

In December we learned that the US Army Materiel Command was coming to campus to recruit graduating seniors. This was the military agency responsible for procurement of napalm, which we knew was despoiling the Indochinese countryside and burning the flesh off any man, woman, or child in its path. In 1967 alone, the United States defoliated 1.7 million acres in South Vietnam. A coalition of campus antiwar groups staged a sit-in not only to stop them from recruiting but to publicize more widely the use and effects of napalm. Our position was that the USAMC was an illegal organization, as its procurement of chemical weapons violated the Geneva Conventions.

That Friday, seventy-five students piled into the office of the director of the campus Job Placement Center, where the interviews were to be held. We sat down on all the chairs, floors, and desks available, throwing the staff and Army recruiters into confusion. They asked us to leave. We stated that we would leave only after the two recruiters left the campus.

After a while, the dean of Student Life arrived. When his attempts to persuade us to leave failed, he warned that "undoubtedly there will be some disciplinary actions. I will write down the names of those I recognize." The rest of us debated amongst ourselves about giving him our names. Finally, doing what I thought was the honorable thing, I was one of twenty-six who did. At five o'clock, the recruiters left the campus, escorted by a group of chanting students ("one, two, three, four, we don't want your dirty war") and to cheers from the rest of us.

A few days later, the thirty-four students whose names were recorded were notified of charges against them. A hearing before a student-faculty disciplinary committee would be held the following week. To plan strategy and tactics, SDS met several times at the home of two of our members, Larry and Miriam, who lived in a railroad flat in a tenement down on Houston Street. We had long, heated discussions about how to use the situation to organize fellow students against the war. We wanted to throw a monkey wrench into the workings of the systems that supported it, in this case our college administration which, in our view, was collaborating in the war by allowing the USAMC to recruit on campus. The hearing would be closed to the public to divide us from supporters and prevent disruptive demonstrations. However, we would each be allowed to bring one person in as an "advisor."

As the date of the hearings approached, the SDS people agreed on a strategy of going in as each other's advisors. We knew that the committee hearing the charges would try to keep the focus on the issue of campus discipline; we decided not to answer their questions directly but instead, to turn the focus of the proceedings back to the war wherever possible. Meanwhile, we leafleted the campus and stood on the steps of Cohen Library, taking turns with a bullhorn, exhorting crowds of passing students to support our actions.

On the night of the hearing, we milled around the corridor outside Shepard's Great Hall in muted fear and excitement. We were called before the committee in groups of eleven or so students, each with his or her advisor. When it was my group's turn, I remember looking around as we filed into the front row of auditorium seats. The Great Hall was a room of enormous proportions, pseudo-gothic in design, with dark wood paneled walls and a huge cathedral-like ceiling. The committee of nine was seated on the platform before us in ornately carved, high-backed chairs behind a trestle table.

Our advisors sat in the row behind us, where we could

confer by turning around in our seats. I had asked a guy named Ian to be my advisor. He was a little older, with levelheaded positions in tune with my own. I was keyed up but determined not to let my fear outwit me. As the questioning began, the panel focused on students one by one, asking questions such as, "Did you participate in the obstruction of business in the college's Job Placement Center on the day of December 8, 1966?" The six students before me were quite lame in their responses, answering the questions straight, in timid voices. Why weren't they doing what we had agreed upon? Because of fear, obviously. Would I be able to do better? My pulse pounded in my ears as the attention of the panel moved down the line toward me.

I answered the first few questions in a shaky but suitably truculent voice. Yes, I was there on that date. I turned to Ian twice to get his opinion about how to word my responses. But once I was into the process, my anger outweighed my fear and I felt able to hold my own. The energy in the room, which had been heavy with disappointment, picked up, and I could feel my comrades' interest and support as their heads and hope turned toward me.

My opening came when Professor Mack, chairman of the committee, angrily reworded a question I had sidestepped several times.

"On that day, were you or were you not asked to leave the premises of the Job Placement Center by a responsible member of the faculty?"

I pounced. "No, I was not. A *responsible* member of the faculty would have been doing what I was doing—opposing the recruitment of students for an immoral and illegal war."

My comrades clapped, whistled, and stomped the floor in jubilant approval. As the panel moved on to the more seasoned activists, matters improved. They had a hard time getting a straight answer out of anybody. For the moment, the committee was stymied. I felt great, elated by my part in our small victory. Jim and I celebrated that night by going out to dinner (quite a departure from our impecunious norm).

In the end, however, thirty-four of us were suspended from classes for eight days. Fortunately, many of my professors sympathized with our action and found ways to help me keep up my course work. I was able to complete the semester without my grades dropping.

NOT LONG AFTERWARD, I was on a Trailways bus going to Woodstock, to join Jim for a weekend in the country at the home of some actor friends of his. Soothed by my anonymity and the motion of the bus, I looked out at trees ablaze—orange and gold and heart-stopping red. An unfamiliar sensation welled up within me. For the first time I could remember, simply and for no particular reason, I was glad to be alive. I smiled at my reflection in the window.

I CONTINUED TO SEE Dr. Heimarck twice a week throughout college. A lot of anxiety was coming up in my relationship with Jim. I had begun to feel stifled, impatient with his stubborn stance as an angry victim. This was the very sense of myself I was working so hard to overcome. In response to my complaints and efforts to enlighten him, Jim's sexual desire for me cooled. This was extremely painful to me; I still had a fundamental need to be wanted by men as a prerequisite to any sense of self-worth. I clutched and cried and Jim couldn't help but be turned off. That old familiar knot.

Toward the end of my junior year, we broke up. But it didn't take long for us to renew our friendship with many late-night calls, sharing confidences and cat stories. We remained friends until Jim died in 2000.

Jim Friedman sent this to all his friends on his birthday

I FULFILLED MY LAST science requirement at City with a popular course nicknamed, "Physics for Poets." In a steeply tiered lecture theater in Shepard Hall, Professor Harry Soodak made the history and ideas of physics come alive. Grateful as I was that he was such a good teacher, I was delighted when Soodak joined the contingent of several hundred CCNY students and faculty who marched downtown *en masse* to support the student uprising at Columbia University. There, at a rally at the Sundial, where hundreds of students and supporters filled the quad, I saw my old high school chum Lewis Cole (later called "mastermind of the Columbia Revolt" by the press), giving a speech from a balcony high above the crowd. It was the first time I recall hearing the term, "up against the wall, motherfucker" used in a political context.

During my last semester at City, spring 1969, the college was closed down by student strikes for open enrollment. Black and Hispanic students had organized to claim the right of any New York City high school graduate, regardless of grades, to be admitted to the City University. I was not active in the strike though I supported it in principle. I attended some classes at the homes of my professors; others were simply cancelled and Pass/Fail grades issued.

I did not achieve my goal to never get a grade below B, earning a C in Archery and also in a three-credit music appreciation course I opted to take because I had hoped to learn how to better listen to classical music. Nevertheless, I graduated *magna cum laude*. To my surprise, I was elected to the Phi Beta Kappa Society, an organization which I cherish and continue to support because it promotes the timeless benefits of a liberal arts education as a platform to a well-lived life.

CHAPTER 10

Alan

I took a break from political activism when I fell in love with Alan Rosenfeld in the summer of '68. We met through Laurie, who had been friends with Alan at NYU. He was twenty-nine, about 5'9" tall, and slightly rotund, with wavy brown hair and cornflower blue eyes. He was funny, warm, attentive—and straight as an arrow. I found him attractive despite the fact that he fit too well my stereotype of "a nice Jewish boy." Politically and culturally, he was so much more conservative than I was. He didn't even smoke dope.

Alan had a master's in communications from UCLA and was looking for work in television. When we met, he had just returned to New York from Pittsburgh, where he'd directed an award-winning series for teenagers on public television. He told me he was recovering from a broken engagement; he was sad. In fact, he said he had two previous relationships in which he wanted to get married but the girl had ended it. I didn't pay much attention. I was—unexpectedly—having fun dating him. I admired the fact that he was principled about his career. He was determined not to take purely commercial jobs, so his search was taking a long time. I was going into senior year, taking two interesting courses in summer school and temping as a secretary.

I remember that summer as warm and leisurely, full of

trips to upstate lakes and dinners on restaurant patios. Alan was surviving courtesy of American Express, pending future employment. We ate only at better restaurants since, in those days, only the finer restaurants took credit cards. This was a welcome change—Jim and I almost never ate out.

Alan taught me how to drive with a stick shift in his convertible sports car, a little red Triumph which he loved unnaturally. He had a lusty sensuality as well as a boyish romanticism. He called me "my honey" and brought me little stuffed animals, which I hated and told him so. He also played the guitar and wrote a pretty love song for me. I was flattered and touched, and told him so. We spent a lot of time with Alan's two best friends from UCLA, Russ Aldrich and Peter Brown. Russ, tall, slender, and fastidious, was a director of commercials for a big ad agency. He was dating Astrid, a very blond Lufthansa stewardess who lived down the hall in Russ's elegant eastside brownstone. (From Astrid I learned that if you do not want to drink at a party but wish to *appear* to be drinking, you can put an olive in a glass of water and everyone will think it's a martini. For my part, I always preferred the real thing.)

But my favorite dinner partners were Peter and his fiancée, Veronica. Our well-lubricated *soirées* were always fun and often raucous, whether in one of our favorite restaurants, like Martell's on Third Avenue, or in Peter's bachelor pad. We spent one evening there doing a reading of my old favorite, *Who's Afraid of Virginia Woolf?* Alan and I read George and Martha, though our affectionate relations resembled theirs not at all. Alan loved the theater and supported my dream of becoming an actress after graduation. I felt I had finally found a man who would not disappoint me, whose love I could count on. Life was a round of delightful pleasures.

Then, in July, Alan asked me to marry him.

I had never wanted to get married. After all, the unions with which I was most familiar were my parents' marriages, and I certainly didn't want anything like that. More to the point, I was afraid of being trapped in a relationship with no escape, as I had felt trapped in life with my mother. As much as I loved Alan and wanted to be with him, I told him I just wanted to live together. But cohabitation without benefit of wedlock was still somewhat scandalous to mainstream America in 1968 and Alan was determined to do it the traditional way. When I said no to his repeated proposals, he just said OK, in a way that meant he was not going to give up. His motto was, "He conquers who endures." Secretly, the way he wanted me so much turned me soft inside.

• • •

IT IS AUGUST, AND the late afternoon sun is warming my suntanned body, still wet from our last swim. Alan lies on the plastic lounge chair beside me, droplets of water glistening in the hair on his chest. We have the pool all to ourselves. It's Saturday and his grandmother has lent us her cabin in a Catskill Mountain bungalow colony for the weekend. We are only half a mile from the Granville, where I attempted suicide four years ago. The scars on my wrists are still pinkish.

My eyes are closed but I am keenly aware of the maleness of Alan's presence. I love knowing I can touch his body any time I want. A feeling of languid well-being envelops me. When the sun finally goes down, we will shower and go out for dinner. Later, I know we'll make love and fall asleep, our bodies purring with satisfaction, in each other's arms.

I am utterly content.

Just then Alan says, for the umpteenth time, "So when are we going to get married?" His eyes are still closed.

Without thinking, I answer, "I bet if I said yes, you'd drop your teeth." This is a line straight out of the movie *Love with the Proper Stranger*, starring Natalie Wood and Steve McQueen.

"Try me," says Alan, without turning his head from the sun.

And I say, though shocked to hear it come out of my mouth, "Yes."

From that moment on, I'm swept along in a flow of events that seem to unfold with a life of their own.

• • •

WE WERE NOW ENGAGED and somehow, that changed everything. At first, I was filled with a joyful sense that at last I had found a safe harbor. But my happiness began to ebb away as I noticed that everyone started behaving differently toward me. I was surprised and saddened when Noni and Bill, the aunt and uncle who loved me like a daughter, acted as if I were, somehow, a more legitimate person now. I expected this reaction from my father but not from the Singers, who knew me so well and who had always treated me as an individual, someone special and worthy unto herself. And of course my mother, who had moved to Las Vegas with Don, was thrilled. I could feel her excitement through the telephone line when I told her the news. To Bonnie, as we know, getting married was the be-all and end-all. My discomfort began to grow.

At a small engagement party in his apartment, Russ gave me *The New York Times Cook Book* as a gift. I loved to cook but this frightened me. Into what kind of a pigeonhole were they all trying to squeeze me?

In September, I took a full program of fifteen credits at City. Alan finally got a good job as a director for an independent production company outside Washington. During the fall semester I went down there on weekends and school breaks. We drove around DC and all its suburbs, hunting for an apartment for Alan, the place where we would live when we got married. We finally found a modest one-bedroom in one of the big postwar complexes of boxy brick buildings in Alexandria, Virginia. We shopped for furniture. For the bedroom, Alan insisted we use his parents' old bed, in storage since his widowed father had remarried. The Freudian implications of sharing his dead mother's bed were a bit much for me. I argued vociferously against it. But once Alan set his mind to something, he wouldn't relent. He conquers who endures. Telling myself it wasn't that important, I gave in. On the other hand, Alan was encouraging me to apply to the apprenticeship program at the newly formed Arena Stage Repertory Company after we got married. So he certainly didn't expect me to settle for the role of housewife, I kept assuring myself.

We explored Washington together—I hadn't visited there since JFK's funeral. We went to all the tourist sights, which was fun, but Alan kept insisting that his beloved red TR4 be in every picture. "Me and my car in front of the Washington Monument, the Lincoln Memorial, the White House." Despite the fact that I amuse myself by indulging silly fetishes of my own, I started feeling turned off by these inanities. It seemed that the closer I felt to Alan, the less tolerant I became. With increasing urgency, I analyzed my fear of intimacy with Dr. Heimarck.

At first, Alan agreed to have a simple wedding at City Hall, which I wanted. A month later, he decided we must be married by his childhood rabbi from the Bronx. Reluctantly, I said OK. Though I refused to admit it to myself, part of me found comfort in Alan's traditionalism. It made me trust him—as much as I was able to trust any man. We went to visit this gentle, caring rabbi in his musty old apartment on the Grand Concourse. After talking for a little while we set a date: June 15, 1969.

As the weeks went on, Alan thought of more and more

people in his life who would drop dead if they were not invited to his wedding. This wedding kept getting bigger, looming like a huge boulder rolling down a hill, straight at me. A small, insistent voice started up in my head, saying, "Don't do it, don't do it, don't do it, don't do it . . ." This terrified me more than anything. Was I going to sabotage my chance for a healthy, loving relationship because of my neurotic fears?

As winter deepened, new anxieties gripped me. I began to imagine people were following me down the street as I walked home after dark. I analyzed this endlessly in therapy, where I could hardly keep up with the fast-breaking events in my fervid psyche. I started to get migraines and, by the end of March, I had one constant headache. Dr. Heimarck and I talked about all the possible causes: my anxiety about graduating from college, my fear of intimacy and its childhood roots, etc., etc., etc. Once, Alan came to a therapy session with me to talk about it. But the voice in my head only became more insistent: "Don't do it, don't do it, don't do it, don't do it, don't do it . . ."

The headache got worse.

The last straw came when Alan's aunt and stepmother called, sorry for me because my own family (knowing I would hate it) was not planning a bridal shower. Kindly, they offered to give one for me. The velvet-gloved vise of bourgeois convention was closing around my temples.

• • •

I'M MAKING DINNER IN my tiny kitchen, referring to the recipe in my *New York Times Cook Book*. The headache makes it hard to concentrate. I'm nervous, but my mind is made up. Lady Flea is standing at my feet, gazing up expectantly. By the time I fill her bowl from the can of Friskies tuna, the downstairs bell is already buzzing. Weekend traffic from DC must have been light.

"Hi, honey," chirps Alan as he walks in. I'm annoyed by his everlasting cheeriness. But I don't want to be annoyed; I want to be kind.

"Hi," I answer without turning around as he hangs his jacket in the closet. He comes up behind me, circling my waist with his arms and peering over my shoulder. "Looks good. What is it?"

"*Carbonnade à la flamande.*"

"You put beer in it?"

"Yes, it's Belgian—you know, '*flamande,*' Flemish." Can't miss a chance to lecture, can you, Riqui? Give him a break, at least tonight.

"See, I knew you'd use that cookbook. You got so freaked out when Russ gave it to you."

"Well, that was because of them seeing me as a housewife. Don't you understand that yet?" Hold on, hold on, Riqui. "Anyway, I think it's gonna be good. Why don't you relax—it'll be ready in a few minutes."

Alan goes into the main room and leans on the turquoise bolster, stroking Lady Flea until we eat. She stays put—she loves his touch as much as I do. At dinner, I ask him a lot of questions about work, avoiding any talk of the wedding. Afterward, I bring out my "psychedelic" Peter Max mugs and we sit on the couch, sipping coffee.

"I have to talk to you," I say, quavering a little.

"Uh-oh, what is it?" He's using that affectionate, patronizing tone that pisses me off.

"I can't marry you."

"Mm-hmm. How come?" He doesn't believe me.

"You know I never wanted to get married. I can't stand being shoehorned into a bourgeois convention I don't believe in. I feel like I'm suffocating."

"Have you talked to Dr. Heimarck about it?" He's looking at me now with cocked head, a hint of uncertainty in his voice.

"Of course, I've talked to Dr. Heimarck about it. I've talked and talked." Lower your voice, Riqui. I swallow and resist the temptation to touch his arm. "You know I love you—it's not that. It's just I can't marry you and move to Washington."

His face grows paler; he's holding his half-full mug at a dangerous angle.

"Look, I know you're scared. We don't have to get married right away. We can wait a while."

My headache is at a crescendo. Am I doing the right thing, or ruining my best chance for happiness? I don't know, I don't know.

"No. I'm sorry."

I feel as if I'm amputating my own arm, without anesthesia.

"Honey, you can't be serious," he says, putting his cup on the coffee table. "This is nuts! Where is this coming from all of a sudden?"

"It's not all of a sudden. You know I've been having these horrible headaches. And now this wedding shower, I hate wedding showers . . ."

"So tell them you don't want the stupid shower!" He's starting to tear up.

". . . and the rabbi and all the people and your mother's bed. I can't do it! We have to end it." Tears wet my cheeks.

"So we'll cancel the wedding and get married at City Hall. Riqui, please . . . I can't believe this." He pauses. "What about acting? You're going to try out for the Arena Stage." Tears fill his blue eyes and spill through his thick lashes. We're both crying now. I reach over and put my arms around him, holding him awkwardly as he sobs.

"I'm sorry, I'm so sorry," I wail. "I can't help it. I know you must be angry. I can't blame you for being angry."

In a small voice, Alan says, "We'll just live together, then."

"No." We've gone too far for that, somehow. I have to do what I have to do. I feel so hot and my head is pounding.

"Why not?" I'm relieved to hear the truculence in his voice. Anything's better than seeing how much I'm hurting him.

"You'll just resent me, and be passive aggressive, the way you get. It won't work."

"I will *not* resent you. I love you. You know how much I love you."

"I know, I know. But we're so different, we have such different values. You want a straight, middle-class life and I don't. I feel like I'm suffocating . . ."

We're silent for a while—the tears have stopped. None of this is news. We've known it all along, haven't we? Yet it's so unfair to Alan.

"I'm sorry," I repeat. He leans into me and we lie back together on my single bed. At first, I think he's fallen asleep; his body weighs heavily on my side. It seems like hours lying here; I just wish he would leave already and this would be over. I can't believe I'm thinking this—I've just blindsided him in the worst possible way.

I shift my weight and Alan stirs.

"I know you must be angry. It's important to express your anger." His anger would be such a relief—for both of us, I think.

"What makes me angry is when you keep telling me I'm angry," he spits, sitting up and picking up his cold coffee. Suddenly, a thought occurs to him. "Why didn't you tell me before we had that whole dinner?"

This confounds me. "Well, I wanted you to have a good dinner after your trip," I stammer. "I didn't want to just throw it at you right away."

"Well, you should have," he snaps as he stands up, raises the coffee mug, and slams it to the floor, where it shatters into garishly colored pieces.

Lady Flea darts under the bed. Alan goes to the closet, yanks his jacket from the hanger, and stalks out of the apartment, slamming the door behind him.

I stay seated on the couch for a long while. In the ensuing silence, my headache vanishes.

In all the years since, I've never had a migraine again.

ainful memories of ruptured relationships blur my view of upstate towns, fewer and farther between as the bus starts the long upgrade to the Catskills, slowing down even more. The trees along the highway are bare now, still wintry.

Men. How many times have I gone through that unique hell of losing a man with whom I was once happy, who I hoped would save me? With all the therapy and even after the sea change of the Women's Movement, my gut twists as I recall breaking up with Alan, the agony of losing Steve. Even with Jim Friedman, I felt so rejected.

I shift in my seat, trying to get more comfortable without disturbing Olga.

I don't want to think about that pain. I go back to counting bus trips . . .

CHAPTER 11
A Mind Blown . . .

"A mind blown is a mind shown," Robbie said again in his mellow California way as we headed toward Montreal. We were on the road north in a chocolate brown '64 Volkswagen microbus with no reverse gear. It seemed Robbie had dropped reverse on a dirt-road side trip somewhere in Kansas and couldn't afford to fix it. What, I wondered, had I gotten myself into? It was July 29, 1969.

Linda Arkin, a friend of Roberta's, introduced me to Robbie one afternoon shortly after my graduation from City. She was friends with his sister. Since breaking my engagement in April, I had been wandering around the city in a kind of trance of pain. The open enrollment strike which shut the school down meant my college career had ended not with a bang but with a whimper, which only added to my sense of disorientation. In sympathy for my state, Linda invited me out to the movies that hot summer day. She had been hanging around with Robbie for a few weeks while he was in New York, visiting his family and buying camera equipment. He was planning to be a photographer.

Robbie was a wiry little black guy, about five foot seven. Although he had grown up in the Bronx, he had a California cool cultivated in San Diego, where he settled after his discharge from the Navy. He had vowed never to go through an

East Coast winter again. His light-coffee-colored face was warm and open. His hair was long and rather odd looking, flying around his head in strings. He told us that on his trip east he had stopped in a black barbershop in Texas. He'd flopped in a chair and said to the barber, "straighten out my Afro," meaning please trim my hair. Then, exhausted from his long stretch at the wheel, he fell asleep. He woke to find to his dismay that his nappy hair had been chemically straightened, in the now-scorned fashion of the older generation. He related this tale rather wistfully.

"Nice guy," I thought of Robbie, "but what a jerk!"

After the movie—Robert Downey Sr.'s *Putney Swope*—we walked up sizzling Second Avenue to Drake's Drum for their trademark burgers on English muffins and a cold beer. Sitting side by side at the empty bar, we basked in the dark cool of the conditioned air. Robbie was saying how he really wanted company on his drive back to San Diego, which he planned to take across the Trans-Canada Highway.

"Why don't you go?" Linda said to me, suddenly. I blinked. As I bit into my rare burger, I considered this. I could not think of one good reason not to go. The wedding was off, and in my state of guilty misery and gnawing suspicion that I had made a terrible mistake, I couldn't imagine going to auditions. My only semblance of a plan for the future was to go to that Woodstock Music Festival, but I hadn't bought tickets yet. I looked at Robbie more closely. I wasn't particularly attracted to him but he seemed like a good guy and I liked how enthusiastic he seemed about his photography.

Wiping ketchup from my chin and swallowing hard, I said, "I'll go with you."

"Far out," said Robbie with a big smile.

A week later, we were on the road.

The back of the bus was outfitted with a narrow platform

laid with sheepskin rugs—the only bed. He had a Coleman stove, plenty of grass, and rock music on bulky tape cartridges. The rest of the space was taken up by bags filled with cameras, lenses of varying lengths, and a tripod. Robbie said he'd sleep on the floor in his sleeping bag, he didn't mind. But that felt weird. As Katie Coleman said about those times (years later, in a program called *The Sixties*), for our generation having sex was like shaking hands. On our second night out, having smoked some of that good grass, I drew Robbie up onto the platform bed, my way of trying to get more comfortable with him. I did get more comfortable, but not much more. We were from such different worlds.

Having been radicalized by his tour of duty in Vietnam, Robbie shared my political views. But his mildness of manner made me extremely nervous—it was so not my edgy New York way. He'd chat pleasantly with perfect strangers at every rest stop while I sat in the bus, antsy and fearful, wishing he would come away. In his affable manner, he often suggested to obviously straitlaced, conservative people vacationing in their Winnebagos, that perhaps the government wasn't telling us the whole truth about the war. And they would actually engage in civil conversation with Robbie, the friendly little black guy—a Navy veteran! As we got on the road again, he would observe with satisfaction, "A mind blown is a mind shown"— which, by the fourth time he said it, made me want to scream.

By the time we got to Montreal, I was popping my prescribed Valium at the minimum intervals. (Dr. Heimarck had noted with some understatement that, once again, I was acting impulsively.)

In Montreal, we crashed at the barely furnished basement apartment of some young Quebecois longhairs. Robbie approached them in the street to ask if they knew where we could get a shower. As in the United States, there was a great brotherhood of young people all across Canada, a community in lifestyle as much as politics. In Robbie's company, I gradually started to feel like one of them. We recognized each other easily: the men had long hair, beards, afros; the women wore long skirts or dirty bell-bottom jeans. Everyone wore bright colors and loose, flowing fabrics or fringed leather. When we passed each other on the road, we flashed the peace sign: two fingers in a V-formation. There was no problem distinguishing Us from Them—the crew-cut older generation who were, as so many of us saw it, trying to kill us with their unjust war.

We usually parked the bus in a campground overnight, cooking simple meals on Robbie's Coleman stove. One night in Ontario, I spread the sleeping bag on the grass and, despite Robbie's warnings, spent the night under a dome of stars more amazing than I had ever seen outside the Hayden Planetarium. I awoke at dawn covered with insect bites, but it was worth it. My grief over losing Alan was starting to abate.

In cities, we often ate at soup kitchens run by the Diggers. These Diggers were hippies, namesakes of the nineteenth-century English anti-capitalists who created alternative systems of economic community. They gave away food and clothing wherever they could.

Rock music was everywhere and as we traveled west, Robbie and I heard reports of astonishing happenings at Woodstock: thousands of us in the open air, smoking pot, sharing LSD, and making love in the mud and sunshine to the soaring sounds of free music. We knew it was a milestone. Society was on the brink of the Age of Aquarius and we would change the world, no question.

The further west we drove in the little brown bus, the looser I became.

Robbie always picked up hitchhikers, and there were many. It seemed that our whole generation was on the road that summer. My favorite hitchhiker was a guy named Gino, a curly-headed Canadian with a huge smile and boundless enthusiasm. We picked him up right outside Sault Ste. Marie and he traveled with us through most of Ontario. Gino said the three of us looked like the Mod Squad. Tooling along the highway, we smoked some grass and he and Robbie talked for hours about all kinds of stuff. I sat in the back, tuning in and out of the conversation, listening to music that made my heart rocket with a sense of expanding possibilities: The Steve Miller Band's *Children of the Future*; Blood, Sweat & Tears's *Child Is Father to the Man*; and of course, Steppenwolf:

> *Get your motor running,*
> *Head out on the highway,*
> *Lookin' for adventure,*
> *In whatever comes our way . . .*
>
> *Like a true nature's child,*
> *We were born, born to be wild . . .*

God, that backbeat!

About a week after we dropped Gino off, we spotted him again, thumbing a ride somewhere on the endless prairies of Saskatchewan.

"Gino, Gino . . . ," we cried as we pulled onto the shoulder of the highway. It was like meeting a long-lost friend.

When the bus broke down in Winnipeg on the three-day Canadian Labor Day weekend, we looked for kindred spirits in a city park. It was raining, so we asked around for a crash pad. Every town of any size seemed to have one, an apartment or house where you could just go and stay for a few nights and maybe eat, if you or someone else brought food.

We were directed to a house in a working class neighborhood. There were ten or fifteen mattresses and sleeping bags on the floor in different rooms. Incense burned all day and sequined Indian print cottons, spread on chairs, windows, and beds, helped alleviate the impact of the dishes piled high in the sink, scraps of food on the table and floors, grime and dust balls in every corner. At night, we sat around in a circle with maybe eight other people, some travelers, some who lived there or nearby, passing joints, talking, listening to music. Later, we could hear couples and new acquaintances making it on various mattresses around us.

On the road again, the boring plains finally gave way to mountains. The Canadian Rockies were breathtaking in more ways than one, since I was terrified when it was my turn to drive through them. The bus, which couldn't do more than fifty-five on a flat surface, inched up the mountain roads with their steep drop-offs. When another VW bus passed in the opposite direction, it took all my nerve to take one hand off the wheel to flash the requisite V-sign to the other driver.

We reached the coast about two and a half weeks after leaving New York. Robbie did most of the driving down the rugged coast of Washington and Oregon, so I got to enjoy the ocean views. When we got to the redwoods, I was awestruck. Walking among the towering trees in California's Muir Woods, I couldn't understand why Robbie had lugged all his camera equipment into the peaceful forest. Some kind of ego trip, I harrumphed to myself.

"Can't you just enjoy being here, now?" I demanded, self-righteously. He was silent but, as usual, my intolerance hurt his feelings. I could see it on his face. Nevertheless, he proceeded to set the camera on a tripod, strip off all his clothes, and seat himself in a cross-legged pose in front of the giant ferns and trees. Dour, I agreed to snap the shutter. Later, when I saw the magical picture Robbie created—primeval man in the primordial forest—I was ashamed of myself.

We reached San Francisco toward the end of August and crashed with some friends of Robbie's. There, I dropped LSD for the first time. Until then, I had feared that acid would puncture the ego strength I had worked so hard to build in my five years of therapy. Now, after all my recent challenges and adventures, I felt free enough to take the chance.

• • •

I'M ON THE PASSENGER side of the vinyl bench seat of the VW when the LSD starts doing its work. Robbie told me he has dropped a lot of acid; he is used to tripping. Still, I am amazed he can drive so normally up and down the hilly streets of brightly painted Victorian houses. My senses are running riot as we ride around the city. All at once, it seems the universe is revealing to me a glory I had never imagined. We stop in an open-air café for an apple turnover. In the restaurant bathroom, I am astonished to feel my entire alimentary canal from the inside, including every inch of my intestines from beginning to end.

In Golden Gate Park, nature's amazing palette of greens makes me weep with joy.

"A mind blown is a mind shown," says Robbie softly.

I look over at him and see that he is absolutely beautiful; a liquid love fills me entirely. Simultaneously I am aware that if one could *really* see any other person with perfect clarity, as I am now, they too would be absolutely beautiful.

We continue to drive around the city and insights flood my consciousness. The stone wall of my limitations, at which I have been chipping away in therapy with a hammer and chisel, is becoming loose gravel. I know I can sweep it all away if I am quick enough. Incredibly excited by this possibility, I start talking fast, trying to tell Robbie what I'm seeing. He pulls over and sits quietly, listening to my stream of consciousness, exuding love, acceptance, and a sense of wonder.

Back at the house where we're crashing, we sit in the living room, rapping with our hostess Joanie about what to eat. In response to a suggestion from Robbie, I hear her say, "Mmmm, vegetables," as if they're a delicious treat. This surprises me inordinately; I have never heard anyone speak of vegetables this way. California people are definitely different.

There's a knock on the door and Joanie leads two guys and a chick into the room. (I'm picking up the lingo, I see.) I get a bad feeling about these people, which quickly expands into a sense of dread. Are they actually real?

Suddenly, my mind is spinning in fear. Is that me crying? Somewhere in the distance, Joanie is trying to talk me down from my panic but I am desperate to get away from these strangers. With soft words of reassurance, Robbie leads me out to the parked bus, where we lie on the platform bed. I cling to him for dear life. The air around us is alive and Robbie and I are mere points of energy, an assemblage of seething particles of blue light. I cannot breathe. If I don't hold on to Robbie, I'll fall off the edge of the universe. I hold on.

Hours pass—or is it minutes? Gradually I realize, intellectually at least, that this feeling is just a fear. I'm calm enough to go back into the house, though I must still hold on to Robbie's hand for the rest of the day, even while he goes to the bathroom. He accepts this with gentle tolerance. By evening, with the bathroom door closed, I'm able to let him pee alone while I gaze into the mirror over the stained sink.

With wonder, I think, "I'm looking into the eyes of someone in a psychotic state." This makes me laugh. I'm so grateful to Robbie for sticking with me.

I have fallen in love.

．．．

FROM SAN FRANCISCO, WE gave a ride to a pretty French girl we met in Haight-Ashbury. She was planning to hitchhike through Central America, following in the footsteps of her compatriot Régis Debray, the revolutionary who joined the guerillas in the mountains of Bolivia. I was jealous of Robbie's attentions to her, but he told me in his diffident way that he loved me.

I stayed with Robbie in San Diego, meeting his friends and reveling in our new love as he showed me around. I had planned to return to New York in September, but when the time came, the thought of separating from Robbie was too painful.

"I'm thinking of moving here," I told him. His face lit up.

I spent a month in New York, saying good-bye to friends and family and to Dr. Heimarck, who was highly skeptical about my impulsive move. I asked Roberta to keep my books, sold my furniture for a pittance, and gave my dear Lady Flea to Uncle Bill and Aunt Noni, who promptly renamed her Ketzele.

I returned to San Diego three weeks later to start my new life.

CHAPTER 12
Brave New World

As I walk off the plane at Lindbergh Field, my heart pounds with excitement at the prospect of seeing Robbie again. I search the small group of people at the gate. No Robbie. Disbelieving, I look again. And again. He's really not here. My throat constricts.

"He must be parking, a little late, car trouble . . . ," I tell myself.

The minutes tick by and I battle tears of panic. My underarms are clammy in my sleeveless blouse. I know no one else in this strangely sunlit city. I'm afraid to leave the gate area to look for a phone. What if he comes to find me and I miss him? Already, I'm experiencing the familiar nightmare. And already I'm planning how to cope with imminent disaster. . . . If Robbie doesn't want me, I can turn around and go back to New York. I can stay with Bill and Noni until I find a job, or . . . where is he? An accident? Oh, God, no, don't think of that . . .

Finally—fifteen or twenty minutes may have passed—I start a frozen walk down the corridor toward the main terminal, carefully scanning right and left as I walk so as not to miss seeing Robbie running to find me. As I reach an open waiting area, I spot him, asleep, slouched in one of the molded plastic chairs facing a television, arms folded across his chest. I touch his shoulder and he leaps into motion, alarmed.

"Riqui, you're here!"

"Where were you?" I say. "I've been here for half an hour."

"I was up all night, cleaning the apartment. I got here early. I guess I fell out."

"How could you?" My cry is equal parts rage and relief. "I didn't know what to do."

As the tears finally come, Robbie hugs me. He is all apologies and profuse explanations. He has a new haircut, a still-short natural, and he looks handsome. His brown denim bell-bottoms are clean and his short-sleeved shirt looks pressed. He hugs me nervously and I can see he feels confused and anxious. I allow myself to be comforted, trying to capture some of the joy of reunion I had anticipated during the long flight. But a cold fear has settled in my stomach.

This little scene turns out to be a template for our domestic relationship.

Welcome to San Diego.

. . .

ROBBIE'S APARTMENT WAS IN the basement of a Victorian house in the Hillcrest neighborhood, near Balboa Park. Curlew Street was lined with houses like ours—big, old, moderately well-kept, with no winter weather to withstand. All kinds of flowers brightened even the plainest homes during most of the year. The apartment entrance was down around back of the house, through an overgrown yard that looked out over one of the wild canyons that streak the city. You came into the kitchen through a screen door, then sidled between a Formica table and the stove to get to the living room. Robbie had removed the sofa and chairs, leaving only a richly colored, if threadbare, Persian carpet and some large cushions to lie around on. Later, we painted a scavenged industrial spool to use as a table, with two canvas director's chairs. On the wall-mounted shelves were some books, a hookah, and Robbie's stereo and record collection. The bedroom was ample with a double bed, a desk, and a lamp on the night table and a high window at ground level.

The bathroom was the second largest room, with a cement floor. Besides the usual fixtures, it doubled as a darkroom, complete with a dry mount press which Robbie used for his haunting eight-by-ten black and whites, portraits mostly, many of which hung on the paneled living room walls. He earned extra money with photography jobs, when he could get them.

In those first disoriented months, Robbie taught me how to develop photographs and create certain effects with the enlarger. I spent hours, stoned, making pictures in that cavernous, red-lit room. I would experiment with different looks and exposures while listening to records over headphones. I loved the music Robbie turned me on to: Chicago Transit Authority, Canned Heat, Santana.

Using his veteran's benefits, Robbie was taking nineteen credits at Mesa Junior College. He immediately got involved in student politics and "rapped" at the campus rally on October 15, National Moratorium Day, which saw rap sessions and anti-war rallies across the country. Robbie was later elected president of the student body for the spring semester.

Even now, when I picture Robbie's face, his gentle eyes and smooth brown skin, I feel an extraordinary tenderness. During those first months in California, my world centered on him. I had no other connections in town, and little sense that I might make any. For one thing, I had no car. Public transportation was sparse and pedestrians virtually unheard of. One day, as I walked up Curlew Street to pick up some milk, a five-year-old neighbor playing in his front yard called out: "Where are you going?"

"To the store," I replied.

His jaw dropped in amazement: "Why are you walking?"

Ever affable, Robbie had many friends, men and women, black and white—all of them, apparently, easier to talk to than me. He was always making new friends as he bopped around town in his trusty brown bus, whose reverse gear had finally been restored. We had agreed to be sexually monogamous, an arrangement considered quaint, if not downright reactionary by most people we knew. Still, Robbie would greet every attractive young woman with a seductive, "How ya' doin', sweet thing?" This always made me flinch.

When I first moved in, Robbie's friends were in the habit of dropping by all the time, walking into the kitchen without knocking, which I experienced as an invasion of my one safe space. I insisted that visitors knock and wait to be admitted. His friends thought Robbie's new ol' lady was pathetically uptight. I didn't conceal the fact that I hated the term "ol' lady" because of the way it utterly discounted me as a person. His friends started dropping in a lot less.

To me, San Diego was a cultural wasteland, where everyone had even white teeth and suspiciously easygoing manners, as if they'd been warm all their lives. I missed Dr. Heimarck and dreamt of him often. I was a stranger in a strange land.

Between his busy schedule and the uneasy burden of living with someone who looked to him as her only source of wellbeing, Robbie often came home hours late. Waiting, I freaked out as the hand on the clock passed the hour when he said he would return, and then the next, and the next. Emotional echoes were triggered from early childhood hours spent in misery, waiting for my chronically late father to pick me up on his visitation day.

Roberta, the original pack rat, saved my letters and postcards.

November 16, 1969

Dear Roberta,

Well, I'm furious, for a change. Robbie went out two hours ago, saying "I'll be back in an hour." This is after Friday night when he went out at 8 to do some publicity shots for a rock group at a beer joint. I was going to go with him but I decided not to (since he hadn't invited me). He kept saying he'd be back early. At midnight, I decided that instead of exploding I was going out. This is quite a trick in San Diego, at midnight, without a car. But I got all prettied up, called a cab and went to this bar & picked up two guys & got stoned in their car & got home at 2:30—and Robbie had just gotten home and didn't even know I was out. Then he got upset at the thought of how he would have felt when he walked in the bedroom & I wasn't there!...

He just came home and when I asked him why he'd said he'd be back in an hour, he apologized. He's always apologizing, which puts me in the role of a nag.

Frustrated by Robbie's inaccessibility, I shrieked, I sobbed, I ranted and raged. Once, I threw a chair in his direction. He just stared at me, wide-eyed in apparent fear, silent in the face of my violent emotions. When I was spent and we had found our way back to the gentle sweet connection we shared, Robbie tried to reassure me by saying, "Don't you think I love you?" But why did he always put it in the form of a question? Our sex life dwindled under the stress.

In a grasp at some kind of independence, I started attending open meetings at the Synanon Club, which was within walking distance from our house. Here we "played the Synanon Game," a sort of leaderless group therapy, invented by junkies in the late fifties. Synanon had been effective in getting people off heroin, and was now open to non-junkies—"squares"—billing itself as "an education process, a lifestyle and . . . a social movement." I attended the jargon-laden sessions, where everyone was harangued to "get off their bullshit" and tell the healing truth about themselves. In college, I had been in a couple of T-groups, unstructured laboratories for group dynamics, and I felt more or less comfortable with the confrontational *modus operandi* I found at Synanon. Anyway, I enjoyed the drama. After the first couple of meetings, I felt a bit less isolated.

The group was large, about twenty people most nights. Half the participants were addicts in recovery, clad in the overalls that were a kind of uniform. The junkies had the most prestige because they had really been there, down and dirty. They were practiced at "pulling people's covers," exposing self-deception. On my third or fourth night, when it was my turn to talk, I copped to still smoking grass. I knew the first rule of the Synanon Game was a commitment to use no drugs at all. Still, I couldn't see lying. The group was outraged, and I was strenuously attacked. I was kicked out of Synanon. But I hadn't connected enough with anyone there to care much.

ONCE A MONTH, ROBBIE and I drove downtown to a government distribution point to pick up cartons of government food commodities from a Department of Agriculture distribution center. These included supplies of beans, rice, Spam, butter, macaroni, a big orange block of cheddar cheese, and assorted canned goods. Almost everyone we knew got commodities: students, communes, the many people who hung out more than worked, people who believed in ripping off the system, which I guess I did too. Robbie hated doing it—it reminded him too much of the humiliations of his childhood. But since he didn't receive his first VA check until December, the food helped us make ends meet.

At the end of October, I went to an employment agency, hoping, I wrote Roberta, to find "a hip job," perhaps at a radio station. As the young employment counselor reviewed my application—BA in psychology, *magna cum laude*, Phi Beta Kappa, continuity director at WHN—the first question she asked me was, "Can you type?" Later, preparing me to interview with a prospective employer, she told me, "He's a bit of a Jew, but he's all right."

I was dumbfounded—no one had ever said such a thing to me before. Swallowing hard, I said, "What does that mean? I'm Jewish." She became flustered and backpedaled furiously. "Well, I mean, I'm sorry, it's just an expression. . . ."

I got a boring job as a receptionist at a construction firm.

MY MOTHER, NATURALLY, WAS relieved that I had a man. Bonnie was no racist—she'd had several black friends back in New York. It had taken her time to get over my broken engagement with Alan, who was both Jewish and financially secure, but she was happy I now lived close enough to visit her in Vegas. Robbie and I drove there for the weekend soon after I moved to San Diego.

When we arrived on Friday afternoon, Robbie showed my sister Heather and toddler Danny the bus you could sleep in. They thought this was the coolest thing and he hung out with them while they played in it. My mother took me inside where I found, in platters all in a row on the kitchen counter, a fully cooked turkey, ham, and brisket.

"Ma, what's this?" I asked, eyes popping and mouth watering. "We're only here for two days."

"Well," said Bonnie. "I didn't know what he liked."

At times, you just had to love her.

She, Don, and their kids were in a pretty good phase. I always liked Vegas and it felt good to be on home ground with my family for a while. I almost dreaded going back to San Diego. Sometimes, I went to Vegas on my own to meet Laurie, my old partner in troublemaking, when she came to town on gambling junkets. Now a successful business owner, she gambled often enough to rate a free room at the brand-new Caesar's Palace hotel. While I lived in San Diego, she several times paid for me to fly in and spend the weekend with her. In sharp contrast to my countercultural life with Robbie, I enjoyed spending hours at the blackjack table, with the plentiful free food, cigarettes, and booze. We almost never stopped playing long enough to go to a show. Often, we'd play all night and just have a sandwich at the blackjack table so as not to miss any action.

On those weekends, I didn't even let Bonnie know I was in town. I'd allow myself fifty dollars to lose, folding a five-dollar bill into a corner of my wallet in order to be sure I'd have cab fare to the airport on Sunday afternoon. I was often flat broke as I walked across the molten tarmac on McCarran Air Field, reddened eyes squinting against the desert sun to climb the metal staircase and board the plane to San Diego. Robbie would pick me up, shaking his head with disapproval and disbelief that I enjoyed these decadent weekends so much. I probably answered by quoting something Jim Friedman often said, which Jim liked to attribute to the Buddha: "Do I contradict myself? Then I contradict myself." Turns out, that was Walt Whitman.

IN DECEMBER, I BOUGHT an old, blue Volkswagen Beetle for $200. With my own wheels, I was at last less dependent on Robbie. Consequently, I became less clutching and our relationship improved. Later, when my little bug was totaled while parked on the hill in front of our house, I bought my own VW bus, hand-painted pastel pink, from our friend Cecil. It came complete with platform bed and sheepskin rug, and was enough of a hippie-mobile to get me stopped one night in archconservative La Jolla (one of the wealthiest communities in the nation). At thirty miles per hour I was ticketed for driving too slow! (Read: "We don't want your kind around here.")

Another time in La Jolla, Robbie and I were walking on the cliffs above the beach, tripping on mescaline, holding hands and enjoying the beauty of ocean and sky. An old man dressed in an expensive suit walked slowly toward us, leaning heavily on a cane. He looked around eighty. Feeling very expansive, I smiled at him. As he passed, he looked at Robbie as if he were a worm, then at me in my long, patchwork skirt, and made a disgusted, grunting sound. I gasped, feeling I'd been punched in the stomach. Robbie just nodded at me knowingly. I tried to imagine what it was like to receive that kind of treatment all one's life—to be looked at as if you were an insect.

Suntanned, blond-haired Cecil was one of Robbie's friends with whom I *did* connect. When he stopped by, we'd sit in the kitchen, roll joints from the open bag on the table, and drink herbal tea from delicately painted Japanese tea cups. Like many Californians I met, Cecil was a vegetarian. While incredibly fastidious about what he ate, he would ingest anything at all to get stoned. I also liked Robbie's two close buddies from school, Tommy and Tommy. They, too, were Vietnam vets in their mid-twenties, starting college on the GI Bill. Together with their fun-loving wives, we shared many high times that autumn, going to concerts in Balboa Park or barbecuing at one of our houses. Once, I flew up to Oakland after work to spend a weekend at the home of Tommy Acuna's parents. The other five had gone up the day before. Robbie was an hour late picking me up at the airport and I was furious, sorely tempted to turn around and fly home. But, after making an angry scene at the airport, I let Robbie talk me into staying. It was great to spend time with Tommy's Chicano family, as I learned to call Mexican Americans. As far as I was concerned, being exposed to the warm Chicano people and their culture—not to mention their food—was the best thing about California.

Horsing around with Robbie, Cecil, and Boris

During those first months in San Diego, I would waken for work with a leaden feeling to hear the clock radio painfully prodding me into my boring days and insecure nights. It seemed Peggy Lee's throaty voice was singing inside my head:

Is that all there is?
Is that all there is, my friend?
If that's all there is, then let's keep dancing . . .

Life brightened at home when we adopted two stray cats, dubbed by Robbie "Boris" and "Natasha." But I needed a sense of purpose, some intellectual stimulation. I decided to go to graduate school.

I HAD LET GO of my dream of acting and had only vague ideas about jobs or a career. My history left me with a profound skepticism about my ability to set a goal and then achieve it. I had often discussed becoming a psychotherapist with Dr. Heimarck. I felt that therapy had saved my life and I found the exploration of the mind fascinating. Now, I decided to apply to PhD programs in clinical psychology. It felt like my default position. I would need certain undergraduate prerequisites which I had declined to take at City. So, in February 1970, I enrolled in Experimental Psychology, Psychological Testing, and Physiological Psych at San Diego State. Attending classes on the sun-drenched campus at State was a different experience than going to CCNY, to put it mildly. Here, it was not unusual for long-haired students to bring a dog to class, as one bearded student in my Experimental lectures did. The yellow mutt with mournful eyes and a red cotton bandanna for a collar lay peacefully at the bare feet of his master as we learned the basics of empirical methodology.

California.

In the autumn of 1969, San Diego had not yet surpassed San Francisco as the second largest city in California. With a population of 697,000, it was still small-town enough to have daily listings of local divorces and annulments in the *San Diego Union.*

The naval base, with ships and troops going back and forth to Southeast Asia, dominated mainstream society. Much of the established community was reactionary. San Diego and neighboring Orange County were home to militant right wing groups like The John Birch Society and the Minutemen. Ronald Reagan was governor of the state.

As much as anywhere in the country, San Diego was polarized, culturally and politically. In contrast to the conservative mainstream, there was an active counterculture which could be divided into two overlapping subsets: hippies and politicos. Mission Beach and Pacific Beach were filled with hundreds of grungy young people smoking grass, dropping acid, and, more and more, frying their brains on amphetamines, speed. That year, Operation Intercept, a federal effort to shut off the flow of drugs at the Mexican border, was tying up traffic from nearby Tijuana for hours; it succeeded in driving the price of pot up to fifteen dollars an ounce in LA. Meanwhile, the Nixon Administration recommended lowering penalties for smoking grass as Margaret Mead testified before a Senate subcommittee that marijuana should be legalized for people sixteen and over.

In San Francisco, four hundred American Indians occupied Alcatraz Island. They stayed for months in an attempt to claim the island from the federal government under an 1868 treaty. In Chicago, the conspiracy trial of the Chicago Eight (for disrupting the city during the Democratic Convention) dragged on, while the National Guard was called in to quell violence fomented by the newly formed Weather Underground during their Days of Rage. Fred Hampton, the Illinois state chairman of the Black Panther Party, which had begun as a community-centered movement toward self-reliance for black people, was killed in his bed by police on December 4. Activists everywhere referred to cops as "the pigs."

Across the country, bombings had become commonplace. The FBI estimated there were sixty-one serious incidents involving arson or bombing on college campuses in 1968. At 1:00 a.m. on November 12, 1969, four days after my twenty-fourth birthday, simultaneous explosions went off at the offices of General Motors, Standard Oil, and the Chase Manhattan Bank in New York. Credit was claimed by a small revolutionary group. From Vietnam, the daily diet of body counts was augmented by the nauseating news of an American massacre in a village called My Lai 4. Israel was at war with Egypt. Airline hijackings were all the rage. Up in LA, authorities were slowly unraveling the gruesome murders of the pregnant Sharon Tate and her friends by Charles Manson's weird hippie family. The extent of the pollution of Earth's water and air was gradually being disclosed to the public. A 1969 report to Congress by American Public Health Directors stated:

A large proportion of the 22 million blacks, 5 million Mexican-Americans, and 500,000 Indians and millions of others, live day in and day out in conditions we would not let our animals endure.

Note the "we," spoken in a context where all decisions were tacitly understood to be made by white men.

Whether I focused on it or not, the violence in the world was a constant undercurrent roiling my guts. I had to do something about it.

The long-term goal of all my political activities was the creation of a society in which the well-being of individuals, not property rights, was the paramount value. It seemed obvious to me that the basis of such a social system had to be an equitable distribution of the earth's resources—which, I believed, belong to us all—to people according to their needs. In other words, social justice and cultural change would necessarily follow a change in material conditions. How can people rise to a vision of universal brotherhood, I reasoned with Marx, when their children are hungry?

There was no SDS chapter at San Diego State, so I joined

the Radical Student Union, a small group of activists whose ideology was congruent with my own. We met at the apartment of Jesse and Sherry Smith, graduate students from back east. I learned a lot from their solid commitment to radical social change and their habits of careful political analysis.

On Friday, May 1, 1970, the nation learned of the United States' invasion of Cambodia, and large demonstrations took place on campuses nationwide. When, on Monday, four students were killed by the National Guard during a protest on the Kent State campus in Ohio, it was way beyond intolerable.

On Tuesday, I was one of thousands of students attending a rally at the Main Quad at State. We voted to strike on Thursday and Friday with picket lines to begin at 7:00 a.m. Pre-strike information tables were to be set up around campus and rappers were designated to raise the issues in every classroom. We RSU activists threw ourselves into the work, but the strike was preempted when Governor Reagan announced the closing of all State and UC campuses until the following Monday. (A number of universities closed for the year, including Boston, Brown, Tufts, and Princeton.) On Curlew Street, our days started early and ended late as Robbie and I passed one another coming or going to meetings at one of our respective schools. We were in a state of permanent arousal to action and felt closer than ever as part of this huge movement toward the good. Our sex life improved considerably.

Anti-war activities in San Diego centered on the citywide march planned for Saturday to coincide with protests across the nation. There was a tremendous amount of work to do: making placards, writing, mimeographing and distributing leaflets, making arrangements with the authorities, getting permits, etc. RSU met to decide how we could be most effective to help "educate" the greatest number of people about the systemic causes of the current situation.

Robbie flew back east to attend a meeting of the National Student Association. Meanwhile, San Diego's planning meetings, open to everyone, were held at night in the Aztec Student Center at State. Scores of people attended and discussions went on for hours, leading to votes on strategy and tactics. Off-campus groups participated, including the combat-booted guys from the Movement for a Democratic Military.

MDM was a group of anti-war veterans and active servicemen agitating for rights for people in the military, such as the right to petition for redress of grievances. Their communal house near Camp Pendleton had recently been riddled with bullets from a passing car, wounding a Marine deserter who was staying there. In February, one general had called MDM "a serious threat to the defense of the country." I was impressed, on the whole, by these tough men who made their stand in the belly of the beast. However, I opposed their present position, most vigorously advocated by a hairy guy called Jay King, which was to aggressively provoke the authorities whenever possible. He particularly pissed me off when he argued for vandalism at the college—like filling all the door locks on campus with some kind of gum. I saw this as a pointless distraction from meaningful actions.

Jay was the boyfriend of Pam, one of the women who lived upstairs from us on Curlew Street with three other friends of mine. Their vociferous lovemaking often kept Robbie and me up at night. Jay had long black hair and a matted beard and, like most of the guys from MDM, he always wore camouflage fatigues. There was something about him I just didn't trust and I was one of those who argued vehemently against his proposals at the meeting. The majority of people at the planning meetings were students and faculty who wanted to keep the march non-violent in order to enlist the support of the widest possible range of people opposed to the war. MDM was voted down.

. . .

ON SATURDAY, I AM woken as usual by Boris when he stretches his oversized yellow self out on my right side, puts his wet puss in my ear and purrs loudly. This is his subtle way of letting me know it's breakfast time. Who could resist? Only five hours sleep—again. I swing out of bed and go to the kitchen where Natasha mews placidly, ever the lady, waiting to be served.

"Yes, yes, poopers, I know," I coo as I spoon out the Friskies and fill their water bowl. I pour enough dry food to last all day. The morning is chilly. I put on Robbie's frayed brown denim bell-bottoms which I've lately co-opted. They fit like a glove. I grab a sweatshirt and leave the door unlocked behind me. The canyon out back is lush with greenery.

I park my pink chariot a few blocks from the Horton Plaza and arrive just as the final meeting is starting. RSU has opted to focus on organizing and participating as monitors to maintain order and avoid confrontation. There are eight teams of monitors, eight to ten in each. Jesse Smith, who is coordinating the teams, is addressing the group through a bullhorn, briefing everyone on how to handle disruptions—we are prepared for many. Teams are assigned to clean up both Horton Plaza and Balboa Park after the crowd has gone. At the end of the meeting, we pick up folded white cotton head-bands stenciled with the word "Monitor." Despite the sleep deprivation, I feel strong and determined to do my part to make the march a success.

A couple of thousand people gather in the plaza and march out at noon. The day has warmed into San Diego's usual perfect weather. By 1:00 p.m., almost 10,000 people are walking slowly through downtown streets toward Balboa Park, by far the largest anti-war demonstration San Diego has seen. It's not only students and hippies but middle-class families with strollers, Chicanos, elderly people carrying placards and chanting, "Peace Now, Peace Now." One sign reads, "When they silence the majority, who will speak out?" Team captains are walking back and forth, carrying walkie-talkies. Volunteer medical people circulate and volunteer lawyers are on call in case of need. There are fewer counter-demonstrators than we expected. When we come upon a group of hecklers in hard hats, the first team of monitors moves quickly to fan out in front of them and link arms. Facing the marchers, they exhort everyone to "just pass by."

I am standing in position at the top of Fifth Avenue, watching the huge press of people moving peaceably in my direction. My sweatshirt is tied around my waist. I feel great—at last Middle America is standing up against the war.

Suddenly, I hear the approaching sounds of abrasive voices. Gradually the MDM contingent—fifteen men wearing yellow shirts with their usual fatigues and combat boots—comes into view. Very deliberately, they are walking too slowly over the I-5 Bridge—a gap is widening between MDM and the marchers ahead of them. Jay King is front and center, arms linked with the other guys. Under my thick headband, perspiration breaks out as I watch the whole MDM group sit down in the middle of the street! The marchers behind them, thousands of people, are brought to a halt.

"Motherfuckers!" I mutter to myself, walking quickly toward the bridge.

Jesse shows up within a couple of minutes, speaking urgently into his walkie-talkie. Many monitors rush to join us from ahead and behind; we huddle quickly, then link arms around MDM and form two corridors to allow the marchers to move in a narrow column past the seated men on either side, thus foiling their attempt to disrupt the march.

"Just keep moving," I repeat with the others as calmly as I can to the people walking through.

Jay King starts to chant and the others join in: "The monitors are pigs, the monitors are pigs." But the march remains nonviolent to the end.

• • •

A FEW MONTHS LATER a couple of the guys from MDM were at the hospital to visit a sick friend when, to their surprise, they spotted their buddy Jay with a woman being admitted to Maternity. The story is imperfectly recalled hearsay, but the central fact was verified: Jay King was an undercover cop named John O'Brien. He worked for the San Diego Police Department. The woman he brought to the hospital that day was his wife. Their baby was born the next morning.

When the two guys—with whom "Jay" had lived and worked for the past ten months or so—returned to their car in the hospital parking lot, marijuana had been planted in their glove compartment and cops were on hand to bust them. The story was all over the radical community within hours. I was outraged on behalf of Pam. As her downstairs neighbor, I was uniquely situated to know how often she and Jay had boisterous sex. She was livid. I admit I also felt vindicated, relishing that delicious "I was so right not to trust him" feeling.

Agent provocateur.

IT TURNS OUT THAT my entire FBI file, which I obtained under the Freedom of Information Act, centers around my association with MDM, whose members were known to visit the "New Left type commune" on Curlew Street, in which they said I lived with "other known subversive persons." The file, fourteen pages with more than half the text redacted with thick black lines, records my parents' names and addresses, my educational history back to PA, including college grades, and my New York employers. Two "confidential sources" in New York are cited. (One I know was my old roommate Laurie, a Republican; she called me after agents came to question her about me.) On May 18, 1971, the San Diego office of the FBI recorded its intention to "continue to follow the activities of subject."

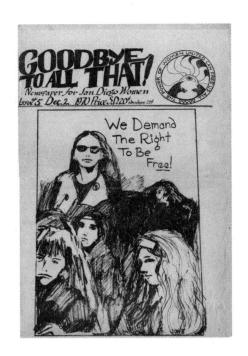

CHAPTER 13

Goodbye to All That

I n January of 1970, Congress held hearings on the dangers of
that great liberator, the birth control pill. Evidence of various
health risks was presented, and it scared me. I had been taking
the pill for about five years. With all the stress in our relationship, Robbie and I had an erratic sex life at best. I harbored the
irrational belief that I could never get pregnant because, I think,
I still felt like damaged goods on some level. I had certainly
risked pregnancy often enough in the past. Why jeopardize my

health, I asked myself. I stopped taking the pill and got a diaphragm, which I used less than religiously.

When the doctor at the new Free Clinic confirmed that I was pregnant, I learned that, according to a liberalized 1967 California law, I could get a legal abortion if two psychiatrists attested "there [was] a substantial risk that continuance of the pregnancy would gravely impair the physical or mental health of the mother." The clinic referred me to psychiatrists sympathetic to a woman's right to free choice. I said the appropriate things to the doctors to allow them to recommend abortion.

Meanwhile, to my surprise, I loved being pregnant. It gave me a sense of well-being, fullness. Robbie, too, was obviously happy about it. However, I never considered having the child. I knew I was still too unstable to be a good mother and I was convinced that to bring a child into this world was no favor. The room on the maternity ward had four beds, but only one was occupied, by a woman who was overdue and might be having a saline-induced birth. Her husband and mother came to see her at the start of afternoon visiting hours; I could hear the talking through the curtain drawn around her bed. I waited for Robbie to come. The minutes passed, then one hour, then the next. Echoes of waiting at the window for my father. Shadow memories of lying on the floor of Ellen Schwartz's apartment, waiting to hear Steve knock on our door to say he was sorry. Robbie didn't come. That night, desolate, I called Jim Friedman in New York and we had one of our long conversations. I confided my disappointment in Robbie, my sadness and loneliness. Consoled by Jim's ready sympathy, I went to sleep prepared to face the morning.

After the D&C, I ran a slight fever so the doctor kept me in the hospital a second night. Robbie finally came to visit that afternoon. He had various pretexts for not showing up the day before, but I got that he had just been too sad to come. He pointed out to me that I had never asked him how he felt about the abortion. I had assumed he saw the options as I did, not taking into consideration the implications of the fact that Robbie had been raised Catholic. And he had said nothing about it to me, feeling he didn't have the right. Sitting together on the hospital bed, we held each other and cried. For our lost child. For our difficulty in understanding one another.

MY PSYCHOLOGY COURSES AT State were dry but challenging. I was meeting people and making my own friends. At last I had a full life, independent of Robbie. But it was through Robbie that I met Juliet Wittman, the closest friend I made in San Diego.

Juliet lived in the People's Commune with about twenty people who published a first-rate underground newspaper, the *San Diego Street Journal*, a sorely needed alternative in a city where both dailies were published by the conservative Copley Press. The group shared two big houses in our Hillcrest neighborhood. They were experimenting with new approaches to family and community, attempting to implement the sexually liberating ideas of Wilhelm Reich. They shared spouses and lovers. Children were considered the responsibility of the whole community.

With all the hippie culture of her house, however, Juliet was a *landsman*. The daughter of Czech Jews, she was raised in England and had come to the United States to attend the University of Delaware. She'd been an actress in New York and had lived on the Upper West Side. At last, I found a friend in California who spoke my language and shared my frame of reference as well as my political ideals. I was curious about commune life, and she talked about replacing the loss of the traditional extended family. I took a new look at the nuclear family, which I had always romanticized from my outsider's vantage point, nose pressed pathetically against the window as I peered in at *Father Knows Best*. Now, as I stopped to think about it and looked at the facts, I began to see the nuclear family as less than ideal for raising healthy, civic-minded members of society.

When Robbie introduced us, Juliet was recovering from hepatitis. I visited often during her recuperation as she rested on one of the house's lumpy sofas. Her fellow communards, including children and dogs, came and went through the cluttered living room where we talked for hours.

It was in this setting that the light of feminism dawned in my life.

The new wave of Women's Liberation had been in motion since 1965, when female New Left activists joined together to protest the relegation of women in the Movement to the traditional roles assumed to be women's natural sphere: mimeographing the position papers, making the coffee, supporting their "heavy revvy" men. In one infamous quote, Stokely Carmichael said that the place of women in the Movement was "prone."

While I was still back at CCNY, a friend told me about women at Sarah Lawrence who were forming groups to talk about their own oppression. I didn't connect with anything I heard at that point. Now, after my struggle with emotional dependence on Robbie and the insulting dismissal of my job credentials with "Can you type?"; after needing to have a psychiatrist say I was unstable in order to terminate an unwanted pregnancy, I was ripe to hear Juliet's analysis of her own difficult experiences with the male "non-leaders" in the People's Commune. They were effective muckrakers and committed radicals but they also displayed the pervasive *machismo* that affected Movement men everywhere—until "their" women woke up. (One of these men was Lowell Bergman, who went

on to a long career of effective muckraking at *Ramparts* magazine, *60 Minutes*, and *Frontline*.)

Juliet and I shared war stories and examined how the
feminist perspective related to our understanding of the Movement and society at large. Also, we laughed a lot and made
fudge. When Juliet, Pam, and Jan, a single mother with two
kids, moved in upstairs at our Curlew Street house, Juliet and I
got even closer. She came down to drink herb tea at the
kitchen table or Robbie and I went upstairs to share meals.
This was the "New Left-type commune" the FBI observed.

The discovery of feminism caused an explosive expansion
of my worldview and an almost blinding illumination of my
personal history. This is difficult to recapture; so much that
was revolutionary in impact then is conventional wisdom—at
least by lip service—now. Most immediately obvious was how
my sense of my own value, like my mother's, had always centered around my relationships with men: father, boyfriends,
teachers. I saw how brainwashed I had been by my beloved
movies of the 1950s, which left no doubt that a true woman's
life revolved around her man and doing whatever it took to
snag and keep him. Now, during those long hours of conversation with Juliet, I realized that I was, on many levels, a victim
of sexism.

Of course, black, poor, and Third World women were
much worse off. Just for starters, black women have always
been at the bottom of the salary scale. But I also saw how
playing women off against each other by race and class was a
classic case of divide and conquer. The more I learned (or just
reexamined things I had taken for granted, like calling adult
women "girls"), I began to see other women as sisters in oppression. I was outraged to learn that, in many states, a married
woman still, in 1970, had neither property rights nor legal
recourse if she was raped by her husband. Another eye-opener

for me was that women made, on average, only sixty cents for every dollar earned by men. (In 2015, that figure rose to seventy-nine cents. We've come a long way, maybe, but not far enough.)

As usual, my analytic bent and training in philosophy came into play as I sought to drill down to the deepest implications of this new awareness. I saw the subtle influence on my mind of the linguistic convention that refers to humankind as "man" and God as "He." The subliminal message: males are primary and, oh, there are females, too. This devaluation of the feminine was, I realized, part of the warp and woof of my own low self-esteem. When I looked at the history of civilization from this perspective, I concluded that, historically, the domination of women by men is the very prototype of oppression (that is, relations based on unequal power, both personal and institutional). I became convinced that freedom for all—still, always, my overriding goal—would never be achieved until this fundamental inequality was rectified.

The confluence of the personal and political opened, for me as for so many other women at that historic moment, a wellspring of rage and fervor which fueled my rebellion. Every day brought new revelations of how sexism permeated every aspect of society and my own psyche. As I examined my unconscious assumptions, it became clear that I had taken the concepts of female weakness and inferiority as truth. On a deep level, I felt powerless and excruciatingly vulnerable as a girl. (No wonder I had, at an early age, subtly identified myself as a boy.) I would prove I was just as good as any man, using sexual conquest as a spear and my intellect as a shield.

Yet this, in turn, aroused deep anxiety. If I really succeeded, what man would want me? "Who then will take care of me?" quaked the vulnerable inner child, whose voice I continued to repress.

Still, we are multileveled creatures, and as I spent time talking about these things with other women, I reveled in a new sense of liberation. I began to see myself as a woman among sisters who were exploring and affirming what it meant to be female. What were the *real* differences between the sexes, apart from cultural conditioning? It was a question that would preoccupy me for the next five years.

THE DISTORTIONS, OMISSIONS, AND disinformation of the government and mainstream media in the United States were well documented by 1970. For example, the Women's Movement was consistently trivialized by the press as a bunch of bra burners and lesbians. In response, around the country, a homegrown alternative press sprang up. In 1969, there were 440 underground newspapers in the United States. By the mid-seventies, there were an estimated 250 "local, indigenous feminist publications," according to Susan Brownmiller's *In Our Time.*

In the summer of 1970, Juliet, Pam, and I, with a group of women from UC San Diego, started a paper called *Goodbye To All That.* The title was taken from an article by poet Robin Morgan, which Brownmiller called a "rhapsodic farewell to the male-dominated New Left." Our first issue, twelve pages put together by about ten women, came out on September 15. We identified ourselves as "students, artists, housewives, and mothers." Above the masthead, we declared our intentions:

> *We view Women's Liberation as part of the struggle of other oppressed people; true liberation can be achieved only when workers, blacks, Chicanos, and homosexuals are free to fully develop their capacities. . . . We believe that this presupposes a radical restructuring of society, including alternatives to the nuclear family and an end to exploita-*

tion of human labor for profit. GTAT will be published by women working together in a truly collective way—no editors, hierarchy, or big-wig "non-leaders."

There were no set roles or jobs; everyone pitched in to share the work. Copy meetings were open to all. We wanted every woman in San Diego to feel the newspaper was responsive to her concerns and input. Sitting on the bare living room floor upstairs at Curlew Street, we reviewed the submissions of news stories, political features, poetry, essays, and art. Copy meetings were long and boisterous. There was lots of passionate disagreement and compromise. I knew nothing about how to publish a newspaper, and delighted in learning. I typed copy, did layout and paste-up, and ornamented columns with drawings and decorative self-adhesive borders. I even had my photos published. We also subscribed to the Liberation News Service, the underground's answer to the wire services, which regularly sent out packets of news releases and photos.

The paper had a decidedly handmade look. The quality of the writing was uneven, to say the least, due to our non-elitist editorial policy. But I was proud of our principled practices. It was incredibly energizing working with women committed to respecting and supporting each other *as women.* It was, in a word not yet trite, empowering.

A sampling from early issues of *GTAT* included an interview with a woman who spent eight months in the San Diego County jail awaiting trial for possession of marijuana; a personal account of a visit to a gynecologist; and Juliet's comprehensive two-part report on job discrimination. The latter presented and analyzed Department of Labor statistics showing, for example, that while in 1955, the median wage for women was 63.9 percent that of men, in 1965 it was 60 percent. (In 2014 it was 83 percent.)

Everyone sold ads and tried to persuade various shops around town to carry the paper. You could buy *GTAT* at stores like Yab Yum Artifacts and the Get It On Shoppe (which also sold "posters, black lights, head items, and Zap Comics"). We hawked the paper near college campuses and on the streets in Mission Beach. On Saturday nights at the Unicorn Theater, we went up and down the line of people waiting for admission to the underground movies shown at midnight.

The newspaper cost twenty cents a copy. Each issue included a call (some might say a plea) for women to join us and/ or send money. Ever broke, we regularly took donated items to sell at the local swap meets on weekends. Our group was fluid. A core of seven to ten women was always at meetings and willing to do the work. Others came and went, perhaps twenty altogether. During production weekends we spent long hours at the typewriter and light table, sustained by burritos and quesadillas brought upstairs from the mama and papa taco joint down the street. We all worked on the layout and paste-up of the three broad columns per page. When the paper was ready to go to press, someone had to drive it up to Riverside, a two-hour trip. No San Diego printer was willing to print *GTAT*.

I loved working with women as a group and when, every two weeks, I held in my hand that tangible thing, a newspaper, I felt great satisfaction. *GTAT* was our baby.

ON OCTOBER 13, *GTAT* was up to fifteen pages and included our response to radical men's accusations that we were "counter-revolutionary." I got a lot of this at home, where Robbie snorted and fumed a lot about women's issues being secondary to those of the truly oppressed. He bridled at my new insistence that he acknowledge the inequities between the sexes, not only in society, but in our relationship. We fought about whose job it was to clean the house. But, since all the women he respected were singing the same song, he gradually came to see the merit of our arguments and began the difficult process of changing his ways. I was, admittedly, less than patient. As I felt more independent, Robbie and I grew apart.

The Halloween issue of *GTAT* was down to eight pages again, reflecting our constant financial struggles. The full-page cover illustration showed a vagina schematically drawn, with a border of smaller designs and captions in homage to "Witch Power." Inside was a historical analysis of the demonization of female shamanism and a long article entitled "Witch Hunt for Angela Davis," the black activist who had just been jailed in New York. On the back page, decorating our weekly announcements, was a whimsical little sketch I made of a witch on a broomstick, saying "boo." Non-artistic me! I was tickled. I pasted it up myself, rubber-cementing it next to notices of medical classes at the San Diego Women's Center, women's and men's consciousness-raising groups, a board meeting of the incipient San Diego State Women's Studies Program, and sculpture classes. Later issues contained extensive reports on the Indochinese Women's Conference in Canada and the People's Peace Treaty.

In January 1971, *GTAT's* cover story was about a local group of businessmen. The purpose of their club was to help disadvantaged children and they had invited two women, feminists from one of the colleges, to speak to them about women's liberation. When the women started speaking, however, the audience of about a hundred men heckled and jeered the speakers. Then someone fired two shots—blanks, from a real gun. The frightened women were escorted out of the room to catcalls of "bring out the rape squad."

The story in *GTAT* was collectively written by some of our staff. It named the two club members who alone spoke up against the hecklers. We also published the complete member-ship roster of the club, including addresses and phone numbers. I thought this was great. However, I was troubled by the drawing proposed to accompany the article. It depicted a placard that said, "Today's Chauvinist Pig is Tomorrow's Bacon." Keenly aware of the power of words on the unconscious, I had never been comfortable calling men "pigs." I believed this dehuman-ized the speaker as much as the target of the name-calling.

But my sisters were adamant about using the graphic; I was voted down.

For the next issue, I wrote an article titled "When is a Man a Pig—the Paradox of a Humanist Revolution." I argued that while individual men may act like animals,

> it's a terrible thing to kill a human being—much more terri-ble than it seems when you call it "offing a pig." . . . The only way to build a humane society after the revolution is to preserve our respect for human life at every step along the way—even in taking it.

Virtually everyone at the copy meeting opposed my posi-tion. They insisted that I sign the piece, a practice we usually eschewed, to make it clear this was only one person's opinion. In addition, the other women collectively wrote a response to my piece which was set on the same page. It was called "Yes, But . . ." and it detailed police brutality after a Chicano Mora-torium rally in LA the preceding week. One person had been killed and some forty others wounded with buckshot. "Some of us on the *GTAT* staff feel that pig is the only name for these brutal men . . . ," they wrote. "[We] will continue to use this term as a gesture of solidarity with those oppressed sisters and brothers who don't have time for moral scruples about using the word 'pig.'"

I was deeply disturbed by this episode. It revealed a rift between me and my fellow radicals. Even Sherry Smith, whose political analyses I'd always respected, refuted my piece in detail at a citywide women's meeting. Some of our more liberal readers complimented me on the article, which didn't sit well with me either since I opposed liberalism as a band-aid approach to societal problems that required radical surgery.

Juliet had the last word on the issue in a piece which she entitled "Sow Speaks." It took the form of a letter to the editor, signed "Sally Sow," registering porcine upset with

> . . . your last issue and its careless and arrogant de-animalization of pigs. Pigs do not carry weapons. . . . We don't invade other animals' territory to exploit, bomb, burn, or defoliate it . . .
>
> Your misuse of animal names and total lack of understanding of our natures is just another example of your monumental stupidity about the natural world you so freely abuse.

Right on, Juliet! Though she disagreed with me too, Juliet's humor took the edge off the conflict and made me feel less isolated.

When I had to sign my article, I used my *nom de plume*, RiK. As was customary on some underground papers, many of us used pseudonyms which we handwrote on the back page. The staff on Issue #9 included "Ruby Tuesday," "Madame New," "Maud Gonne," and "Medusa." Later, I changed my alias to "Cass Traitor," which tickled my (angry) funny bone more than anybody else's. I figured since this was what radical feminists were always accused of, I might as well take it head on.

One morning, as I climbed into my bus to go to work, I found a sticker pasted in the middle of the driver's side of my windshield. It had a graphic showing a black circle with crosshairs inside it: the view through a rifle sight. The caption was printed in bold, black letters:

TRAITOR BEWARE!

Right now someone may have a rifle aimed at the back of your neck . . . These patriots are working night and day to protect America from traitors like you . . .

The Minutemen

I viewed that sticker as a badge of honor.

CHAPTER 14

Brains

I n my Physiological Psych class at State, I met a woman named Olena who shared my newfound interest in neurophysiology. Through Olena, I got a job as research assistant to her mentor, a psychologist named Carol A. Schulman. Carol was a petite, forty-something woman with a permanent suntan and an infectious smile. With the help of an engineer back east, she had designed a special-purpose computer to test the hearing of newborns before they left the hospital, using heart rate as a measure of response. At that time, many children had hearing defects that went undetected until the age when they would normally begin to speak, and Carol had received a one-year grant from the State of California to see if her machine was feasible for use as a mass screening device for newborns.

We worked in the neonatal nursery at the University of California at San Diego Hospital, and I loved those tiny babies. Using Carol's prototype computer—a clunky blue metal machine on a rolling cart, with numerous dials and a small oscilloscope—I would paste three electrodes on the baby's chest to read its heart rate. The EKG would appear on the scope. I then placed earphones on the downy little head. This procedure was completely painless—often the baby didn't even wake up during the test.

When I switched on the computer, a pulse of white noise was delivered through the headset, starting at a low level and then gradually increasing in volume. After five trials, a stylus printed out the averaged heart rate of the baby on graph paper. When there was a significant change in heart rate in response to the noise at a certain decibel level, this was considered the child's hearing threshold. Newborns have very high thresholds, the better to let them sleep a lot, my dear. I was fascinated by how different newborns are from one another. Even at two days of age, they all have unique personalities.

Now that I was earning enough to support myself ($8,000 for the year), I was able to rent a furnished studio a few blocks from the hospital and from Curlew Street. Robbie and I parted amicably. With many of the other Movement men, he came to see how women's liberation was congruent with his ideals and he worked at integrating feminist values into his behavior. And I was more accepting of him, now that I felt I was standing on my own two feet. We continued to see each other, and some of our best times together were our occasional meetings during the year that followed.

Meanwhile, I did a lot of reading about sensory perception. University was a teaching hospital, so there were weekly grand rounds and symposia of various sorts that I was able to attend. From the beginning, Carol Schulman was generous, encouraging me to learn as much as I could and sharing her many interests with me. She was fun to be with—playful, committed to her work, and interested in a wide range of related research. She took me to visit the laboratories of neuroscientists at UCSD, and to the prestigious Scripps Institute in La Jolla. I was excited by this new world of research and awed by scientists, well-known in their fields, who spoke with barely concealed lust about "the Nobel."

Since I did not believe in God or in a soul, I now concluded that the secrets of human complexity must be found in the nervous system. Neuroanatomy became a favorite reading topic; I even had the opportunity to coauthor a paper with Carol about this research, which didn't hurt at all when I applied to grad school. Life was feeling good.

. . .

ON A COOL DECEMBER evening after work, I park the pink chariot outside the People's Commune. Juliet and I have come to support Joy as she gives birth in one of the upstairs bedrooms. She's doing it at home, so the baby's arrival won't be recorded for the purposes of Uncle Sam and the draft. A sympathetic MD is on call in case of any complications. I'm not really friends with Joy, but can't resist when, in true communard spirit, she lets it be known that visitors are welcome. I've never seen a woman in labor before and feel more than a little trepidation upon entering the bedroom. Four or five people are sitting around and Robbie is taking pictures, but he leaves soon after we arrive. Joy, wearing only a sweater and looking like the proverbial beached whale, lies on her back on a rumpled double mattress on the floor. Richard, the father, lies beside her with his head propped on one arm. Dressed all in black, and wearing a beret, Che-like, he's calmly watching as Joy tokes on a joint between contractions, then passes it over to us by way of welcome. She's already been in labor for several hours but doesn't appear to be in pain. She's talking to us in a low voice when she stops suddenly and puts her hand around her belly, blowing in and out rapidly through her mouth. My own breath tightens as I watch her. I wish I was more comfortable with her nakedness, her vagina in full view, this scary, elemental process.

"Breathe into it, babe," coos Richard.

Sweat appears on her upper lip, but after a few minutes the contraction passes and Joy relaxes without comment. We continue to talk and the contractions keep coming every twenty minutes or so. I'm impressed by her stamina—she seems so unruffled! People come, sit for a while and move on.

After another hour or so, I leave, flashing Joy the V-sign. I have work tomorrow. As I fire up the bus, I wonder if the grass is impeding her labor.

• • •

IT TURNED OUT THE baby was slightly out of position. After thirty-six hours of labor at home, Joy was admitted to University Hospital and the newborn Max became a denizen of our nursery. He was in excellent health and his hearing threshold was normal.

The Christmas issue of *GTAT* ran a picture of Joy lying naked on the rumpled bed, hand on her still–*in utero* baby, with bearded Richard beside her. The caption read, "*Tidings of Great Joy—a REVOLUTION is born.*"

DURING THE CHRISTMAS HOLIDAYS in 1970, I flew to Michigan to visit Aunt Ruth in East Lansing. Ruth was now practicing Transcendental Meditation, which had become popular when the Beatles and other celebrities took it up. She took me to a meeting where, for the first time, I sat quietly in a darkened room full of people meditating. There was an intangible energy in that place that I found calming.

Maharishi Mahesh Yogi, the Indian teacher who brought this ancient practice to the West, had a scientific background and so the meditation he taught was presented in secular terms, supported by empirical evidence of the physiological benefits. This appealed to me. I could see the value of reduced blood pressure, changes in blood chemistry and characteristic brain waves indicating that the body rests deeply during twenty-minute periods of meditation. Maharishi taught that all you had to do was practice his simple technique twice a day for twenty minutes.

Upon my return to California, I decided to take the weekend course to begin my own meditation practice. One fine day in January, with a sense of venturing into the unknown (one of my favorite things to do), I tooled over the new Bay Bridge in my old pink bus to a private home in Coronado where the class would be held. As instructed, I brought a flower and a piece of fruit. I suppressed any cynical thoughts about "primitive rituals" as I entered the bedroom, fragrant with incense, where the meditation teacher sat next to a makeshift altar with a photo of Maharishi's own guru.

The instructor was named Jonathan, a well-groomed young man who wore, as all the TM teachers did, a suit and tie. This made it seem all the more incongruous that he sat cross-legged on the floor, intoning Sanskrit words as he offered my flower and orange at the altar.

Transcendental Meditation, I had heard at an Introductory Lecture, was a simple, natural process of focusing your attention on a mantra, a syllable or syllables which were said to have special power inherent in their particular sound vibrations. In this initiation, I would be given my own personal mantra which I was never to say aloud.

When Jonathan finally whispered the mantra in my ear, I felt disappointed. The two-syllable mantra didn't seem exotic enough to me. But I was determined to follow through to see if I could reap some of the benefits Aunt Ruthie had raved about.

Three other people were initiated that day. We practiced our newly learned technique together in that spacious, well-appointed living room with cathedral ceilings. After Jonathan guided us into meditation, it was unbelievable how many thoughts took form in twenty minutes: Will I see Robbie tonight? Bonnie's ham, turkey, and brisket on the counter side-by-side (mouth waters); wait, the mantra . . . that incense smells too sweet. My nose itches . . . image of Heidi the dachshund wagging her tail . . . Oh, yes, the mantra . . . Wanna finish my article tonight for the next copy meeting . . . oh, no! Why can't I keep my mind on that mantra? I've always had good focus, after all, Phi Beta Kappa . . . Damn, back to the mantra!

Afterward, we discussed our experiences and asked questions. I mentioned that my mind had wandered incessantly, as if on automatic pilot. Jonathan said this was natural and that, when you become aware the mind has strayed from the magic syllables, you should "gently bring your attention back to the mantra."

One of the first things I realized from meditation was that being gentle with my mind was not my usual practice.

When we discussed our experiences as a group, I saw that all sorts of phenomena typically occur in meditation: anger or sadness come up, or perhaps strong physical sensations. Jonathan explained these as signs that the inner stress we normally carry in our bodies was being released. Whatever; I only knew that I felt subtly refreshed after each session.

• • •

THE SECOND MORNING OF the initiation course. My little group is once again sitting in the living room in Coronado. I am in a deep armchair, facing the glass doors overlooking the bay, alive with weekend pleasure boats.

In his soft voice, Jonathan tells us to close our eyes for meditation.

As instructed, I focus on the mantra. Once again, the mind

does its dance of random movements. Again and again, I return my attention to the magic syllables.

Now, all of a sudden, I find myself up near the ceiling! I can see the entire room below and the tops of the heads of the meditators. Out of the corner of my eye, I notice dust on the ledge above the glass doors. I feel marvelous—so light! Looking down, I see *me*, sitting in the armchair with closed eyes.

"My God," I think, "I'm out of my body!"

Thwaack! I am snapped back into my seat as though released by some giant rubber band. Disoriented, I continue to sit in the chair for the rest of the session, focusing and refocusing on the mantra.

After twenty minutes, Jonathan says, "You may open your eyes now."

Then he asks, as he does after each meditation period, "It was easy?"

When I describe my experience, he says calmly, "It's another sign of unstressing."

This explanation strikes me as incomplete. But since I have no other plausible way of understanding what happened, I let it go.

In the years that follow, this out-of-body experience remains a vivid memory.

• • •

DURING THE EARLY MONTHS of my TM practice, I gradually became aware that I was gaining stamina from sitting through whatever mental and physical sensations came up. For example, I often became acutely uncomfortable during meditation, with an antsy feeling that made me want to jump out of my skin. Normally, I would stand up to do something, anything, to alleviate this discomfort. Now I learned that if I just followed the discipline of sitting there—returning my focus to my mantra as often as I could—the agitation subsided. This was quite a revelation. I saw that I did not have to get drawn into every passing thought or emotion. And as I maintained a regular practice, it became easier not to react reflexively to whatever happened to be going on in my mind. How liberating!

Not only that, but I became less nervous and high-strung. My friends and coworkers remarked on this. My friendships and relationships at work improved. I continued to practice TM for the next five years.

Up a tree in San Diego

AS SUMMER APPROACHED, THE People's Commune broke up and our community diffused. One group of activists, including Paula, a friend of Juliet's who had occasionally worked on

GTAT, rented a small house near the beach. One afternoon, as Paula stood near a window, she was shot in the elbow by someone in a passing car. The Minutemen? We were never able to find out. And even though I was told that her injuries were not too severe, it was scary as hell. I was more than ready to return to New York. (My job at the hospital was ending because Carol's one-year grant expired.) Almost everyone I knew was leaving San Diego, including Robbie, who was moving to San Francisco. A number of people from the commune were going to Eugene, Oregon. Juliet was moving to Boulder to study journalism at the University of Colorado. She wanted to visit friends in New York before starting school so we arranged to drive back east together. We got to go for free by transporting the car of a San Diego family who was relocating to Amherst. Their '68 Volvo was a far cry from the reverse-less brown bus in which I'd first arrived two years earlier. Good-bye, San Diego.

WHEN JULIET AND I crossed the George Washington Bridge three weeks later, I almost wept to see that beloved skyline. We parked the Volvo and I actually knelt down and kissed the sidewalk on 95th Street in front of the old Thalia theater, where I'd seen my first foreign films. After we delivered the car to Amherst, Juliet flew to Boulder. (She went on to become an award-winning journalist and author of *Breast Cancer Journal*, a beautiful book which was a finalist for the National Book Award in 1993.)

Well, I was back . . . And since becoming an actress no longer seemed an option for me—the idea of auditioning for some men who'd have the power to give or not give me what I wanted was anathema—I did the only other thing I could think of: I applied to grad school. Meanwhile, to save money, I went to live with Noni and Bill again, in Teaneck.

CHAPTER 15

Adelphi

C ompetition for admission to PhD programs in clinical psychology was intense, so I applied to eight different universities, composing long essays about why I wanted to be a psychologist. (I didn't mention that being a therapist was my fallback position.) While waiting for their replies, I registered with a temporary agency and worked as a full-time secretary in Manhattan.

Politically, I was exhausted. The New Left had splintered into a bewildering array of factions. Some of them, like the Weathermen, advocated terrorism as a means of struggle. To me, this was tantamount to becoming the enemy. Gradually, I came to believe that if there was ever to be the society I longed to live in—a society where all individuals can live in equality and dignity (including, for example, universal health care)— people's consciousness would have to change first. No matter how high the ideals that inspire a revolution, the result cannot surpass the level of humanity of the people who make it. I thought of Rousseau's concept of "enlightened self-interest," meaning (as I understood it) the awareness that one's true well-being is inextricably connected with the well-being of others.

Although I attended protest marches in New York and Washington for women's rights and against the war, I had lost the sense that my whole generation was on the same idealistic page. I no longer believed a revolution was possible in the United States. And if the revolution *did* come, I was certain that some of my erstwhile brothers and sisters would have me up against the wall for revisionist humanist heresies.

But how did I justify going to work in corporate America? Easy: I needed money and I couldn't face waitressing again. Besides, it was only temporary.

I worked for five months in the Advertising Department of GAF Corporation on West 50th Street. As in my days at WHN, I enjoyed playing in the business world, with easy tasks and plenty of men around to feed my ego. Despite my feminist beliefs, I was still so needy; being seductive was second nature to me. My rhetoric, to quote Robin Morgan, was way ahead of my reality.

So I went back into therapy with Dr. Heimarck. I was feeling strangled by my bottomless need to be desired. I came to understand that, because from a very early age, I'd experienced my mother as inconsistent, even dangerous, I'd learned to look to men (and sex) for nurturance and validation. But I also feared and resented men for their perceived power, and I competed with them. I usually chose men who were emotionally inaccessible, like my father. And when someone offered me the nourishment I needed (like Alan or Dr. Heimarck), I eventually found reasons to reject him.

Intellectually, I understood the dynamics of these patterns, yet too often my insights stayed on that level. The old feelings from childhood, kept in darkness for so long, felt like powerful ogres; when I dared approach them, they'd automatically shut off, as if a wall dropped down to block me from experiencing my deepest self. I was so frustrated when I could *see* the ways in which I hobbled myself, yet not feel able to change my behavior. I was determined to be free of those self-limiting patterns, one way or another.

I WAS JUBILANT WHEN I received an acceptance letter from my top choice of grad schools, Adelphi University, one of the few purely psychoanalytic programs in the country. Now, with the money I'd saved from my temp jobs, I was free to set off for Europe.

. . .

I'M STANDING ON A long line to check in at Hartford International Airport. The FAA is cracking down on fake "charter" flights like mine which have been underselling the commercial airlines. Early this morning, I received a call informing me that the flight would leave from Connecticut instead of New York's JFK.

Looking up from reading my new bible, *Europe on $5 a Day*, I notice a young man watching me from the next line. He's five foot nine, slender with trim brown hair and beard, wearing jeans and a khaki army jacket. The intensity of his brown eyes is magnified by his rimless glasses. We chat comfortably and learn that we're both taking this trip to Europe prior to starting grad school in the fall. Like me, determined not to rush around like the stereotypical American tourist, Doug has no itinerary, just a stake and a Eurail pass.

His stake is from his recent discharge from the army after returning from Vietnam.

Oh.

"I've been opposing the war for years," I tell him.

"I don't blame you," he answers grimly, looking away. Clearly, he wants to end it there.

I find Doug quite handsome. His reserved manner and my leeriness about his participation in the war keep me from flirting with him in my usual seductive way, but his sensitivity and quiet intelligence appeal to me.

We agree to sit together on the plane.

By the time we finally lift off, darkness is falling. Flying across the cloudbanks above the Atlantic, Doug and I talk easily all through the foreshortened night. We talk about our travel plans, and about wanting to be therapists. Later, I ask him about the Army. He tells me that he's from a family of Army men going back four generations. In college, it was unthinkable for him not to join the Reserve Officers Training Corps; afterward, he had been unable to make the break involved in refusing to fight. Through tight lips, his brow furrowed over his dark eyes, he says, "I was a lieutenant in the Artillery." He stops speaking and looks away again. Dark intimations of what he must have seen or done. I feel sadness for him—and I like him a lot.

. . .

Doug was staying with a friend in London, I in an attic room at a B&B in Clapham. For breakfast, I was seated at a table for two, one of several in the little dining room, which I shared with a balding gentleman in his forties. He was an MP from Scotland who made our economical guesthouse his home whilst Parliament was in session. We chatted cordially. He asked me questions about American politics and the Movement; I asked him about Scotland, which I hoped to visit soon.

I went around London on my own, visiting the major tourist spots and museums. With ticket prices at about $1.50, I saw a play every night. Doug and I met in the city several times to see the sights.

One morning, as I fished some egg out of its pool of bacon grease and contemplated the baked beans with some distaste, my breakfast partner said to me, "What do you think about Wallace being shot?"

"Pardon me?"

"George Wallace—he's been shot."

Swallowing with more than the usual difficulty, I blushed for my country as the man told me about the assassination attempt. Of course, I had no love for Wallace, the segregationist governor and would-be presidential candidate. But would the violence never end?

ONE NIGHT, DOUG AND I went to see the London production of *Hair*. It was strange to see this quintessentially American show in England. We agreed that traveling abroad made us feel somehow more American and thus experience the pain of our torn country even more acutely.

We continued to get along well, though we were a bit formal with each other. He had planned to rent a car to drive to Scotland and asked if I wanted to share the trip with him. So, on May 17, this brave young man let me drive us out of London traffic in an orange Volkswagen Beetle whose stick shift was on the wrong side; its gears were in positions deeply perplexing to me, a person with a dyslexic-type right-left confusion. I supposed that, after Vietnam, riding around Piccadilly Circus with a panicky driver, on the wrong side of the road, was nothing to Doug, though I did see his jaw muscles working.

We spent six days touring the Lake District and Wales. I believe we saw every house Wordsworth ever lived in. While it was never warm, it was quiet and Doug and I had some lovely rambles in the fields. But he suffered when it rained. He said it reminded him too much of monsoon in Vietnam.

He and I had similar rhythms. Doug would go off to do some serious photography with his Nikon, while I meditated in a country church, or sat on the stone ruins of an abandoned castle, marveling at the peace of Wales, a place with more sheep than people. We each wanted a fair amount of time to be by ourselves and we both took pleasure in recounting our experiences over dinner or a beer, or as we shared the driving along the lightly traveled country roads. We became lovers more or less as a matter of convenience. We both appreciated that sharing a room made it possible to take better accommodations than we could afford as singles.

But, discouraged by the frequent rain, we gave up on our plan to drive north to Scotland. Instead, Doug decided to come to Amsterdam, which I had planned as my next stop.

After a queasy ferry crossing from England, I felt for the first time the chilling actuality of World War II when I saw Rotterdam, an entirely modern city because it was bombed to smithereens in 1940.

We took the train to Amsterdam, where we found a room in a narrow hotel with a view of the canal, a sixteenth-century house on the Herengracht. There we stayed for ten days, to see all the sights and also take time to relax and hang out. I liked freewheeling Amsterdam with its easy ways, the down-to-earth Dutch and scores of hippies of all nations sitting around the Dam Square. But during the day, more and more, Doug and I went our separate ways.

On our last night in Amsterdam, we splurged on a fancier restaurant than usual, and shared a bottle of wine. For the first time he spoke at length of his time in Vietnam. He described the misery of the jungle during monsoon, when he thought he would never be dry again. He spoke of seeing a frightened eighteen-year-old boy under his command turn in one instant from a regular kid talking about rock and roll, into a reckless killer, firing into rustling bushes when he had no idea who was there. Doug talked late into the night, at last articulating the heartsickness he felt about the whole adventure. He had come to Europe to get the taste of Vietnam out of his mouth. I just listened, mourning again America's lost innocence and the pain of my generation, my brothers forced into these terrible life-and-death choices. We grew closer that night, and Doug decided to continue on to Paris with me, though the sexual part of our relationship had faded away.

In Paris, we took separate rooms on the fifth floor of a modest hotel in the Latin Quarter.

I ALWAYS SAY IF I had gone to Paris first, I would never have made it anywhere else. To my delight, my French was serviceable enough; only a few Parisians pretended not to understand my middling pronunciation. Speaking another language made me feel like a slightly different person—very freeing. But I barely tolerated the constant come-ons from men in the streets on the Left Bank. I could not believe their persistence. The standard response to my "*Non*" to whatever invitation they made was "*Pourquoi?*"

"*Parce que.*" Because, asshole!

"*Mais, pourquoi pas?*" (But why not?)

Aaargh!

One day, however, I allowed myself to be picked up by a tall, lanky man, an Armenian expat with a chiseled nose and unkempt salt-and-pepper hair. Artine lived in an outlying arrondissement, a tiny room in a large building with littered stairwells and rudimentary toilets in the hall. He showed me how to find cheap meals in student cafeterias and arranged for me to purchase hashish, with trembling hands, in back of a bistro on Boul' St. Mich. When we got stoned with some of his student neighbors, all of whom spoke several languages, my French was put to the test. But who cared? Was I not delighting in *la vie bohême* in Paris?

Doug and I met a couple of times at a café by the Seine, enjoying a view of Notre Dame as we compared notes on our experiences. In mid-June, my money finally ran out and it was time to go home. Doug was leaving Paris too, fed up with the ongoing wet weather. He planned to use his Eurail pass to get on a train and stay on until he reached someplace warm and sunny—Spain, perhaps. We parted fondly.

I took the ferry from Calais to Dover and spent a couple of lonely days in London, before flying back to New York. It gave me great satisfaction that my seven weeks in Europe cost me only $500, airfare and hash included.

In October I received a note from Doug with a picture of the Notre Dame illumined at night. *Let us sit together once again on the Rue St. Jacques sipping espresso as we contemplate the great Cathedral . . .* , he wrote—or something like it. I threw out his note in the great clearance of my past which I did after the *est* Training. But I did save his photograph of the golden spires and buttresses flying above the trees on the Ile de la Cité. I never saw Doug again.

CLINICAL PSYCHOLOGY WAS A hot field in the seventies and Adelphi's PhD program was considered one of the best in the country. Of the twenty-two clinical students in my class, seven were women, four were black, one was a Catholic priest, and another, a middle-aged Venezuelan, was a former executive for Shell Oil. More than half the men were married but only one of the women was. She was the wife of a faculty member.

The program was highly structured. Every student attended full-time, and almost all our courses were required; there were few electives. The prospect of facing three years of the same rigorous professional training together was conducive to cohesiveness, camaraderie, and competitiveness within this small group of people, most of whom were quite competitive to begin with. I know I was.

Besides the desire to help others, most of us shared the belief that Freudian thought was the deepest probe we had into the workings of the human psyche. For me, the feminist critique of Freud's Victorian-era sexism could not invalidate his more profound discoveries, especially of the unconscious mind and its mysterious ways. I firmly believed that personality is formed during the first five years of life. It troubles me that debunking Freud has become so popular. Whatever his short-comings, his genius and courageous self-exploration—which I only began to appreciate when I actually read his works—brought about a fundamental shift in the Western understanding of what it means to be human.

When I started grad school, I learned from Fanya, my father's ex-wife, that a twenty-four-year-old cousin of hers was a second-year student in Adelphi's clinical psych program and was looking for a roommate. Ellen turned out to be a balanced, fun-loving person, graceful and easy to get along with. Together, we found a modest two-bedroom apartment in a spiritless brick building a couple of miles from campus in Hempstead, Long Island. I benefited from her second-year perspective on the faculty and on the ins and outs of the program when it was all so new to me. What's more, Ellen was generous with her car, letting me borrow it to go into the city on weekends while she stayed at home with her boyfriend, Howie.

On my first day at Adelphi, in a class called Psychodynamic Behavior, a heated discussion developed when the instructor averred that the ultimate basis for behavior is psychological. I had to challenge him; hadn't I been contemplating this subject since my forays into neurophysiology? I reminded Dr. Belasny that Freud himself always believed that, some day, empirical science would uncover the biological causes for the phenomena that psychoanalysis described.

"If you don't believe in the soul," I said—and I knew few sophisticated intellectuals then who *did* believe in the soul —"the brain must be the source of human complexity." This notion, that psychology was a function of physiology, was rejected as reductionist by most psychoanalysts back then. Dr. Belasny responded to my comment with distaste. I argued the point and, as usual when one of my pet ideas was involved, got quite het up about it. When the hour ended, five or six of my new classmates surrounded me in excitement to continue the discussion. Wow! These people felt the same enthusiasm I did about understanding the nature of the mind. And, they were clearly smart and well read. This was exhilarating as hell. I couldn't wait to plunge into my studies with this new group of intellectual peers.

•   •   •

THE COURSE IS PSYCHOLOGICAL Testing. I'm sitting in the front row of the classroom. A virgin notebook lies open to the first page on the square ledge attached to my chair. Dr. Fisher, a trim, silver-haired man in his fifties, introduces himself.

"Call me Marty," he says, nervously.

He tells us how, after a career as a successful haberdasher, he became a psychologist, inspired by his own psychoanalysis. His language is informal, laced with earthy slang to show that he's hip. He goes on to give us an overview of the clinical value of psychological testing in making differential diagnoses. However, he warns, a therapist should never become too attached to a diagnosis. Each person presents a unique profile and to make the right therapeutic interventions, an analyst must listen closely.

"If you are really listening to your patients," says Marty,

"you'll often be surprised. A therapist should always retain the ability to be surprised." I like this perspective immediately. From my experience as a patient, this strikes me as fresh and true.

Marty now begins to discuss the principles of projective testing, demonstrating a point by holding up one of the drawings of the Thematic Apperception Test or TAT, in which subjects are asked to make up stories about a series of pictures. One drawing depicts a woman lying in bed, her breasts uncovered. By way of description, Marty offers: "This is a picture of a girl with her tits hanging out." He proceeds to give examples of various types of responses to this drawing and what they might reveal about the respondent's personality and inner conflicts.

I sit, frozen, as if a bucket of ice water has been dumped over my head. Am I really hearing this here, in what I hoped would be a high-minded temple of humanism? I look around the classroom to see if anyone else is reacting. A few men are grinning; the women look impassive. I feel cornered. If I allow this to go by without comment, I could be facing three years of sexist affronts. Yet, like everyone else in the room, I want to make a good impression on our small, elite faculty. Finally, as Marty rattles on in his good-natured way, I raise a sweaty, trembling hand.

"Yes—what's your name?"

"Riqui Kreiter. Um, I just want to point out that describing that picture as 'a girl with her tits hanging out' is demeaning to women, offensive."

I hear people behind me shift in their seats. During a pause which feels endless, I catch sight of an intense-looking woman of my age, whose brown hair falls to her shoulders over her cotton turtleneck. Caroline appears to smirk as she watches to see how the teacher will react.

"Is that so?" Marty says at length. "Well, I certainly didn't mean to be *offensive* . . . "

I feel hot—I know my face is red. I cannot focus on anything else that is said in class and can't wait for it to be over.

Afterward, as I fumble with my books and handbag, Caroline comes up to me and says in a heavy Bronx accent, "That was quite interesting. When you challenged the professor, I said to myself, 'She's either very brave or very stupid.'" Annoyed by her condescension, I retort, "Well I just felt it was too important to let it pass."

Caroline shrugs. In the corridor, Wayne, a heavyset guy with thinning hair and wire-rimmed glasses, asks me if I want to go to the Union for coffee before our next class. As we cross the campus lawn, he says to me, "Riqui, I don't agree with what you said, but I must say, you've got balls."

• • •

MARTY NEVER SPOKE LIKE that in class again. Or rather, he did, but then he would look at me and correct himself. Or he would ask me when he made one of his faintly scurrilous remarks, "Is that sexist, Riqui?" In this way, I became the bearer of the cross of Class Feminist, which relieved everyone else of any need to respond to the still pervasive knee-jerk language of male dominance. This role made me squirm, but I also welcomed it as a way of differentiating myself from the other women in my class whom I perceived as benighted, despite their strong intellects. They seemed to me shamefully apolitical in a field where the textbooks still commonly referred to the therapist as "he," and the patient as "she." Of course, the Catch-22 of my bravado was that when I made a valid point about the many biases toward women in psychology, it was easy to dismiss with an unspoken: "There goes Riqui again." Still, I like to believe my militancy, however unmodulated, forced the point into the awareness of students and faculty. I felt they were, on the whole, people of good-will.

In addition to learning how to administer projective tests like the TAT and Rorschach Inkblots, we had a first-year course in clinical research to start us thinking about approaches to our dissertations. We were also assigned field placements with psychologists in local schools. But most satisfying to me were our studies of Freud's own writings as well as those of the post-Freudians who elaborated on the master's work, exploring the complex functions of the ego and its pathology. One professor alerted us to the dangers of "Medical Students' Syndrome." Not infrequently, he said, doctoral candidates fell into the trap of detecting in themselves the symptoms of the illnesses they were studying. Unfortunately, despite this warning, it was all too easy for me to identify with the neuroses we analyzed in class. This tendency created a gnawing sense of discomfort which soured, to some extent, the joy I was finding in the intellectual work.

I THREW THE FIRST party for my class that October. Counting dates and wives, there were perhaps thirty people to eat crudités and pass joints around our long living room. Thus, I launched my career as class social director, a role I have reprised in other groups over the years. While my deeply rooted sense of distrust often made me uptight in one-on-one relationships, I felt safe enough as part of a group to allow my goodwill to shine. I was very fond of my class and I wanted them all to like each other, too.

I was elected to serve as class representative on the student-faculty council which governed our PhD program. One result of the student struggles of the sixties, in schools across the country, was increased student input into decisions that affected their education. At Adelphi, the three student reps had a full vote in all matters, except personnel decisions. The biggest issue I voted on was whether or not the program should begin to award master's degrees to students who completed two years of coursework and clinical placements. The argument against it was that a doctorate was and should remain the entry-level degree for a clinical psychologist. The PhD was awarded upon completion of the three-year training, a one-year internship, and the dissertation. The persuasive argument for giving students an MA was that the university would receive a certain amount of money from the state for every degree awarded. I voted for the change, never dreaming this would be a fateful decision for me.

During the break after my first semester, Ellen and I flew to Nassau to attend the winter meeting of the American Psychological Association's Division of Psychotherapy, where we did a presentation called "Women as Therapists and Patients." My roommate was one of several female students in the other classes who were less sanguine about sexism than my classmates. Our paper was a critical review of current professional literature. In addition to shedding light on the covert sexism in our field and adding to our resumes, we got to spend four days in the Bahamas with a group of psychologists who were notorious for their wild parties.

•   •   •

IT'S 7:00 P.M., AND the small hospitality room at the Freeport Holiday Inn is packed with perhaps thirty psychotherapists sitting on every available surface, most on the floor. We have been meeting in this laboratory "leaderless encounter group" for hours, making observations on our group dynamics as they occur. As usual, I have been in the thick of it, though it is difficult to tell what we've actually been talking about all this time. These shrinks are masters of mind games and of course I love to play.

"Let's break for dinner," says the middle-aged earth mother type who's been knitting the whole time. Her long, beaded earrings dangle as she shakes her head. "We're way past the point of diminishing returns." Immediately, someone accuses her of resisting the process. People argue this for a while until finally, a consensus to adjourn is reached.

As the group rouses itself and moves toward the door, a bearish man with an early Beatles haircut, thick mustache, and smoky voice comes up to me and introduces himself. His name is Barry.

"I'd just like to say I think you are very honest, and I appreciate that very much," he says earnestly. Then, lowering his voice, he steps close enough for me to feel his heat. "So many of these people are so full of shit," he whispers.

"I'd like to make it with you, too," think I.

One of the other men calls out, "Whoever would like to, can come to my room to turn on before dinner. I'm on the other side of the pool; Room 110."

Barry and I walk around the pool together with about ten others. He confesses that he is a behavior therapist. With a partner, he runs his own clinic in Manhattan.

A behaviorist! One of those who deny intrapsychic dynamics, treating only behavior as real. Anathema! But he is so sexy, exuding this dynamite masculine energy. Room 110 is crowded, humming with several conversations. Barry and I sit next to each other on the bed as two joints circulate. Our mouths are talking about his stunning success in treating phobias—our eyes are on a completely different topic. When everyone leaves the room to go eat, Barry and I stay behind and fall upon each other with gusto. Mmmmm, a behaviorist!

• • •

FROM SEXY BARRY, WHOM I dated for a while upon returning to New York, I learned that behaviorists can be truly caring people, notwithstanding the fact that B. F. Skinner reputedly raised his daughter in a box. In specific cases, as in the treatment of phobias, I saw that behavior therapy can be a lot more efficient and helpful than psychodynamic approaches. Another prejudice bites the dust. For myself, however, I could never be satisfied practicing a purely cognitive or behavioristic approach. In my view, psychoanalysis, with all its Talmudic complexities, offered a much more comprehensive theory of personality. And I was more interested in theoretical understanding than in psychoanalysis as a clinical method.

While I wanted to help others as I had been helped by therapy, what I was really after was knowledge of the deepest processes of consciousness. At school, I immersed myself in the readings and discussions, but when it came to the practical training—administering test batteries to clinic patients, writing reports and recommendations, and, later, treating patients under supervision—I was unsure of myself and anxious. I didn't trust myself not to screw people up. I saw potential pitfalls on all sides. I especially feared falling into power trips, which develop all too often in therapist-patient relationships.

Then, in the fall of '73, I had a field placement at Creedmoor Psychiatric Hospital. As part of a psychiatric team, I visited an inpatient for a couple of hours once a week, on an informal basis. I was always uneasy when I was admitted to the locked ward with its day room full of psychotic people, virtually all on heavy medication. Some talked aloud to themselves, others stared blankly into space. The patient to whom I was assigned was a nineteen-year-old schizophrenic named Linda. She was blond and thin and she moved in a tense, jerky fashion, like a tightly wound top that could easily spin out of control. This may have been a side effect of her medication, but I found it disturbing. She was bright and she functioned normally some of the time. She had only recently been hospitalized after running naked on the steps of St. Patrick's Cathedral. She told me she had done this in order to liberate bystanders, people who were all stuck in their own ideas of propriety. (Of course, this didn't seem that outlandish to me.) I remember she often sang to herself, under her breath, the popular song, "She's Come Undone," sounding a note of self-awareness that made me feel sad for her.

Even after four or five visits, I could not find a comfortable or real way to relate to Linda. The distance between her inner world and my own looked dangerously short. I felt like an impostor, and I was aware that schizophrenics often have uncanny insight into those around them. One day, when I suggested to Linda that some fantasies she was describing indicated repressed anger, she said, "Those are *your* impulses, Riqui."

My stomach clenched and I felt exposed. I mumbled something like, "Well, you may be right," but it frightened me that I was so easily read by her. The inner pressures were mounting again.

As my studies progressed I began to see, to my dismay, that the edifice of self-knowledge, self-esteem, and impulse control that I had so painstakingly built up in my five years of therapy had a crack in its foundation. Underneath, buried in the dungeon of my own heart, was another me: an infant, bereft and crying inconsolably.

*O*lga has slipped from meditation back to sleep, snoring lightly. The sky is striping gold and red as the sun inches down toward the rounded foothills. Lovely.

As the bus descends a long incline into a valley, I suddenly remember this part of the road from the summer of '64, when two waiters from the Granville gave me rides back to the hotel on my days off, when I had fled to the city. When only the city was the real world and, thinking myself hip, I'd joke that the fresh air was making me ill. Oh, well. Everything in its own time.

CHAPTER 16

On 72nd Street

Six months of living on Long Island were enough to make me yearn for Manhattan. I found a place with neighbors of a classmate in a large prewar building on 72nd Street off Riverside Drive. They had a sort of semi-communal arrangement and were seeking a fifth roommate to share rent.

I moved into the maid's room off the kitchen. It was the typical tiny rectangle found in many of New York's prewar buildings, with an adjacent half-bathroom (like the room where I'd first had sex with Steve). I never minded living in a small space—I felt cozy and safe there.

I was elated to be living back in the city with a new circle of friends. The door to our fourth-floor apartment was always unlocked and there was usually something social happening in our ample living room, or a meal to share around the big dining room table. We hung out and played parlor games, listened to music, had earnest discussions. We threw big, bring-your-own-bottle parties where my psychologist classmates and their spouses mingled with friends of my roommates—Broadway dancers, Catholic activists, dental students, and all manner of crashers coming and going through our unlocked door. Joints were passed around rooms alive with conversation.

Later, when the crowd thinned, we'd roll up the blue shag carpet and dance in the living room.

In 1974, with my roommates and other friends, I participated in a women's consciousness-raising group that met in different apartments. We'd sit in a circle drinking wine and sharing Brie and crackers as we discussed a new topic each week. We'd go around the circle, speaking in turn, perhaps about menstruation or our first sexual experiences. Gradually, the usual social defenses fell away as we discovered deep commonalities in our lives as women. During that year of affectionate bonding, the CR group became a source of strength and support for me.

But the tension of my inner conflicts escalated during my last two years at Adelphi. More and more I sought escape by getting high and aggressively asserting my "freedom" from male dominance in my relationships and at school. My old habit of sexual conquest still provided a temporary illusion of power and liberation. But that illusion was wearing thin. Beneath my bravado, I feared that my sexuality was the most I had to offer in a relationship. Secretly, I longed for a prince to cut through the thicket of my defenses and carry me off on his white horse.

Realizing I needed help, I went back into therapy. I began a Sullivanian analysis with Marcia Pollak, whom I could afford because she saw me under the auspices of the NYU clinic as part of her post-doctoral training. I went three times a week, which was exponentially more powerful than the twice-a-week sessions I'd had with Dr. Heimarck. I found that lying on the couch made me more vulnerable and open. From this position, without the social cues of my therapist's facial expressions, I could go deeper into the fertile intrapsychic territory of the unconscious.

•   •   •

I'M STRETCHED OUT ON Marcia's brown leather sofa. A few inches past my stocking feet I see the cream-colored shade of the lamp on the end table. Beyond that, a bit of spring evening light is visible through the ground floor window.

I'm telling Marcia, a disembodied voice from the armchair behind my head, about an upsetting time I had with the guy I was seeing. I'd gone to his house for an unscheduled date and we got into one of our frustrating impasses.

"I called him from school and he asked me to come over," I say, looking at the cracks in the ceiling. "I just knew it wasn't a good idea, but since I wouldn't see him for two weeks, I said yes. Then, when I got there—"

"Wait," Marcia interrupts. "What do you mean you 'knew it wasn't a good idea'?"

I think about this, picturing myself in the phone booth yesterday as Jack said, "Do you wanna come over?"

"Well," I tell Marcia, "it's like a little voice in my head said 'don't go see him today,' but I just ignored it."

"Ah," she says. "So what is that little voice?"

As I reflect on this, I suddenly realize that this "voice" has a quality different from my other thoughts. I have the sense that it's always present and that it knows what's good for me, though I habitually drown it in a flood of emotions and lists of pros and cons. I feel as if a door has opened, and light invades a dark and cluttered room in my head.

• • •

AFTER THAT, I PRACTICED listening for this voice, through all the cacophony in my mind. I learned that, when I pay attention and follow its prompts, I'm invariably led in a direction of greater well-being. On all the paths I've tried since then, tuning in to that inner voice and staying connected with it has been my goal. Thank you, Marcia Pollak.

• • •

IT'S AROUND 3:00 A.M. The apartment is quiet. I hear only the occasional car making the turn onto Riverside Drive four flights below. I am lying in bed with the lights out, stoned but not really sleepy. My mind is busy, ranging far and wide.

All at once I'm engulfed by a visceral memory: I feel very small and I seem to see bars on the side of my bed as I lie in the dark. An excruciating pain, almost physical, grips me. My adored Daddy has been taken from me, wrenched, it seems, from my arms. I double over into a fetal position, sobbing in agony. But part of my mind is clear and detached, observing this little baby, and marveling.

That was ME in that small body! Exactly the same me I am now.

Experiencing this directly feels utterly different from re-membering in the ordinary way that this child was myself. It is a new way of knowing. I'm astonished. *I* was in that crib. I am perceiving the world as if from inside that small body and mind, even as the adult me is watching.

I cannot stand the pain much longer—I am so small and it hurts so much.

Daddy, Daddy, Daddy, Daddy . . . I have no defenses against this heartbreak. The part of me that is watching feels so sorry for the poor little girl.

As this continues, I have a growing certainty (in the adult part of my mind) that a burden I have carried all my life is being lifted. I'm finally experiencing this pain directly instead of ana-lyzing it with a therapist. And I'm simultaneously aware that I am *not* still that helpless child. I am the one watching her. I can feel that I will henceforth be free of, at least, this particular chunk of pain.

When my tears subside, I feel washed clean, light as a feather. I fall asleep smiling.

During my final year of coursework at Adelphi, my hedonism increased in inverse proportion to my groundedness in my studies. I was constantly anxious. I procrastinated on my dissertation as I focused on treating (under supervision, of course) four young people who sought therapy at the university clinic. I was also co-leading a therapy group with my friend Wayne. Discussing the work with my clinical supervisors, it was apparent that, when I played the role of therapist, all my self-doubts were exacerbated. I felt guilty about, even ashamed of, my inexperience. No amount of reassurance alleviated my discomfort. I was having serious doubts about my ability to be the kind of therapist I wanted to be—i.e., perfect. And so, I partied.

I had finally overcome my old inhibition, at least when high, and loved to dance all night, cabbing from party to party with friends on weekends. Still driven by my hungry inner child, my motto at this time was "Everything in excess is best." But when a neighbor gave me a tab of acid for Christmas, I just put it in my jewelry box, under all the dangly earrings and strands of multicolored beads made of coffee beans. Remembering my psychotic episode of five years earlier, I figured I'd wait 'til I was ready to try tripping again.

My deeper interests were now finding a new focus.

I was still meditating twice a day for twenty minutes; unlike many people I knew, I had not dropped TM just because I still smoked pot. Meditation made my mind steadier, better able to hold its course in the stormy sea of emotions which could flood my thoughts so easily.

Since two roommates moved, I now had a large bedroom, painted lemon yellow with a partial view of the river. I spent winter break lining crates with orange contact paper to make end tables and sanding and staining pine boards for bookshelves I propped in place with scavenged bricks. I did temp jobs to supplement my financial aid. When I worked for a week in the office of John Denver's business manager, I got a bunch of free records of which I grew fond.

I continued to work hard in my analysis with Marcia. Three days a week I lay on her couch, struggling with the anger I had carried since childhood, with my fear of that anger, and with all the conflicts that continued to make graduate school so difficult for me.

It was exhausting.

ON MARCH 23, 1975, I was sitting on my bed, thumbing through my well-worn copy of *Be Here Now*. Almost everyone I knew owned a copy of this book, first published in 1971 and still in print forty years later. In it, Richard Alpert, a colleague of Timothy Leary's at Harvard, describes their pioneering experiments with psychedelics. Working with LSD, he says, he dropped layer after layer of his identity and was transformed by these experiences into a spiritual seeker. Then he traveled to India, found a guru, and changed his name to Ram Dass.

Now, as I flipped through the brown pages filled with undulating drawings and spiritual insights, I went over to the jewelry box where I'd kept the small blotter for the past three months waiting for the right time, the right company, the right circumstances in which I could safely take it. Without a second thought, I placed it on my tongue. The pink dot of LSD dissolved into my system.

. . .

I START TO FEEL the effects of the acid as I rock gently in the Bentwood chair in the living room, listening to John Denver's plaintive voice.

Suddenly, I'm hearing it as if for the first time:

Hey, it's good to be back home again . . .

Yes, yes! I feel that. It is good to be back home again, *so-o-o* good . . .

My thoughts start sliding around and I feel happy. After a while, I return to my room, with its high ceilings and wood floors. Opposite me as I sit on the bed is a small desk in a corner, perpendicular to the window. The rest of that wall is lined floor to ceiling with the homemade bookshelves. When I lean back, I can see the Hudson out the window, an inky ribbon between the moving lights of the West Side Highway and New Jersey's looming Palisades.

There is a riot going on in my head. I pick up my Sony and press the record buttons, taping over therapy sessions with my clients, and start talking. I have no blank tapes and I *must* somehow capture this kaleidoscope of thoughts and feelings. One question recurs: What is the real Reality?

I try to speak everything, saying whatever comes into my head. Throughout the night, I feel like I'm swimming in insights and realizations.

*If there is a God, please God, please, I wanna remember this,
if I don't die. Because* [laughing] *my mind is breaking, my
head feels like it's going to explode. . . . What the hell is
making me do this? Why am I undertaking this, this whole
questioning?*

Round and round I go, sentences peeling, ideas intersecting.
As I continue to talk, I begin to get intense headaches. I soon
become aware that this occurs at exactly the points where, in
my own therapy sessions, I would normally stop the inner
exploration. These headaches, I now see, are signposts of my
resistance to the process. But instead of quitting, I talk myself
through, saying, "I have a splitting headache. I really want to
stop now. My temples are pounding . . . " and so on, until the
headache disappears. I have to laugh at how difficult this is.

*Just talking makes me feel like I have to keep up a certain
front. . . . The headache comes from trying to put into words
what I'm experiencing all the rest of the time. Trying to
capture it on one line, capture reality on one line, and the
headache gets worse as I do this. Oh, gosh.
    . . . OK, I'm trying to confront every fear honestly.
That's why I'm making the tape. It always comes down to
time . . . This whole tape is a running after myself in time . . .*

At some point it occurs to me that I have arrived at the
same point at which I freaked out during my 1969 trip with
Robbie. Now, as then, I find myself on the edge of the unknown, peering into the darkness beyond my concept of what
is real—and, again, it feels like a terrifying abyss. But this time,
instead of caving in to the fear that I will fall off the edge of the
universe, I take a breath and step forward, continuing to watch
my train of thought. Each time I do this, I find myself in a field
of light and some new vista opens before me . . . until I come
to the next abyss.

One of many issues that arises several times in different forms—this surprises me—is my experience of being Jewish:

Oh, oy. [High voice] *Oy. There's like this Jewish old man in me. . . . Oh, god, being Jewish is such a big puzzle, and at this moment seems like a big game, really. . . . To be Jewish means to think about the worst thing that can happen, all the time.* [Hearty laugh]

An hour later:

. . . Oh, embarrassment about being Jewish. OK, back to working through my Jewish karma. Oh, yes, it's so much more lovely not to be Jewish, that's the thing. O, God, yeah. It's so much lovelier to be, um, non-Jewish, like a gentleman or um . . . Oh, and [for me] shame is very much part of being Jewish. Shame . . . God, that stops a lot of words—shame. Incredible how many levels one can realize things on . . .

Several times I see the image of a wizened old Jew in an embroidered skullcap, cackling in mirth. The third time he appears in my mind's eye, I realize to my surprise that this is an image of my mother! I suddenly remember how she complained bitterly that, when she was a child, only boys were permitted to study Talmud.

Through the long hours, insights come up again and again, gaining depth and texture each time they present themselves, in a sort of upward spiral. Each thought reverberates inside me, stirring up multiple ideas that stream off in different directions like a bouquet of fireworks. I see with new admiration Freud's genius in realizing the power of untrammeled free association to reveal the workings of the unconscious. Many people appear in the field of my awareness: lovers, roommates, therapy clients. I feel that I can see through their disguises, realizing what they mean to me on many levels. For example, I visualize one girlfriend as ugly, then realize that I habitually distort her pretty face in my mind out of jealousy. As each person comes before me, I see what I have projected onto them, images of them that I have taken to be who they really are: transference. "Freud was so right," I crow, for the fifth time that night.

In this way, I withdraw my projections one by one and see each person with new clarity, as if a filter has been removed. The re-owned projections give me a sense of fullness and strength, since I now experience inside myself the energy I was using to maintain those projected images. And I'm witnessing the whole process as it happens—an intoxicating feeling.

As the hours pass, the miscellaneous contents of my mind seem to drop away in clumps. I feel lighter. All along, I keep repeating how astonished and grateful I am for this experience. And over and over again, I return to the question, "What is the real Reality?"

When I run out of tape cassettes, I continue by writing furiously in a spiral notebook. Sometime in the middle of the night, I come to the liberating perception that, ultimately, nothing actually matters at all, and I crack up laughing.

IT'S ALMOST 6:00 A.M. Sitting cross-legged on my bed, I lean back against the wall and gaze out at the Hudson. The last two fingers of my left hand are stained deep blue.

Now, all at once, the entire landscape of my life appears before me in high relief, like a topographical map. I see it as if from above and observe that every minute detail has its place. I perceive that it—the whole complex story of Ricky-Rickie-Riki-Riqui—has a perfect order: each wild occurrence, every miserable "mistake," fits precisely into a coherent whole. From this vantage point, not one of my choices could or should have been different! It's also obvious that, since I can now see the unique perfection of everything that happened, all the worrying I have done was totally superfluous to this higher order. Amazing.

The first rays of sunlight reach across the river. Quite unexpectedly, time stands still.

I cannot explain this, except to say that it is so. Time stops, but somehow *I*, as I know myself at the subtlest, most intimate level, am fully present.

How can this be?

I am huge but light, like a vast space, much greater than this individual person. This *I* is boundless yet absolutely familiar, the intimate "I" I've always been. This is the same me who always looked out through my eyes: as a baby in my crib; in Ardsley, at the Krauses'; as I cut my wrists at the Granville, this *I* was watching; when I marched in Mississippi, this exact same *I* was seeing it all. It—*I*—was fully present, unchanged, through all the sane times and all the crazy times . . .

So who, exactly, is this "me"? The answer rolls up from inside with absolute authority:

I AM THAT I AM.

For a moment, there is only silence, a timeless pause. A blanket of unspeakable peace settles over me. Then a thought forms in my mind: so this is what was meant when Moses heard those words at the burning bush.

An all-encompassing gentleness envelops me like a soft cloud. For some reason, it seems to me this Gentleness is Christ. I see with certainty that silence and peace—and so many other gifts—are always available. It's only that we don't notice them.

I am fresh and wide open as a child, filled with gratitude and awe.

. . .

I WANTED MORE THAN anything to stay in the state of peace and fullness I had reached on my trip. For the next week, I carefully considered every move I made in a vain effort not to come down to the ordinary awareness whose limitations I had seen so clearly. My relationship with my body shifted. I had the sense that I was *in* my body but separate from it; I perceived that I could consult my body, for example, about what to eat. If I asked myself, "What should I eat?" and then closed my eyes and waited quietly, an answer would come, suggesting something that felt like just the right food. That morning, I ate only an orange and some herbal tea. In the afternoon, I went on to rice, yogurt, nuts. Later in the week, I added vegetables.

I read the Gospels for the first time and felt I could see where Jesus was coming from, that vast space beyond words. I was astonished by how simple and obvious were the many truths of his teachings: seek and you shall find, for example, and unless you become like a child, you cannot enter the "kingdom of heaven," which I now perceived lay within one's own being. I felt exalted by the holiness of that week which brought Passover, Easter, and Muhammad's birthday.

Yet despite all my efforts, each day I came down a little more. I was shaken to my foundation and everything in my psyche felt susceptible of being rearranged. I sounded more than a little strange when I tried to explain the trip to my friends.

Marcia was understandably alarmed. In my session on Tuesday, as I exerted great effort to communicate to her the profound realizations I had had, my speech was stilted and self-conscious. In my attempts to be crystal clear, I kept saying "OK" intensely as I finished one thought and moved on to the next. I felt that she couldn't grasp what had happened to me. I could hardly fault her for that. But I did.

IT TOOK ME YEARS to fully admit that this experience changed my life. Conventional wisdom has it that drug experiences are, by definition, deluded. But after this acid trip, I turned a corner. For one thing, having seen that perfect order to my personal history, I could never take my worrying quite as seriously as I had before. While I still had much psychological work to do, I had glimpsed the light beyond the more or less repressed psychic pain that had always been the background to my everyday awareness. I knew that the boundless space I had entered so briefly was real.

In the weeks following the trip, I formalized my new sense of self by officially changing my name back to Rifka Batya. It felt like a perfect affirmation of several things at once: my identity as Jewish; my femininity; and my self as Batya, "daughter of God." Best of all, it was the name my mother, Hannah, gave me at birth that I had never used—my own name when I was newborn. It was a first step on the long road to forgiveness. In time I would see I could never attain the freedom I craved without forgiving Bonnie.

As the spring progressed I found that, through my transference to Marcia, I was getting dangerously close to core issues in my relationship with my mother: the fused identities, my deep shame and rage. But I froze with fear when we approached this stuff in our sessions. Though I knew it was necessary, I could not bring myself to descend into that cauldron with Marcia as my guide. In fact, I began to feel I would never allow myself to trust any therapist enough to do the work that would heal the wounds left by the old traumas. The LSD trip convinced me that there were alternative routes to liberation, though I didn't think that taking more acid was the way to get there. It posed too many dangers to my psychological balance.

In *Be Here Now*, Ram Dass recounts his own efforts not to come down from his psychedelic highs. But no matter how much LSD he took—and he took huge amounts—he always did come down.

> *It was a terribly frustrating experience, as if you came into the kingdom of heaven and you saw how it all was and you felt these new states of awareness, and then you got cast out again.*

Like him, I wanted results that would be stable and lasting. He went off to India to find "the next chapter of this drama." I, too, accelerated my forays into the booming spiritual marketplace of 1975. I had to find a way back to the state of consciousness I had tasted at the end of my trip.

CHAPTER 18

Rinpoche

Many people of my generation had moved on from psychedelics to the spiritual quest. There was such a plethora of paths and teachers in New York, I hardly knew where to begin. Some were ancient, traditional paths, Asian or Native American. Others were upstart New Age trips which were difficult to evaluate.

I was a regular listener on Sunday mornings to a show called *In the Spirit* on WBAI, New York's radical public radio station. Here I was introduced to many forms of spirituality that were new to me. When my trusted inner voice responded to something I heard, I followed up on it. This was how I first came to see Rinpoche.

Chögyam Trungpa was a thirty-six-year-old lama who was the former abbot of a monastery in Tibet. After fleeing his country at the time of the Chinese invasion, Trungpa lived in India and the UK, studied at Oxford, and settled in the United States in 1970. He presented Tibetan Buddhist teachings in widely read books like *Cutting Through Spiritual Materialism*, speaking in the American vernacular about the dangers that confront seekers:

> *Walking the spiritual path properly is a very subtle process; it is not something to jump into naively. There are numerous sidetracks which lead to a distorted, ego-centered version of*

spirituality; we can deceive ourselves into thinking we are
developing spiritually when instead we are strengthening our
egocentricity through spiritual techniques. This fundamental
distortion may be referred to as spiritual materialism.

I first saw Rinpoche (the honorific term of address for a
Tibetan spiritual teacher) at a lecture he gave at the Cathedral
of St. John the Divine. I arrived early to get a seat up front. He
arrived two hours late. As we waited, I spoke with some of the
people around me who were already students of Rinpoche's.
They said he was almost always hours late because he lived
spontaneously. This sounded like bullshit to me, but I swal-
lowed my annoyance and waited.

When he finally appeared, Rinpoche walked without fan-
fare to a chair on the platform. He was a short, thickset man
with bronze skin and glossy black hair. He wore a suit and tie. I
watched and listened in fascination as he spoke, addressing us
quietly in an utterly calm voice.

The point of view he expounded was, in part, a highly sophisticated psychology, including an acute analysis of how the
ego—one's sense of identity as a limited individual—turns everything to its own purpose. Rinpoche seemed to confirm what I'd
learned on my trip. The Buddha, he said, discovered that human
beings are seduced by:

> . . . *a fundamental myth: that we are solid beings. But ulti-*
> *mately the myth is false, a huge hoax, a gigantic fraud, and*
> *it is the root of our suffering. . . . We cannot in any way*
> *free ourselves from the domination [of this myth] unless we*
> *cut through, layer by layer, [our] elaborate defenses . . .*

Rinpoche termed this basic human condition "neurotic."
The means to enlightenment he offered for working with this
was the classic one:

The method that the Buddha discovered is meditation. He discovered that struggling to find answers did not work. It was only when there were gaps in his struggle that insights came to him. He began to realize that there was a sane, awake quality within him which manifested itself only in the absence of struggle. So the practice of meditation involves "letting be."

This was a clear exposition of a way different from the psychotherapeutic approach. Perhaps I did not have to resolve my childhood traumas one by one. I could work with the energy that fueled them, as I had on LSD.

And I liked the down-to-earth simplicity of his approach.

Periodically, as he spoke that night at St. John the Divine, Rinpoche paused to pour sake into a little porcelain cup from a Japanese carafe standing on the table beside him. In complete silence, he lifted the cup to his lips, took a sip, then replaced it deliberately on the table. This must be what the Buddhists call mindfulness, I thought. I was shocked to see a spiritual teacher drinking alcohol so publicly, but his lack of pretense appealed to me immensely. The Buddhism Rinpoche taught was free of value judgments. There were no certainties on this path.

IN APRIL, I WENT to a four-day retreat at Rinpoche's farm in Barnet, Vermont. With about forty other seekers, I meditated for hours each day in the local Town Hall, sitting cross-legged on a thick, round cushion on the floor. We sat with half-open eyes in soft focus, maintaining our attention on the breath as it went in and out of the nostrils. Once each hour, a brass gong sounded and we rose to exercise the body, walking silently in a slow circle while continuing to focus on the breath. I had never before meditated for so many hours; it was not easy. All kinds of thoughts, feelings, and sensations went through me, some of them very intense. My legs were killing me and my back ached. It took a lot of will to persist in meditation, always returning my attention to the breath.

At the end of each day, Rinpoche gave a talk on the theme of the retreat, "From Cynicism to Devotion." He taught that "we must make a real commitment to being open with our teacher; we must be willing to give up all our preconceptions," and be naked before the guru, adding:

> I am afraid the word "guru" is overused in the West. It would be better to speak of one's "spiritual friend," because the teachings emphasize a mutual meeting of two minds. It is a matter of mutual communication, rather than a master-servant relationship between a highly evolved being and a miserable confused one.

I had a very strong resistance to this concept of devotion to a guru. It was one thing to appreciate and admire a teacher, as I did Ram Dass. But this . . . I always considered my fierce independence my greatest strength. One afternoon, during the question and answer session, I raised my hand and asked Rinpoche, "Is it necessary for every seeker to have a guru?"

"This is an interesting question," said Rinpoche (and of course my ego puffed up at this). He responded with a metaphor, saying, in essence: Certain birds, when they are ill, are able to get the remedies they need from various trees and bushes, picking and choosing among the seeds and berries by following their instincts.

I was reassured by this answer, thinking surely I was one of those birds. Yet the guru-disciple relationship was central to Rinpoche's Buddhism, as it is to virtually every mystical tradition that seemed true to me. The people I met who had been practicing Tibetan Buddhism for some time seemed grounded and real. So I kept an open mind. Perhaps having a guru would, in the end, bring me the absolute freedom for which I longed. It seemed the spiritual path was paved with such paradoxes.

After the four-day retreat my mind was clear and quiet and I felt like I was standing more fully in my own shoes. Still, when I learned that serious students of Rinpoche's regularly practiced thirty-day or even year-long solitary meditation retreats, I understood why this path was called "the hard way." It was not for the faint of heart.

I RETURNED TO NEW York for my final days at Adelphi. I continued to practice Buddhist meditation, attending sessions at Rinpoche's center on 14th Street. I believed that Tibetan Buddhism could take me to my goal. Why, then, was I still drawn to check out other paths?

More and more, I turned away from the psychotherapeutic approach. I was stymied in my work with Marcia due to a bone-deep distrust that sometimes verged on paranoia. I knew this fear was part of the problem, but I was just done working at it this way. So I quit therapy.

And when, at the end of the school year, I heard about *est*, I decided to enroll in the Training.

CHAPTER 19

est

The Waldorf ballroom, with its cream-colored walls and crystal chandeliers, is set up theater-style with 250 chairs. Although most of the participants are white, they're of a wide range of ages and backgrounds: business executives, hippies, housewives, artists, college students, professionals. A palpable sense of anticipation is in the air.

At 9:00 a.m. sharp, our trainer leaps onto the stage and I feel a surge of energy in myself and everyone around me. He is a handsome thirty-something Texan named Ron Bynum. His well-cut brown hair lies gracefully near his sparkling brown eyes and he wears slim-fitting pants with a soft, open collared shirt. I find Ron sexy as hell as he starts his spiel in a booming voice, projecting as well as any actor to the back of the house. His introductory remarks are laced with expletives. "And for those of you assholes who don't like swearing," he says, "you'll find out that 'fuck' is just another word, like 'spaghetti,'" adding with an impish grin, "but one's better for you."

• • •

EST WAS THE NOTORIOUS brainchild of Werner Erhard, né Jack Rosenberg, a former salesman who had had a spontaneous awakening of consciousness in the late sixties. Werner, as everyone called him, started this large group awareness program, held over two consecutive weekends, in 1971.

Ron told us that *est* was a game and if we played the game by the rules, by the end of the Training we would "get it" about reality—and our lives would start to work. One of the basic premises here was that satisfaction comes from fully experiencing your life, not from understanding it conceptually.

The four days of the Training were structured in three sections. First, the trainer presented certain material: theory and concepts. Then there were exercises like guided meditations, some quite long and intense. In between, there were extended periods for "sharing." You raised your hand and a runner brought you a microphone so you could describe your experience, ask a question, or say anything at all you felt like saying. These sessions lasted until everyone who wanted to had had their say. They could and did go on for hours. The ground rules were that no matter what was said, the rest of us would applaud, not in approval or disapproval, but just to acknowledge the speaker. Similarly, the trainer might just say, "Thank you, I got it," or he might interact with the person who shared.

We had to check our watches at the door each day. Bathroom and meal breaks happened when the trainer deemed the time was right. For meals, we'd traipse out to local restaurants and return at the appointed time to take different seats next to different people. If you were late, you'd find the ballroom doors closed and a volunteer would confront you, asking you to acknowledge that you hadn't kept your signed agreement to be back on time for each session. This gave you an opportunity to notice all the excuses you make in your life for not keeping your agreements. (I still use this to guide my behavior: if I fail to do what I've said I'll do, I take responsibility for it. I then feel a sense of personal power instead of the weakness I feel when I'm blaming "outside forces" for what happens in my life.)

Ron was our trainer for the first weekend; another man

led us through the second weekend. Each day ended only when the trainer felt that everyone "got" whatever we were supposed to get that day. One day it was nine o'clock. Another it was 1:00 a.m.

All the terms used in the Training were defined at length, right out of Webster's. In this way, a powerful language of consciousness, with explicit denotations and connotations, was delineated. Unfortunately, when I and other *est* graduates used these terms later, in settings where they had not been so thoroughly defined, they came out sounding like some facile jargon.

One of the reasons enumerated for this emphasis on precise language was this: words can do no more than point to reality. Truth itself can only be experienced—it is beyond words. I had come up against this frustration after my acid trip, when I tried to communicate my realizations to Marcia and my friends. Hearing the problem articulated so clearly in the Training helped me to just accept this and move on.

On the second day of the Training, a woman raised her hand to complain that the room was too cold.

"How many people think the room is too cold?" asked Ron. About fifty people raised their hands.

"How many people think the room is too warm?" Again, fifty people raised their hands.

This was a real eye-opener. To say "the room is too cold" is a judgment, an evaluation—not the ultimate truth. After all, what makes my judgment any more significant or true than anyone else's? I realized that when I state my point of view as absolute truth, I am not standing on solid ground. What is certainly true is the statement, "I feel cold. I request that you turn down the air conditioning." I feel so much stronger when I say *I* am cold, or angry, as opposed to "it's cold" or "you're wrong." No one can really argue when I simply state my own experience.

If I got nothing else from *est*, this would have been enough.

. . .

THE FOUR LONG DAYS of the Training were, for me, like journeys to distant worlds. Each hotel meeting room was our spaceship and the others in the group were my co-explorers. We dealt with our deepest fears, the nature of the mind, relationships, questions about God, and reincarnation. The Training was a brilliant synthesis of a wide array of approaches to understanding reality: Scientology, Zen Buddhism, Gestalt theory, Synanon, Indian philosophy, and theoretical physics, to name a few. But the whole slick package was definitely greater than the sum of its parts.

It was Werner's intention, we were told, that *est* and its teachings "disappear into our lives." The point was not that the *est* graduates should adopt a new belief system, but that their experience of life would be transformed.

My own experience of life *did* shift radically. I "got it" in my guts that I had made up the story of my life, and kept it going by *choosing* to believe, for example, that I was a victim of a broken home, etc. It was irrelevant that others supported that debilitating belief. I saw clearly that we are always choosing how we experience life, either consciously or unconsciously. After the Training, instead of regarding my life as high drama, I began to see it more as a soap opera, a game to be mastered. This mastery follows when I accept full responsibility for *everything* in my life. I chose to no longer believe that I was a victim— though I could see that, at times, I still felt like one. I found that, by adopting the point of view of the creator, or the observer, those feelings of victimization, which I'd struggled with for years, loosened their hold on me. And the more I practiced making that inner shift, the larger my universe became. Practice proves the truth that:

The mind is its own place, and in itself
Can make a heav'n of hell, a hell of heav'n.
    —John Milton, *Paradise Lost*

After I completed the Training, I was euphoric. I had my hair, which had been shoulder length for years, cut to about an inch all around my head. I felt liberated, so much lighter. I thought now that *est* might be the path that would take me to my goal.

During the summer of '75, I went on a binge of ebullient zealotry, calling everyone I knew to "share my experience" of the Training. I had found something so valuable to me, I just *had* to make them see the light. It turns out it was all too easy to slip from simply communicating my experience, as *est* recommended, into proselytizing. Most of my friends were turned off but indulged me—at least for the first couple of months. I also continued to meditate at the Tibetan Buddhist center on 14th Street. But I was still interested in exploring other avenues. For a while, I attended informal weekly meetings at a Transcendental Meditation center where we studied Maharishi's commentaries on the *Bhagavad Gita.* One of his metaphors has stayed with me. He likened traveling the path to enlightenment to climbing a mountain to capture a fort. Like Rinpoche, he warned there are many distractions along the way as the seeker gains personal powers such as clairvoyance and other psychic abilities. These are like diamond mines on the side of the road which can lure a seeker away into unseen pitfalls or dead ends.

I found value in each of these approaches, but my deep longing for the exquisite peace I'd once tasted remained unsatisfied.

I ended my final year of coursework at Adelphi with three incompletes that I planned to address in the indeterminate future. For the time being, I took a year's leave of absence. I felt powerful, free, and happier than I could remember feeling before. My sense of who I really am, beneath the limitations of personality, character, and life history, had been greatly expanded.

I decided I would go out West to see my mother. Maybe I could finally dissolve the old demons and "complete my relationship" with her, an *est* term which I understood to mean transcending my ambivalence in order to reach the space of unconditional love, one in which you accept someone "exactly as they are and exactly as they are not."

Before leaving the apartment on 72nd Street, I cleared out my room for two new roommates, a married couple named Rosie and John. I wasn't sure when I would return. As part of my *est*-ian transformation, I threw away my old diaries, Playbills, and memorabilia of all kinds, including my acid tapes (except for written transcripts of the first two). I wanted to see if Werner's idea would work: that when you let go of old things you've been hanging on to, you create the space for something new to enter your life. I was ready for something new.

Money was short so, in late August, I hopped a Greyhound bus to start another trip across the country.

*O*lga wakes up and rubs her pretty gray eyes.

"Do you know how much farther it is?" she asks with a smile.

"I'm not sure; at the rate we're going—maybe another twenty minutes?"

She leans into the aisle to check out the road ahead. "I'm deeply excited," she tells me, affirming the obvious. "I've been hearing about Swamiji for so long. I've been waiting to see him for a year. I would've gone to California but I couldn't afford it."

Swamiji is arriving after giving public programs in the Bay Area for the past six months or so. "I almost went to see him when I was out there in October," I tell her. "I ended up seeing Baba Ram Dass that night instead."

"Oh, Swamiji is much higher than Ram Dass," she says with certainty.

"Maybe. But it seemed that was the right choice for me that night. Anyway, I'm glad I'm meeting him now."

"How did you first hear about him?"

"In the Training last year. Remember when Ron referred to Swamiji as an example of someone operating from Source?"

"Oh, yeah. I already knew about him so I guess it didn't make that much of an impression on me." She pauses. "Did you like the Training?"

"I loved the Training," I answer immediately, like I haven't told the entire world this fact by now. "How about you?"

Olga shrugs gently. "I found it too Western—too aggressive."

Resisting the impulse to argue with her, I reply, "I can see that." But I can't resist adding, "For me, it was transformational." Olga shrugs in friendly indifference and we both return to our silent contemplations.

CHAPTER 20

Greyhound Odyssey

I hadn't seen Bonnie for a couple of years, but from our phone conversations she seemed happy enough. I felt sure that, now that I'd "gotten it," I would finally be able to handle our fraught relationship. But first, some adventure! My ticket to San Francisco allowed me three stops along the way. When I was a teenager, an anonymous bus trip across the country had been one of my romantic fantasies of escape, and I did, in fact, enjoy sitting alone on the bus, looking out the window at the farms and small towns we passed through in Pennsylvania and Ohio. I tried to imagine what it was like to grow up there, to have a daily life so different from my own. It all seemed exotic from my inveterate New Yorker's point of view.

My first stop was Columbus, Ohio, where a friend was doing summer stock. She and I went out to dinner after the show, then spent the night in her hotel room where I kept her up for hours as I shared my passion for the Training and how it had transformed my experience.

The next morning, I boarded another Greyhound heading west. I felt very awake, existentially speaking, and drank in the sights and the assortment of interesting characters getting on and off the bus as we traversed Indiana and Illinois. It was my intention to stay open to whatever gifts came my way on this adventure.

· · ·

APPROACHING ST. LOUIS, I'M struck by the beauty of the huge arch by the river, glowing in the light of the setting sun. I haven't heard of this monument before. My main association with St. Louis is that I was conceived here when my father was working for the USO. As the bus wends its way through the seedy downtown streets, I wonder if my parents ever walked on these sidewalks, and what did the city look like in 1945?

The bus terminal is large and well lit, cleaner than the stations we stopped in up north. Still, I am tired and a bit depressed. The initial thrill of adventure has subsided and my body aches from sitting for so long. I buy an egg salad sandwich and coffee and eat, sitting on a wooden bench in the "Ladies Waiting Room," enjoying the chance to stretch my legs fully. I read for an hour, waiting for the earliest opportunity to board the 9:50 for Kansas City. I want to be sure to get a window seat and hope I'll be able to catch some sleep.

Back on the bus, I am about to crow (silently) at having two seats to myself when a nun comes up the aisle and sits beside me. I assume that any nun still wearing a habit after Vatican II is one of the rigid, ruler-wielding types familiar from the school memories of my Catholic friends. I stiffen and look studiously out the window, anticipating cramped hours ahead as the Greyhound makes its way out of the darkened city and onto the interstate. After a while my neighbor—apparently too dense to take a hint—strikes up a cheerful conversation.

"I'm Sister Mary Catherine." I turn toward her and am surprised to see a bright, open face, clear skin, and small features framed by a white wimple. She looks around twenty-five.

"I'm Rifka." It still feels strange to say my new name.

"What kind of name is that?"

"It's Rebecca, from the Bible."

Sister Mary Catherine smiles broadly. "Beautiful," she murmurs.

She tells me she teaches kindergarten in St. Louis and is on her way to visit her family in Kansas before the start of the new school year. "I just love those little kids," she says with an infectious smile. She goes on to tell me some of the funny things children say and do in her classes. I can't help but warm to her.

After inquiring about my destination, she asks what I do. I give the facts and then, hesitantly, tell her how I am not really sure what I want to do. She listens attentively, with sparkling eyes.

"I've been questioning a lot of things," I say shyly. "I used to be an agnostic but I've had some amazing experiences lately." Pause. I am encouraged by her quiet attention. "I'm Jewish but I recently read the Gospels. I had an experience of Christ . . . like a vast gentleness."

I leave out the detail that this happened on an acid trip.

Sister Mary Catherine responds with enthusiasm, telling me how much she loves Jesus but that she does not think of him as the only way. "The only reason I'm a nun is that I was born Catholic," she says. "If I had been born something else, I would have found another way to love God." I am disarmed by her open-minded attitude; another prejudice is overturned. I talk to her a little about *est* and my determination to live more fully in a state of open happiness.

She seems to resonate with this and says, chuckling, "Father O'Day—he's the principal of our school—he says I bubble for Christ."

I cannot resist laughing, too, thinking Father O'Day is right on.

I envy her certainty and her obvious fulfillment in her path.

After a short silence, she says, "I know a book you should read. I mean, you are on a search for God, and this book meant a lot to me before I found my vocation." I'm startled for a moment by her perception of me. I hadn't thought of my journey as a search for God. "It's called *Hinds' Feet on High Places* by Hannah Hurnard," she continues. "She's Catholic, but I don't think you have to be Christian to read it."

I make a mental note of the title. By the time we reach Kansas City, I'm sorry to see her go. When the Greyhound pulls onto the highway heading west, I settle down for a refreshing nap.

• • •

MY MOTHER LIVED IN one of Las Vegas's many developments of two-story stucco apartment complexes, typically laid out with sixteen apartments around a courtyard with swimming pool. Tenant parking and overflowing dumpsters were in the alleys behind the houses. Many of the bedroom windows, like my mother's, were covered on the inside with aluminum foil to keep out the broiling sun so that people who worked nights could get their sleep.

Bonnie made me welcome, moving my twelve-year-old sister into our little brother's room so that I could have Heather's bedroom to myself. Danny was six, blond and irresistible, with freckles and a gravelly voice. Mom seemed pretty happy since he was born—the son she had wanted so much— and I found the family in a relatively idyllic phase. I was delighted to see how both the kids adored their father, who had been sober now for three years.

Don's drinking had taken him on a downward spiral, landing him in an Alcoholics Anonymous halfway house some time in 1972. He had trouble working the Twelve Step program and could not bring himself to believe in a "higher power," the starting point for recovery in AA. But one day, while he was washing pots in the Samaritan House, something happened, he told me with wonder on the first day of my visit. We were sitting with my mother in their pleasant living room, drinking coffee.

"All of a sudden, something clicked," he said, "and it just came to me: 'Everything's going to be all right,' like a voice or something . . . just like that—I don't know why . . ." He laughed shyly.

This experience had been enough to keep Don sober for three years, and counting. I had always been fond of Don and I was happy that he had had such a great experience of "God as you understand him," as they say in AA.

Of course, I told them all about *est* and they listened with interest. It seemed that Bonnie, too, was hoping this visit would heal our old wounds and she liked the idea of "completing our relationship." And when I told her I had had an actual experience of God, she was receptive. Also, unlike the rest of my family and friends who took a long time to start calling me Rifka, my mother switched over readily, and I appreciated that acknowledgement. She often added the Yiddish suffix of endearment and called me Rifkele.

Bonnie herself had always believed in and loved God, albeit One who made her feel terribly guilty if she thought about "Him" too much. Hers was the Old Testament God too often imagined as a judgmental father. She took the children to synagogue sometimes and I went with them during my stay to hear Heather sing in the choir. I knew that Judaism must contain the same truth I was seeking on other paths; surely, through Kabbalah, that experience must be available, I thought. But spiritually, whenever I went to synagogue, I felt like a thirsty person being offered salt water. I had never heard a rabbi speak of God as an immanent, personal experience. Only in the 1990s, when I read *The Jew in the Lotus* by Rodger Kamenetz and *The Receiving* by Tirzah Firestone, did I finally see the spiritual connections between my own experiences and Judaism. Meanwhile, I was sad that I couldn't relate more to my people's religion. But it seemed to have a stabilizing influence on my mother and Heather loved singing in the choir; I was glad of that.

Don had an office job in the Personnel Department at the Golden Nugget. It was a decent job and he was well-liked there. My mother was happy to stay at home and kept the modest apartment very tidy, making inviting meals for the family to share. And she insisted that one of the children say "grace" when we sat down for dinner.

"God is great, God is good, let us thank him for our food," Heather would say sweetly. Don then added his own version of grace, a hand-to-forehead salute with a wry, "Much obliged," which always made the kids laugh.

Like me, Bonnie worked hard to mend our relationship. We had long talks when Don went to work and the children were asleep. As had often happened when I was younger, I found she could be exceptionally insightful, compassionate, and a lot of fun, as long as one of her buttons wasn't pushed. For example, when I talked about my ambivalence about becoming a therapist, she helped me look at some of my fears and affirmed my strengths. If our talk touched on my childhood, however, she was liable to explode. When the mountain of guilt she carried was triggered, she attacked. Her old demons had not disappeared. How could they? She had never tackled them in therapy and, although she gained some insight from the Alanon meetings she went to, she did not really work the Twelve Step program. She yelled at the children, both overweight, if they did not finish the large portions she heaped on their plates. For treats, she encouraged them to get Slurpees—

sugar water over ice—from the local 7-Eleven. Then she'd embarrass them, for example, when posing for group pictures.

"Pull your stomach in, Heather," she'd say loudly. "Stand behind Rifka." "Leave her alone," I'd snap, hugging Heather. "She looks fine." It seemed my old searing pain was right below the surface, though my new sense of identity put me in a different relationship with it. In *est* terminology, the context of my feelings had changed. I felt that I was bigger than the pain, but the content of my feelings in relation to my mother was all too familiar. I identified less with my personality and my history, but not that much less.

Bonnie still loved to drink, and once she succumbed to the temptation to have a vodka or two she was rarely able to stop until blood had been drawn, emotionally speaking. I worried about Don's sobriety but he claimed her drinking did not affect him. Bonnie said that, too.

Several times during my stay, she went on a binge. The family was then forced to live through two or three days of drunken brooding, yelling, and hysterical drama, which frightened children and grown-ups alike. Once, during a fight when we were all in the car, Bonnie reached over from the passenger seat and switched off the ignition in the middle of an intersection. When she sobered up, she was contrite and took up the role of good wife and mother again.

I did my best to comfort the children, but I was often overcome by sadness as I saw them live through what I had endured: a mother whose behavior could swing from caring warmth and wisdom one minute to vicious invective the next. Don was cowed by her and retreated into sleeping twelve hours at a time when things got bad. I lost patience and attacked her, lecturing her on taking responsibility for her own life. I tried to make her see that she was hurting her children just as she had hurt me. She responded by pointing out how my highfalutin statements of what I had attained were belied by my diatribes. Her charges stung all the more because I knew they were accurate.

Once, in the middle of some big brouhaha, she said to me resentfully as a tearful defense of some outrageous behavior, "You know, Rifka, my mother never kissed me goodnight." She spoke as if it were yesterday. Eventually, I came to see how Bonnie's self-image remained that of an abused, love-starved child, a "rotten egg." Whenever I could really get this, it created space in my heart for compassion to grow, even while I couldn't help yelling at her, "That was fifty years ago, Mother. Get over it!"

As if I had gotten over *my* childhood.

I had hoped for greater mastery, that I would be immune to her now, that I could just love her. I had no idea that, for years to come, visiting my mother would be the best reality check I had on how far I had actually progressed toward my goal of freedom from my old patterns. It was amazing how quickly I could become, in her presence, the enraged, judgmental fourteen-year-old I had once been.

Truly forgiving my mother has been the greatest challenge of my life.

I spent almost three months at Bonnie's house in Las Vegas. And, not unlike her with her drinking, I, too, sought relief from these struggles. This was Vegas, after all—there was no dearth of ways to escape.

I GOT INTO GAMBLING in 1968, the first time I visited Bonnie after she moved out west. A friend in New York had taught me a betting system for craps which, he said, should make me some modest winnings. Back then, I played at the Silver Slipper, which Don told me was one of the more down-to-earth casinos on the Strip. My hands shook as I placed my first few bets on the Don't Pass line, betting against the shooter. Gradually, my little pile of chips grew, and I had more and more of the green, ten-dollar discs neatly inserted in the wooden groove by my place at the table. The croupiers kept rolling their eyes, telling me I was just lucky, that my system was no good. I was convinced they were just trying to dissuade me from using my winning strategy.

It was tremendously exciting. I felt powerful, even though my winnings accrued slowly. At eight in the morning, when I had to go back to my mother's to return her car, I felt I was losing money by leaving the casino. I was up a hundred dollars.

I went back every night on that first visit and by the time I returned home, I had lost all my winnings plus my original stake. But by then I was hooked. When I lived in San Diego, I'd spent many weekends at the blackjack tables with Laurie. Now, in 1975, I was looking forward to the prospect, still glamorous to me, of gambling in a casino once again.

As an *est* graduate, I had "gotten" that there was no reason I couldn't win big if I had the clear intention to do so. This, it turned out, was a large "if."

A couple of weeks into my visit, I started going to the casinos regularly. On a typical day, I would drop Don off downtown in time for his 8:00 p.m. shift. Then I'd have the use of the Plymouth for the night. People still dressed up for casinos then, at least on the Strip, and I loved the feeling of dolling up in anticipation of an evening filled with unknown pleasures. I had a fabulous halter-top silk jersey jumpsuit, bright red and backless, with big palazzo pants which flowed around my ankles.

At first, I gambled at Caesar's Palace, where the casino was carpeted in red and consisted primarily of tables for blackjack, craps, and roulette. Really high rollers played cards in the quiet, roped-off area reserved for baccarat. Beautiful waitresses clad in thick makeup and scanty "togas" crisscrossed the room on two-inch heels, balancing trays of cocktails on one hand. Slot machines were in a separate section and did not fill a huge area with their clamorous noise the way they did later. People wore evening clothes, and the atmosphere allowed me to imagine myself some Hitchcock heroine. I still had a rich fantasy life. But it was my old machismo more than delusions of being Grace Kelly that gave me the nerve to sit down at one of the poker tables at Caesar's.

There were some nights when I could not lose. I maintained that detached and widely inclusive perspective which allowed me to view myself and the other players almost like I had in my out-of-body experience years ago. At these times, I knew exactly how much to bet, when to fold, and when to bluff. This could continue as long as I resisted the temptation to drink, substituting a pseudo-cocktail to slake my thirst: club soda with bitters, a cherry, and a slice of orange.

It was easiest to win on the weekends when vacationers filled the tables. But midweek players included hardened regulars (almost exclusively men) who played much better than I. At first, I had the advantage of being a young woman—no one expected me to be as tough a player as I was. I flirted and chatted and enjoyed surprising my opponents with a winning hand. But it didn't take long for these men to turn hostile and become especially aggressive in their play. Over time, this wore me down. More and more often, I succumbed to temptation and drank scotch. Then I'd start to lose. When my game grew cold, I'd leave the poker table and go play blackjack, where thirty dollars could last the whole night.

When I won, I loved walking out of the air-conditioned casino into the golden sunrise. I'd take a few breaths of the dry desert air and stop beside the car to admire the variegated hues of the mountains all around me. When I lost, I got a sinking feeling when I stepped outside and the desert heat and my own exhaustion hit me.

Bonnie was delighted and excited if I won. When I lost money, she got upset.

"Why didn't you leave?" she'd ask in a plaintive voice if I told her I'd been ahead at 2:00 a.m.

I would never say, "Because I couldn't." Instead I'd snap, "Because I chose not to." Which, on the highest level, was true. But it didn't feel true, and she knew it. Part of me—the part of my consciousness that wasn't seduced by all the sense pleasures—watched all this with chagrin.

SEPTEMBER SEEMED TO UNFOLD in slow motion. In the daytime, I slept while the kids were in school. After coffee—Mom always had a pot going in the electric percolator—I'd ride with her to pick up Danny at Clark Elementary. Later, I'd go to the pool to work on my tan, baking in the late afternoon sun in my cotton eyelet bikini, purchased at Bonnie's favorite thrift store. As I lay on the plastic lounge chair, I'd drift off until the heat drove me into the cool turquoise water for a dip. By then, it was time to shower for supper and the cycle began again.

It was delicious for a time. But after a while, I began to feel I was drowning in a sea of sensuality and addiction. By late October, I had lost more money than I had allowed myself. I now avoided Caesar's, with its one-dollar minimums, playing instead in one of the smaller casinos on the Strip where you could bet fifty cents at blackjack. The atmosphere was sleazy rather than glamorous. I was drinking scotch every night.

Bonnie and I were fighting too often as she tried to keep me from losing my money. I began to feel my presence was making life harder for Don and the kids. It was time to leave.

There had been some new openness and communication between my mother and me but on the whole I felt defeated and terribly disappointed.

CHAPTER 21
Odyssey, Continued

left Las Vegas in tatters. My nerves were raw and I felt a little desperate. I was occasionally aware of a subtle sense of freedom and elation which was unscathed by the old patterns, yet along with this came the unsettling fact that I had no more certainties to hang on to. I no longer believed that getting a PhD was better than not getting it. All I knew for sure was that I had to find a way back to the simple truth I had tasted on my trip, that I had understood more fully in *est*—the experience that I was not only Rifka, this individual, but also that vast, all-inclusive being, the creator of my own universe. I was convinced there was a path back to that experience that was right for me and I was now desperate to find it.

Back on a Greyhound heading for San Francisco, I allowed my jagged nerves to be soothed by the desert scenery. Once we arrived, I got a cheap hotel room in the Mission District, then ventured out to walk the hilly streets, needing only my fringed wool shawl (which I wore with jeans) to be comfortable on the sunny autumn days. Haight-Ashbury was still full of bedraggled longhairs but many of them looked burnt out from too many bad trips and speed. The days of Peace and Love were over. This made me sad.

My memory is that I walked around San Francisco muttering to myself in distraction, though I'm not sure this is literally true. It may just be a poetic image I constructed to make myself feel more like Isadora Duncan, whose house I passed on a steep hill one windy afternoon. I had long idealized Isadora as a great artist who lived defiantly outside the confining strictures of society, practicing her art according to her own lights. I stood for a while in front of the Victorian building, reading and re-reading the bronze plaque which said she had lived there in her youth. I wished to emulate her, though her self-destructive aspect seemed less romantic to me now than it had in my teens. As I pulled my shawl around my shoulders and walked on down the street, I was pleased that I *did* feel a bit like I was following her example by taking my life in my own hands, going my own way for better or worse . . .

After my sojourn in Vegas, I knew with certainty that—notwithstanding all my great experiences and understandings with *est*—I'd still not found that path I'd been searching for; the one that would bring me home to rest within myself. So for the five days I was in San Francisco, I checked out other spiritual trips. I stopped in at the Dawn Horse Bookstore, where I saw a film about an American teacher in the Indian tradition called Bubba Free John. His story was intriguing and he had quite a few followers, but I was not drawn to the man I saw in the film. And the idea of giving a teacher authority over me was still, if not anathema, less than appealing. I couldn't imagine trusting anyone enough. I figured I'd find another way, like those birds Rinpoche had mentioned.

Another day, someone stopped me in front of the Scientology office and I went inside to check it out. But, after hearing their pitch, I beat a hasty retreat.

On my last night in town, I went to the Fillmore Auditorium to see Ram Dass. The atmosphere was festive and the air hung heavy with pot. If I was not high when I arrived, I surely got a contact high from sitting in the theater packed with brightly clothed hippies and other seekers. Ram Dass sat on stage in the lotus posture. He was balding and his salt-and-pepper beard was long on his chest. He wore beads and flowing white garments. There were some Indian musicians on stage with him, and they played sitar and tabla at intervals during the evening. When he spoke, I recalled what he wrote at the end of *Be Here Now*:

> *The intensity with which the psychedelics show you "more" makes you greedy to be done before you are ready. This attaches you to the experience of "getting high" which, after a period of time, becomes a cul de sac. The goal of the path is to BE high not to GET high.*

Ram Dass said he was not dropping acid any more, except occasionally to check out his spiritual progress. I believe he also told us that he had seen in meditation that all the LSD he had taken had created certain obstacles in his brain. Hearing what this brave pioneer said that night reinforced my decision not to drop acid again. I also took comfort in his counsel to not allow fear of false gurus—and there were so many around—to keep us from following a spiritual path. If you follow a false teacher and you do it with pure intentions, he said, you may stumble or fall. But eventually, you'll be able to pick yourself up and find a better way. You will still reap the benefits of your own sincere efforts.

The next morning, I boarded a Greyhound one more time. I had made all the stops permitted on my round trip ticket so I had to ride straight through to New York. New York, my home sweet home.

BACK ON 72ND STREET, I began working again for my old temp agency, more grateful than ever for this reliable way of earning easy money. I generally enjoyed the job placements of two to three weeks at a time in advertising agencies where the executives I worked for were creative, if cynical, and the work was undemanding.

I read *Hinds' Feet on High Places,* the book recommended by Sister Mary Catherine. It was an innocent allegory, likening the search for God to climbing a mountain, the same image used by Maharishi. By now I was used to finding similar metaphors used in widely disparate spiritual traditions.

MY THIRTIETH BIRTHDAY SEEMED like a big deal. Not that I had ever subscribed to the dictum "Never trust anyone over thirty." I guess my old conditioning said I should have accomplished more in the world by now. My friends and family were almost universally skeptical about my new direction, especially my leave of absence from the doctoral program. I was restless, feeling that something new and important was coming into my life but perplexed and impatient about how and when. Where was the path that would lead me to the higher consciousness I longed for?

At times, I thought it was Tibetan Buddhism, at times I thought it was *est.* But I still found checking out other paths irresistible.

ecalling that cross-country trip, those endless hours on the Greyhound, makes me squirm in my seat. Three days straight on that bus left some vivid sense memories in my derrière. It's only been two hours since we left Manhattan.

After a long downgrade, the road bridges a small river and ascends once more. The charter exits the Quickway onto a country road I definitely remember. It is nearly dark as we ride past some of the old bungalow colonies. After turning right toward town, I see with a start that we're passing the roadside swimming pool where Alan proposed to me eight years ago. A surge of conflicting feelings rises to my throat. I no longer doubt that I did the right thing in breaking up with Alan but—despite my newfound conviction that everything is, in its own way, perfect, that there is that perfect order to it all—I feel more than a twinge of guilt about hurting him as I did. I vividly recall lying right there and saying yes to his proposal in that automatic way, as if I was in a dream.

Thank God I am no longer that cut off from who I really am. The bus turns left now, on the final leg of our circuitous route.

CHAPTER 22
Are We There Yet?

S itting on a paint-spattered floor, in an artist's studio down in SoHo, I listened to Swamiji's disciples describe their guru as a saint. I'd heard about this meeting on *In the Spirit*, the weekly radio program hosted by Lex Hixon, who interviewed many of the spiritual teachers who were around at that time.

Throughout the winter I had continued to explore different avenues to spiritual enlightenment. I took two consecutive series of weekly *est* seminars, and a four-day lecture series with Rinpoche, but could not settle on either path as my own.

I knew the saying "When the pupil is ready, the teacher appears," and I felt so ready.

One Sunday Lex Hixon invited listeners to his home to meet Khyentse Rinpoche, whom I had heard Trungpa describe as "a fully enlightened being." Thus, on a chilly morning in early March, way before my normal rising time, I got myself up to Hixon's spacious house in Riverdale, a leafy, affluent neighborhood just north of Manhattan. To my surprise, only a handful of other people were there.

Hixon was a student of many religions, a thirtyish man with sandy hair which fell casually over one eye. His house overlooking the Hudson was opulent.

Our small group sat on the carpet of the comfortable living room waiting for the lama to arrive, surrounded by views of the Hudson through big picture windows. In time, Khyentse Rinpoche entered quietly with two younger monks. He was at least six feet tall, huge compared with other Tibetans I had seen; he wore wool robes of orange and maroon. He had thin white hair tied back in a low ponytail and leathery jowls, and there were bags under his eyes. As soon as he walked in, a powerful silence descended upon me. He exchanged pleasantries with Lex and his wife, in a soft voice startling in a man of his stature. From time to time he laughed with disarming candor. The almost palpable quietude I felt in his presence reminded me of the experience at the end of my LSD trip.

Khyentse Rinpoche sat before us on the living room sofa and we were invited to ask questions. Surprising myself, instead of voicing my convoluted spiritual concerns, I heard myself say, "How does Rinpoche like New York?"

For a second I felt his keen eye upon me before it traveled to gaze out the window. Speaking slowly, he replied, through the young monk serving as translator, that he was struck by the "wildness" of the people he saw on the streets of the city. This answer startled me. One of the ancestral gurus of his lineage was said to have lived with hundreds of dogs on an island in the middle of a poisonous lake. And he thought New Yorkers were wild!

But there was a sweetness in this exchange of words; what we actually said did not seem to matter. Khyentse was at once impersonal and friendly. Exceedingly friendly. As I listened and watched from my seat on the floor, I basked in the sense of benevolent peace that seemed to emanate from him. A few other people asked questions. Then the audience was over. We were invited to come up to formally greet the master. One by one, people knelt before him.

At first I felt a little wave of fear and distaste as I watched the others bowing. But I knew no one in that room would care whether or not I followed suit. Khyentse Rinpoche appeared mildly disinterested in this traditional display of respect for a holy man, as if to illustrate Trungpa's point: a true master is one who is "giving up his credentials" in every moment.

I discovered with a sense of excitement that I wanted to bow.

When I placed my forehead on the carpet near the lama's feet, I was surprised at how natural it felt to do so. In honoring the powerful stillness I felt in him, I was in no way belittling myself. On the contrary. I was bowing to him not as a man but as one whom I intuited had risen above identifying himself as a man or woman. I bowed from deep within myself to the vast silence he was emanating.

Looking up, I saw profound kindness in his dark eyes. When I stood, I felt I had crossed some threshold.

NOW, A FEW WEEKS after meeting Khyentse Rinpoche, I'd come to hear about Swamiji. He was spoken of with reverence by many other spiritual leaders, including Werner, Maharishi, Ram Dass, and Zalman Schachter, the mystical rabbi influential in founding the Jewish Renewal movement. And all around New York that spring, you could find posters with a head shot of this Guru's bearded face, a red dot on his forehead between intense eyes looking straight out at the viewer.

The Introductory Program was attended by a motley group, perhaps forty people. Two American women led the program, followed by an Australian man called Madhu. (It was customary for disciples to ask their Guru for a spiritual name as part of the process of shedding old identities. Hell, Ricky— Riqui—Rifka could certainly relate to that.)

Anandi, Sara, and Madhu were in their twenties or early thirties, like most of us in that room. Madhu, a thin, articulate man with black-framed eyeglasses on a beaklike nose, told us that to be with Swamiji was incomparable. We could find out for ourselves when he arrived in New York next week to spend the summer in the Catskills.

"Swamiji teaches us that everything you seek already exists inside you," said Madhu. As he continued, I was reminded of what I knew from my acid trip and *est* experiences: that the baggage of the mind—all the impressions left by past experiences—blinds us to seeing who we really are. Of the teachings I had encountered which felt genuine to me, they all seemed to say this same thing in different ways. Of course, if they all pointed to the same essential Reality, how could it be otherwise?

Swamiji was, Madhu explained, a yogi who, after many years of intense practice under the auspices of his own Guru, now lived in this knowledge which I had only glimpsed. I had read that, in ancient times, a seeker had to live with and serve the Master, usually for twelve years. If, at the end of that period, the student had developed the necessary qualities, the Master would initiate him. But apparently Swamiji was offering initiation to this path without requiring such arduous tests.

Next, Anandi, a delicate and radiant woman with brown hair pulled into a tight bun, described this ancient path. After initiation, she told us, spiritual development proceeds spontaneously, guided from within the seeker by the Guru's subtle power which is—on the deepest level—not different from one's own. She described how her life had transformed dramatically since her own initiation.

Sara, a comfortably unkempt woman, had a less effusive manner, which reassured me after so much gushing. This school of meditation does not conflict with any other religion, she said. In fact, many people reported that it deepened the experience of their own religion. It is the Guru's job, she said, to bring the disciple to the same state of expanded consciousness and bliss that he himself enjoys. She said she had struggled with depression for years but felt the depression had lifted after initiation.

I tended to like these people, though they did seem a little too happy. When it came time for questions, a man gave voice to my skepticism. "You make it sound so easy," he said. "From my experience, the spiritual path is filled with difficult tests and obstacles. Isn't that so?"

Anandi replied. Swamiji's school of yoga is based on grace, she said. While self-effort is certainly required—for example, to sit for meditation—spiritual evolution after initiation happens spontaneously and without fail. But, she said, the "bird of liberation" needs two wings to fly: self-effort and grace.

Birds again! But this was a different angle from "the Hard Way" of working with the mind that Rinpoche described.

It sounded too good to be true; but I had to go see for myself.

CHAPTER 23

Home Free

*I*t's dark when the old bus finally pulls up to the entrance of a low auxiliary building of the hotel, one of the many defunct Borscht Belt properties that have fallen victim to the advent of cheap air travel to distant vacation destinations. I'd never heard of the Lido before.

Olga and I haven't spoken for some time—I may have actually dozed off myself. Now, as we wait for the people in front of us to get their stuff and climb down, I stretch in my seat and tug on my wrinkled blue shirt. Olga turns her head toward me with a dreamy smile.

"I feel like I am here to meet my destiny," she confides.

"We'll see," I say, not wanting to let my own hopes spin out of control. However, I notice my heart is beating a little faster. Stepping out into the night air, I shiver and pull my jacket closed in front as I follow the others through double glass doors into a small lobby, which I guess is the lobby of the Lido's former nightclub.

I'm disoriented by the scene. A crowd of perhaps three hundred people is milling around, waiting for the doors of the hall to open, buzzing with excited expectation. In addition to the hippieish long skirts, some of the American women are wearing saris. *Tsk*, I disapprove to myself. How pretentious. I make my way through the crowd to the coffee shop where refreshments are available. Here I find colored cardboard cutouts of that elephant-headed deity strung across the ceiling and draped with tinsel as if for a children's party. Good grief. This garish sensibility is so different from the refined aesthetic of the Tibetan centers I've attended; I seriously doubt I will find anything I can relate to here.

Stay open, Riqui, I remind myself. Rifka, who made you the judge?

I elbow my way up to the counter and am offered chai, which they tell me is a sweetened, spiced tea. I sip the milky potion standing shoulder to shoulder with the people around me. Mmm, it's good!

A blast from a sharp horn pierces the buzzing talk. There's a man in a suit and tie in the doorway, blowing on a conch shell. The crowd in the lobby behind him starts undulating toward the hall and the coffee shop crowd thins its way out the door. Setting my paper cup on the counter, I follow suit.

We have to remove our shoes before entering the meditation hall, and I try to remember where I'm leaving my Keds among the hundreds of shoes on the lobby floor.

The hall is brightly lit and already crowded. Ushers direct us to sit in rows on the floor facing the stage, women on the left and men on the right of a center aisle. Sexist, snarls the inner critic. Too regimented.

Stop it, Rifka.

The pretty usher with a bun directs me to sit in one of the middle rows, then seats the next woman practically on top of me. Wriggling to give myself a bit more space, I look toward the front. An armchair sits center stage, flanked by end tables with vases of roses. Hanging above the chair is a large picture I recognize as Swamiji's own Guru, a yogi in a loincloth. Incense perfumes the air.

A lanky young black man steps up to a microphone standing

on the floor in front of the stage and introduces himself as Arjuna. He tells us he was a psychologist. After saying a few words of welcome and what a great occasion this is, he announces, "Swamiji's plane landed at LaGuardia about an hour ago. He's on his way."

A great whoop and cheer rise up from the crowd.

"The best way to prepare to meet the Guru is to chant," says Arjuna. "Chanting opens the heart. The women will chant *Hare Krishna*, the men, *Hare Rama*. So let's chant!"

More cheering and clapping as chords from a harmonium rise from up front. Very slowly, the men begin to sing. As the women respond sweetly, "Hare Krishna," the hall monitors come down the aisle, handing out finger cymbals, tambourines, and maracas—maracas!—to whomever reaches for them. So there are ten or fifteen people playing as the volume and tempo of the chant increases with every few repetitions. I join in tentatively. Periodically I close my eyes and just turn my attention inside, trying to stay centered.

Minutes pass, then half an hour. People are swaying and clapping and the sense of fevered anticipation continues to rise as the chanting reaches a crescendo. My mind is in an uproar.

After more than an hour, the door of the hall opens and an energetic brown-skinned man appears in the back of the room, dressed entirely in orange, from his socks and wrinkled skirt, worn below a rust-colored silk tunic, to his tangerine ski cap. Dark sunglasses complete the outfit! The crowd erupts in wild cheers, smiling and waving. The woman behind me is crying and laughing at the same time as she jumps to her feet. I stand with the others, craning my neck to get a look.

Swamiji strides down the center aisle toward his chair. He looks utterly relaxed, smiling and waving back to the crowd.

As I watch, I hear my mind, dripping with Yiddish irony, say, "That's a saint?"

My inner voice—the voice I have learned to trust implicitly—responds in triumph, with complete certainty: "This is it. This is what you've been looking for."

My jaw drops. Really?

Swamiji has reached the stage and he springs into his cushioned chair. Deftly, he crosses his legs beneath him as he draws his lungi down over his knees. We all take our seats on the floor. The whole crowd becomes still as the Guru begins to speak, in Hindi, I assume. His voice is deep and mellifluous and his words seem to come straight through his translator without obstruction.

He begins by saying he welcomes us all, because, he says, God Himself has become this whole universe and is the essential Self of every human being.

He speaks rapidly, gesticulating enthusiastically. In his orange garb, Swamiji feels to me like some kind of holy fire. What a contrast between this and Rinpoche's slow, mindful manner, which I had come to regard as an expression of wisdom. I'm fascinated.

Who *is* this man?

. . .

I REMEMBER NOTHING OF the bus ride home that night or if I sat with Olga. All I knew was that I was going to go back for Swamiji's initiation. I read the free newspaper they'd handed out to learn more about his teachings. The central point was that everything I was looking for lies within. By this, I knew it was a true path. The other thing Swamiji taught—in the words of one of the aphorisms from Indian scriptures—was that the Guru is the means to realizing this truth.

I returned to the Lido on the first weekend in April to take a two-day meditation program. On Friday night, I arrived in

Montgomery at the same bus station where Laurie and I first landed to begin our waitress jobs at the Granville. You've come a long way, baby.

The lobby of the Lido was quiet compared to my first visit there. Everything was remarkably clean, despite the somewhat threadbare carpeting and sparse furnishings. A devotee was vacuuming the lobby as I registered at the desk. I knew doing work, service, was an essential practice in this, as it is in most spiritual paths. I checked in at the desk and was assigned a shared room with four beds, as expected. As I had with *est*, I resolved to accept all the rules and customs in order to see what benefits I could reap from this program. With this attitude, adjusting to three unknown roommates wasn't that hard. So you had to wait your turn for the bathroom.

On Saturday morning, groggy from rising so early, I made my way to the dining room where vegetarian meals were served cafeteria-style. Breakfast consisted of dry toast and a spicy hot cereal, along with that spiced milky tea.

You had to walk down a long breezeway from the lobby to get to the building where the meditation hall and coffee shop were. Having left my shoes (and hopefully my ego) in the shoe room set up next to the hall, I followed an usher who directed me to a seat on "the ladies' side" among perhaps fifty other women. About the same number of men sat on the other side of the aisle. At least today there was more space between people. On my right sat a heavyset black woman dressed completely in white.

"I don't know why men and women have to sit separately," I blurted.

She raised an eyebrow at me. "It's so you won't get distracted," she said. I guessed that was reasonable enough. God knows I'd been distracted by men before. My neighbor and I chatted a little waiting for the retreat to begin. Her nametag said "Ganga." She told me she had flown up from her home in Florida, where she taught elementary school. She hadn't seen Swamiji for an entire year, she said; she was so excited.

Everyone sat in neat rows, most people on cushions or regular pillows, like the one I had brought from my room. A lot of the men and women wore cotton or wool shawls. In the front row, about five musicians sat cross-legged before their instruments: a harmonium, a cylindrical drum, and a few stringed instruments, long-necked gourds polished to a high finish. As I looked around the tiered hall, I reflected that the former Lido nightclub was not that different from the one I remembered at the Granville—except that on these walls were pictures of Indian saints and Gurus wearing loincloths or turbans, photos of modern ones and sepia-toned drawings of historic ones. A thick quiet of anticipation filled the air.

Arjuna, the young African-American guy from the other day, was again the MC. He outlined the weekend schedule, saying Swamiji had designed the retreat as the perfect vehicle for giving initiation. Between sessions of chanting and meditation, there would be explanatory talks and accounts of personal experiences. Each speaker was introduced with a few words about their background. The specifics of who actually said what, when, that weekend are muddled in my memory. The main points are not.

It all revolved around the Guru, understood to be an embodiment of the grace-bestowing power of God. The initiation we would receive would awaken Kundalini, the inner spiritual energy which lies dormant at the base of the spine in the subtle body of every human being. (I had seen Kundalini depicted as a coiled serpent, an image found in many mystical traditions, including Kabbalah. Carl Jung, who'd studied Eastern philosophies, had written that it would take a thousand years of psychoanalysis to awaken the Kundalini.) Once that energy is awakened by a true Guru, the spiritual evolution of the aspirant is guided by the inner subtle intelligence. This is possible because the guru principle is not different from one's own true self. And the experiences shared by the devotees I heard indicated they were reminded again and again that the essence of the Guru lives within themselves. Echoes of the words of Francis of Assisi: "The one you are looking for is the one who is looking." Confirmation of my own most powerful experience: I am that I am.

As I listened to the speakers and soaked in the calm atmosphere of the hall, I felt like I was drinking pure water. My inner voice was cooing.

Arjuna assured us that everyone would receive initiation: Swamiji would go around and touch each person while we meditated. However, the Kundalini awakening might happen any time, he said: while repeating Swamiji's mantra perhaps, or in a dream. One roommate told me last night that she'd gotten initiation simply from seeing Swamiji's photograph, before she even learned who he was.

The next speaker was a former college professor named Elizabeth, a gaunt woman with graying hair drawn into a bun, who spoke about what we might experience during the program. She said that each person receives initiation according to their own nature and capacity.

"Swamiji is like the ocean," she said. "If you come to him with a thimble, he'll fill your thimble; if you bring a bucket, he'll fill your bucket." But in due time everyone would get what they needed to take them to the goal of liberation. We might have very dramatic experiences during meditation, Elizabeth told us. You might feel a rush of energy up the spine or see visions of lights or hear unearthly music such as Swamiji described in writing about his own experiences. Some might feel that nothing in particular happened, only to realize after a few months that their lives were transformed in some fundamental way. Having visions or ecstatic experiences was not the goal: lasting happiness was what this path was all about.

I felt a mounting sense of anticipation: What would happen to me? Would I finally find my way back to that incomparable space I'd tasted last year?

Each speaker assured us we need not take anything on faith. Let your actual experience be your guide, they urged. See for yourself what you experience in the Guru's presence. Arjuna offered this advice, based on his own years with Swamiji: "Watch him like a hawk," he said emphatically. "Try to get an inkling of his state of consciousness." Despite my reservations about the foreign trappings of this path, I had a powerful sense that something great was about to happen.

Swamiji joined us later that morning, dressed in orange silk and still wearing a knitted ski cap. Before taking his seat on stage, he bowed deeply to the enlarged photograph of his Guru, draped with a garland of flowers, which hung above his chair. The mantra Swamiji gave was printed above the picture. He placed some notes on a small podium in front of him and adjusted the attached mic. He was warm and playful as he spoke and his face was remarkably fluid. At one moment he seemed like a sedate wise man, the next he broke up giggling like a mischievous child.

He said a disciple should test a Guru before accepting him. See if you are transformed when you follow his path, he advised. When he spoke of his own Guru, he was humble, singing mystical poems of praise with a haunting tenderness. I watched him with fascination and growing affection.

After a coffee break, we returned to our seats and the lights were dimmed. The harmonium played chords low and slow and Swamiji began chanting the mantra in his broken baritone. A few people up front chanted along with him, then the rest of us repeated the line, chanting in call-and-response fashion for perhaps twenty minutes. When the last strains of the harmonium died down, the meditation session began.

Impelled by my excited curiosity, I peeked through my eyelashes to watch Swamiji as he came down from his seat and moved through the rows of meditators. In the dimly lit room, I saw him in silhouette, bending forward slightly over each person, as he touched the sitter on the top of the head or on the forehead or back. At first, the hall remained quiet.

Elizabeth had advised us that the activated Kundalini caused many manifestations in the process of purifying the seeker. The mind might race during meditation, she said. Strong emotions could surface or spontaneous physical movements might occur. I realized this was what they called "unstressing" in TM.

But nothing prepared me for what happened next. As Swamiji moved through the room, people seemed to take off in his wake. More than one meditator started the heavy yogic breathing called "bellows breath," exhaling rhythmically through the nose. On the men's side, someone roared like a lion—I mean loud! Then a wave of laughter swept the room like a contagion. The air was thick with an indefinable energy.

When Swamiji finally reached my row, I told myself to stay relaxed and open but I was keyed up with anticipation. When he stopped in front of Ganga beside me, the musky scent of the aromatic oil he wore grew intense. I kept my eyes closed and felt the air move as he leaned over her. Ganga began to sob with joy, bending forward to place her forehead on the Guru's toes. I heard him pat her back.

FINALLY, SWAMIJI IS STANDING before me. His thumb presses down on the spot between my eyebrows with unexpected force. Then, his warm palm brushes the crown of my head. A surge of affection seizes me and I have an impulse to hold on to Swamiji's hand to extend the contact. He moves on, and I immediately start repeating the mantra to myself really fast, trying to anchor my mind. What just happened? I feel like one of those cartoon characters whose eyes twirl off in opposite directions after something knocks him for a loop.

Swamiji goes through every row in the room before returning to his seat up front. The sounds in the hall reach a crescendo of noisy yogic breathing, birdcalls, and someone repeating, "Allah Allah Allah Allah Allah Allah . . ." I am barely able to stay focused on the mantra. Among the stream of apparently random images rushing through my mind as I meditate, a vision of Swamiji appears, standing in profile with his orange lungi and buttoned-up cardigan. He appears translucent and, as I continue to watch, in my mind's eye he steps inside my sitting body and disappears.

BOTH DAYS OF THE retreat included *darshan*, an opportunity for each person to go up to the Guru one by one. You could just pay your respects or you could ask Swamiji a question. He held a long wand of peacock feathers with which he brushed people's heads, a way of transmitting blessings. Many devotees brought traditional offerings such as fruit or flowers, which they placed in a basket at the foot of his chair. Others brought vases or clocks, gifts that would be useful in the ashram. I watched as one woman gave him a length of orange silk; Swamiji put down his feathers, took off his cap, and in about three seconds he wound the cloth around his head and fastened it into a jaunty turban! In fact, many people were giving him hats. Wearing different hats was a kind of signature of Swamiji's. He almost always wore one, most often a knitted ski cap, but in the course of time he could be seen wearing turbans, sombreros, and every other kind of head covering offered by devotees from different countries. Sometimes Swamiji gave the seeker a gift too, such as a shawl or something that he had just been given by another devotee. This was all part of the Guru's play or *leela*, the complex dance that whirls around the spiritual master. Swamiji's leela was full of mysterious teachings, as Arjuna had suggested when he said to "Watch him like a hawk." It reminded me of the Chasidic saying: "I go to the master more to watch him tie his shoelaces than to hear him speak."

That afternoon, for my first darshan, I went outside and picked some buttercups and Queen Anne's lace, wildflowers from the roadside meadows near the hotel, presenting them shyly as I knelt before the chair. At such close range, I felt a palpable power emanating from Swamiji. The peacock feathers, scented with that intoxicating fragrance, tickled my face and head. But I could not bring myself to look at him. Swamiji was, to say the least, formidable.

The day ended after Swamiji left the hall with a session where participants were invited to stand up and share their personal experiences. Just like in *est*, you raised your hand and a runner brought you a microphone. A few people talked about their meditation experiences. Then a bespectacled guy about my age, wearing a white shirt, stood up to share. He was Jewish, he said, redundantly; in fact, he had been a cantor. But he had rejected his childhood orthodoxy "a long time ago." Waiting in line for darshan, this man noticed that someone on line ahead of him gave Swamiji a yarmulke. Knowing Swamiji's ways, he was afraid the Guru would pass the skullcap on to him, thus impelling him to reexamine his conflicted stance toward his own Judaism. He was relieved when he saw Swamiji place the skullcap on someone else's head before he reached the chair.

When it was his turn for darshan, the man bowed before his Guru. He was so happy he had turned toward the wisdom of the East. Swamiji flashed him a radiant smile, reached behind his chair, and pulled out another yarmulke! Chuckling, Swamiji crowned the man with the skullcap as he whacked him over the head affectionately with the peacock feathers. Recounting this, the ex-cantor laughed along with the rest of us. He concluded that, in the years he had been following this path, Swamiji always found a way to turn his attention back inside. This yoga was certainly not an escape from facing yourself.

BY SEVEN FORTY-FIVE Sunday morning, after a fitful night full of vivid dreams, I was seated on my pillow in the hall. I had a subtle feeling of well-being as I waited for the second day of the program to begin. I was relaxing more now and looked around me a little more closely. As my gaze wandered around the half-full meditation hall, I was struck again by how much this room resembled the nightclub at the Granville. The proportions of the room were the same. On my left were double doors like the ones that led to the Granville's service bar, where Fred the bartender had instructed Laurie and me in methods of shortchanging customers. Over the past couple of days I had mused that the old Catskill hotels must all have been quite similar in layout. But now, as I pictured how the Lido grounds must have looked before the connecting breezeways were added, it dawned on me that it was *exactly* like the Granville. Could this actually be the same hotel?

• • •

THE MORNING BREAK COMES at ten thirty. As much as I want to follow the crowd to the coffee shop and get a cup of chai, I turn right instead, peeking into the room next to the hall. Yes, it looks just like the lounge where we served drinks after the nightclub show, where I had that intense conversation with Rodney Dangerfield. I go outdoors and cross the quiet road. The early spring sun shines pale yellow above the still-bare treetops and the chill mountain air bites through my light sweater. No one else from the ashram has come outside yet. An old Ford goes by too fast, the stillness more marked when the noise of the engine fades away. The small bungalow before me appears abandoned. I haven't focused on it until now, how it looks just like the staff building at the Granville where I shared a room with Laurie. The two front windows are boarded up but the door, with its peeling brown paint, is unlocked. Just as I remember, it opens onto a narrow corridor that goes straight to the back, with four doors on each side. I walk through slowly, floorboards creaking beneath my feet. There is a strong smell of mold. I remember now the shared bathroom halfway down on the right. An uncanny sense of unreality is descending upon me. Our room was the last one on the left.

The door to the back room is ajar. The room is empty of furniture but the sink is where I remember it, just inside the door. The mirrored medicine chest is gone but I have no doubt. Here I stood on July 4, 1964, cutting into my wrists as Barbra Streisand songs played on the portable Victrola. I glance down at the scars, six crooked white lines across both forearms. I look at the corner where my bed was, picturing myself lying there in a coma before Laurie discovered me.

As I stand motionless in the middle of the room, my mind spins like a tornado, thick with inchoate thoughts. My emotions, however, are still. After long minutes—or is it seconds?—a single thought emerges, my own voice speaking inside my head with crystal clarity. I hear it with surprise: "I love you, Mother."

· · ·

I CANNOT EXPLAIN THIS experience, nor overstate its significance. The closest I have come to describing its impact is this: If all my life I had struggled to make ends meet, at that moment ends met. The circle of my life was closed and I was set free.

AS I WENT BACK to the meditation hall, I kept looking at everything, confirming this was really true. My detachment gradually gave way to excitement. I recalled the breakfasts I'd eaten in the coffee shop, now strung with cardboard Ganeshes, nursing a hangover at 1:00 p.m.

Returning to the Lido's main building for lunch, I saw clearly: that room near the dining hall now used for meetings was the bar where we'd served drinks before dinner. Unbelievably, I was receiving initiation in the nightclub where I had—twelve years earlier—deliberately spilled drinks on nightclub guests in my bitter ire. Twelve—the exact number of years a spiritual seeker was traditionally required to serve the master before receiving initiation.

I AM NOT CERTAIN what teachings Swamiji gave that day in his talk. It is my great good fortune to have heard him speak many times since then, as he sat cross-legged in his big chair, emanating that amazing power of his in a rainbow of colors.

He might have told us there is no need to quit your job or leave your family in order to find God, since this entire universe is nothing but a manifestation of That. In his enthusiasm, he might have interrupted the translator in mid-sentence. Perhaps he then issued a throaty chuckle, which I found irresistible. When his alarm clock pealed, if he hadn't finished what he wanted to say, he probably picked it up and reset it unceremoniously.

He certainly exhorted us to meditate, to honor and serve the great Self who dwells within ourselves and others.

That afternoon, as I stood in line for Swamiji's darshan, it occurred to me that I must tell him what I had discovered. When I reached the front of the line, I knelt down and turned toward the translator.

"Please tell Swamiji, I tried to kill myself in this place twelve years ago."

As the man translated my words, I extended my arms toward the Guru, palms up to show him my scars.

For a moment Swamiji looked down at me kindly, reminding me exactly of a loving uncle. He said with compassion, "You should never do such a thing." Then, without glancing at my wrists, he took them in his hand and drew me affectionately toward him. I felt myself enfolded in warmth. But I was not prepared to accept so much love. I stiffened, pulled back, and sat down on my heels, looking up at the Guru.

Leaning forward in his chair, he peered deeply into my upturned eyes. For some reason, my gaze focused on his left eye; it seemed there was an unfathomable ocean roiling there. When he sat back, there was a playful twinkle in both his eyes.

"This time you got something else," he said, chuckling softly.

He sure got *that* right.

When I rose to go back to my seat, one of Swamiji's attendants who had heard what I said called out to me, "You should share that."

The sharing session was led that afternoon by Madhu, the enthusiastic Aussie I had seen at the introductory program back in SoHo. I raised my hand and stood up when the usher brought me the microphone. Briefly, I told the group that I had worked at this hotel in 1964 and had attempted suicide here. There was an audible gasp. I told them what Swamiji had said to me. Then I paused, uncertain for a moment what I wanted to add.

"I like what they said about how the Guru is like an ocean of love," I said. "If you come to him with a thimble, he'll fill your thimble. If you come with a bucket, he'll fill your bucket. I guess I feel like I have a cup right now . . ."

A wave of friendly laughter greeted this metaphor; the sympathetic goodwill of fellow seekers washed over me as I handed the mic back to the assistant.

"Stick around," said Madhu with a broad smile. "In time, you'll have the biggest bucket you ever saw."

And he surely got *that* right. For I knew, with a certainty that has never faltered, that I had indeed found what I was seeking, the path that would take me all the way to my goal.

ONE OF MY FAVORITE metaphors for that profound initiation is this: An enormous boulder must be cleared from a mountainside. An engineer sets off the depth charge. There is a muffled explosion from within the mountain and the whole rock moves, its great mass lifting up a fraction of an inch from the earth, where it has been embedded for eons. Loud cracking sounds are heard as a network of lines appears, barely perceptible, lacing through the granite. After a second, the boulder shudders and settles down again, appearing exactly as it was before. But the force that kept it locked in place has been shattered. All that remains is the work of clearing it away, piece by piece.

• • •

DURING THE SUMMER OF 1976, I returned to the ashram almost every weekend and spent my ten-day vacation there. I saw Olga often, beaming, all her expectations fulfilled.

One evening during darshan, I asked Swamiji for a spiritual name. He spoke it before the request was out of my mouth. "Urvashi," he said, bopping me with the peacock feathers.

In Indian mythology, Urvashi was one of the *Apsaras*, "celestial dancers" or "courtesans" in heaven (the realm of pleasure), known primarily for her beauty. One legend even details the lengths to which a certain King Pururavas strives to win Urvashi's hand. This seemed to echo the Hebrew meaning of Rifka: "Tied and bound like an animal for the sacrifice; hence, beautiful, voluptuous, desirable." Yet the real understanding and consonance here for me has to do with sacrifice: the ancient Hebrews chose the most desirable animal as a burnt sacrifice to God; and, in the Pururavas story, the trinity of the sacred fires of the Hindu tradition is created. The astrological sign Scorpio, under which I was born, is also associated with an image of fire: the rising of the phoenix from its own ashes.

These synchronicities are like divine hints about the nature of my journey. And on that journey, I have come to simply appreciate the beauty of this person, my individual little self with all her peculiarities, just as I came to treasure the loveliness of the wooded Catskills to which I had been completely blind in the summer of 1964.

Ever since receiving initiation and doing the practices taught by Swamiji, I have had the conviction that, in reality, I have already attained my goal. At times, my dramas look much as they did before. Passionate and painful love affairs. Travels and adventures. Psychological struggles surrounding relationship, achievement, and success. But, on the inside, there is a tenth-of-an-inch of space between *me* and my soap opera, a portal to a place of light and the knowledge of who I *really* am, that great Self I first discovered on an LSD trip in a lemon-yellow bedroom overlooking Riverside Drive. It is ever present, closer than my own breath, the source of limitless happiness.

There have been tests and obstacles to overcome, periods of confusion and discouragement. In my first few years on this path I learned from experience how creatively the ego, with its own desires and preconceptions, resists liberation. I have at times viewed my progress as three steps forward and two steps back. But I keep meditating and practicing the teachings I receive. And the long, deep healing process continues. Even the smallest self-effort on my part is met with an abundance of nurturance and support: Grace. Nothing can repay what I have received from my Guru.

This bird is flying home, free.

AUTHOR'S NOTE

Memory has aptly been called a shapeshifter, and research has documented its malleability. For this reason, and to protect the privacy of the people depicted in *Home Free*, I have changed many of their names.

I do not name my spiritual path or my Guru because my journey is still in progress; I do not wish my still-limited understanding to be taken as a full representation of these great and subtle teachings. For those readers who may be seeking your own way to liberation, I have full faith that you will find the path that is right for you. I send you my heartfelt wish that you attain your goal.

ACKNOWLEDGMENTS

Home Free had its inception when my dear friend Janame, the late, great W. J. O'Connell, suggested we start a writing group. He wanted to write about his planned trip to Tibet. Each week, we'd randomly choose a topic to write about. After a year, I had a number of pieces that seemed to cry out: "We want to be a book." I am eternally grateful for the inspiration and encouragement I received from Janame, as well as Marta Szabo, Diane Fast, Tina Hazarian, Sari Rosenheck, Jean Webster, Julie Mars, Liz Coleman, and Jen Mann.

For indispensable feedback, and support that kept me going through the years, I thank early readers Gail Kotel, Susan Padwee, Rose Brooks, Mary Ann Fitzgerald, Karen Neuberg, Deborah Tuthill, Beatrice Winner, Shelle Sklarsh, Maxine Hayden, Anita Michael, and Elinor Renfield.

The wonderful teacher, essayist, and poet Rebecca McClanahan helped me find the structure to integrate the story. Editor Uma Patti Hayes was, quite literally, a godsend. I am so grateful for her work. For eagle-eyed proofreading, thanks to Janet Bjugan, Beatrice Winner, Lynne Rachlin, and Susan Padwee.

To the other midwives and author's nurses who contributed to finally birthing this baby, thank you, thank you, thank you: Michele G. Weisman, Marc Eliot, Margaret Bendet, Arielle Eckstut, Barrett Briske, and MJ "Bo" Bogatin. And, at She Writes Press, Brooke Warner, Cait Levin, and Julie Metz.

How to thank my closest people, whose contributions are too broad and deep to detail? Roberta Jellinek, my warm and generous friend of fifty years; Lynne Rachlin whose clarity, insight, and values I count on as we share our separate paths through life; and Barry Kotel, who enriches my life every day, as we discover together how love can deepen and grow over years.

Finally, to my beloved meditation teachers, my Guru lineage: my gratitude for your profound and never-ending gifts is beyond words, eternal.

ABOUT THE AUTHOR

photo by Chris Loomis

An astrologer once told Rifka Kreiter that a certain planetary conjunction in her chart signifies "an unusual life, full of unexpected happenings," and this has certainly proved true. *Home Free* recounts her peripatetic early life in New York, LA, and San Diego. She studied acting at New York's High School of Performing Arts, philosophy at City College of New York, and clinical psychology at Adelphi University. She worked as a waitress, hatcheck girl, and hearing researcher. She was continuity director at a New York radio station and assistant convention manager at the Concord Resort Hotel. More recently, she tutored SAT Prep courses and was assistant director of admissions at a rural community college.

Since 1976 she has been following an ancient yogic path and she lived in a meditation ashram for ten years, traveling to India three times.

Rifka currently teaches meditation. At age fifty-five she (finally) met her life partner, an Upper West Side psychotherapist. He and she live happily together in suburban New Jersey. Find her at rifkakreiter.com.